BIG BAD ASS
· BOOK OF THE ·
ZODIAC

BIG BAD ASS

· BOOK OF THE ·

ZODIAC

The Diagram Group

and James Napoli

STERLING INNOVATION

An imprint of Sterling Publishing Co., Inc.

New York / London

www.sterlingpublishing.com

STERLING, the Sterling logo, STERLING INNOVATION, and the Sterling Innovation logo are registered trademarks of Sterling Publishing Co., Inc.

Library of Congress Cataloging-in-Publication Data Available

2   4   6   8   10   9   7   5   3   1

Published by Sterling Publishing Co., Inc.
387 Park Avenue South, New York, NY 10016

A Diagram Book first created by Diagram Visual Information.
195 Kentish Town Road, London, NW5 2JU, England.
© 2010 by Diagram Visual Information Limited.

Distributed in Canada by Sterling Publishing
c/o Canadian Manda Group, 165 Dufferin Street
Toronto, Ontario, Canada M6K 3H6
Distributed in the United Kingdom by GMC Distribution Services
Castle Place, 166 High Street, Lewes, East Sussex, England BN7 1XU
Distributed in Australia by Capricorn Link (Australia) Pty. Ltd.
P.O. Box 704, Windsor, NSW 2756, Australia

Interior design by Alicia Freile, Tango Media

Sterling ISBN 978-1-4027-4786-1

For information about custom editions, special sales, premium and corporate purchases, please contact Sterling Special Sales Department at 800-805-5489 or specialsales@sterlingpublishing.com.

TOC

Part I: Zodiac Types

Part II: Chinese Astrology

Part I:
Zodiac Types

Introduction

P art I, Zodiac Types, is a clear and concise introduction to the signs of the zodiac and the behavioral characteristics they are believed to endow. Each sign and its attributes have been detailed within separate chapters. Many different aspects—from a Scorpio's personality and reactions to situations in the workplace and at home, to a Taurean's behavior when in love—are described with the help of lists, panels, and illustrations.

What is a sign of the zodiac?

Each of the 12 signs of the zodiac is a name given to a 30-degree arc of the sky, as viewed from Earth. As the Earth moves around the Sun, the Sun appears to pass from one 30-degree arc to the next, completing the journey through all 12 zodiac arcs in one year. For example, a person whose birthday is on January 1 is born when the Sun is in the zodiac sign of Capricorn. This is referred to as a person's sun sign (see "zodiac band," page 8). Hence, a person born a month later, when the sun is passing through the next 30-degree arc, would have the next zodiac sign, Aquarius, as his or her sun sign.

Characteristics of the zodiac signs

The popular view is that a person will display the characteristics associated with his or her sun sign. For example, characteristics typical of Capricorn include ambition, faithfulness, weak knee joints, and a long life span. In reality, however, many people born with the Sun in Capricorn may well have little ambition, be unfaithful, have perfect knees, or may have died young.

What is astrology?

Astrology is the study of apparent coincidences between certain events on Earth and the positions of the Sun, Moon, and eight other planets. In traditional terms, the Sun, Moon, and planets (often loosely called "the stars") are said to influence events on Earth. The modern view, first suggested by the psychologist Carl Gustav Jung, is that events coincide with a particular pattern of the stars. This phenomenon is known as synchronicity.

The personal birth chart

When studying synchronicity between personality and the stars, a complete horoscope or birth chart must be made. This shows the positions of the Sun, Moon, and planets at the time of birth, relative to the place of birth. The birth chart indicates many features, only one of which is the position of the Sun at birth.

A sample birth chart

The symbols on the chart are the standard ones used to indicate the zodiac signs, the Sun, Moon, and planets. The chart on page 10 is for a person born on May 25, 1931; therefore, the Sun is in the zodiac sign of Gemini. The position of the Moon at birth, the positions of all the eight planets of the solar system, and several other important features, such as geographical location, are all taken into account when interpreting the chart. For example, in the sample chart, the Moon is in Virgo, i.e., the moon sign is Virgo. The Moon is linked with mood and emotion, so astrologically this person's moods would be Virgoan, rather than Geminian. A person who had been born on the same day, in a different year and location, however, would have a chart that was oriented differently, although it would have several similar features. In very broad, general terms, this is the basis of personal astrology.

A BIRTH CHART

See "Astrological Symbols" on page 13 for the meanings of the symbols shown.

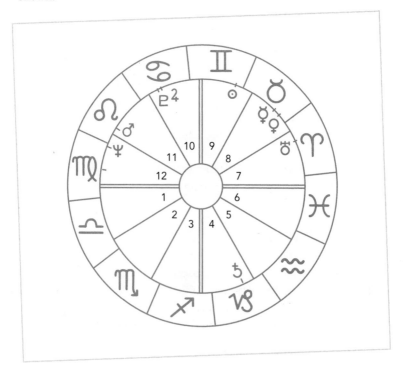

Finding your sun sign

The approximate dates of when the Sun moves into each sign are listed on page 11. They will be correct for most years, but incorrect for others. For example, if your birthday is July 22, some lists will say your sun sign is Cancer, as shown on page 11; others will say Leo.

Sign	Dates
Aries	March 21–April 19
Taurus	April 20–May 20
Gemini	May 21–June 20
Cancer	June 21–July 22
Leo	July 23–August 22
Virgo	August 23–September 22
Libra	September 23–October 22
Scorpio	October 23–November 21
Sagittarius	November 22–December 21
Capricorn	December 22–January 19
Aquarius	January 20–February 18
Pisces	February 19–March 20

The cusp

The exact time when the Sun moves from one sign to the next is known as the cusp or beginning of the sign. Because the movement of the Earth around the Sun is not exactly regular each year, the precise date when the Sun moves from one sign to the next sometimes differs.

Predictions

Future events cannot be predicted. Professional astrologers read trends by comparing a person's birth chart with the day-to-day movements of the Moon and the small planets (Mercury, Venus, Mars), and the longer-term movements of the larger planets (Jupiter, Saturn, Neptune, Uranus, Pluto).

Astrology and free will

In general, astrological interpretations are descriptions of how a person may behave rather than what he or she might actually do. Every characteristic has its positive and negative sides, the interpretation of which is a matter for personal choice; for example, one Taurean characteristic is never to change without very good reason. This could be interpreted either as undying loyalty or as stubborn resistance.

How to enjoy this book

The information about each zodiac sign is a summary of the main characteristics associated with it. If you find that you happen to be typical of your sun sign, it is probably because several planets are in your sign or are linked with it in positive ways.

If you have few or none of the characteristics of your sun sign, it could be for one or more of the following reasons:

1. Other signs are stronger in your chart.

2. Your full potential has not yet emerged.

3. The characteristic has negative "influences" in the orientation of your chart, which you have controlled.

4. Your birth date is the day of a cusp, and the exact time of birth may indicate that your sun sign is actually in the next, or previous, sign.

Reading the sun signs is fun and may be revealing. If, however, you wish to investigate astrology further, the best course of action is to have a full chart made and interpreted by a qualified astrologer.

ASTROLOGICAL SYMBOLS

The symbols used to represent the signs and their ruling planets below.

Sign	Symbol	Ruling planets	Symbols
Aries	♈	Mars	♂
Taurus	♉	Venus	♀
Gemini	♊	Mercury	☿
Cancer	♋	Moon	☽
Leo	♌	Sun	☉
Virgo	♍	Mercury	☿
Libra	♎	Venus	♀
Scorpio	♏	Mars; Pluto	♂ ♇
Sagittarius	♐	Jupiter	♃
Capricorn	♑	Saturn	♄
Aquarius	♒	Saturn; Uranus	♄ ♅
Pisces	♓	Jupiter; Neptune	♃ ♆

1. Aries: The Ram
March 21 - April 19

The FIRST sign of the zodiac is concerned with:
- self-assertion, initiation, new beginnings
- action, daring, challenge, adventure
- exploration, pioneering, discovering
- aggression, creativity, personal goals
- personal control of everything
- competition, winning, being first
- courage, honesty, nobility, openness

Elemental quality

Aries is the cardinal fire sign of the zodiac. It can be likened to a fire, which gives direction, such as in a rocket, a gun, or an engine. Superman and Superwoman, who can propel themselves in any direction, are good metaphors of Aries energy. Fire is a process that causes change and Aries uses energy to bring about changes. Being a cardinal sign, Aries is the most energetic of the fire signs and usually takes the initiative.

THE ARIES PERSONALITY

CHARACTERISTICS

Positive
- Is a leader
- Is energetic
- Helps others to achieve their dreams
- Accepts challenges
- Believes the best of others
- Takes risks for others
- Defends the vulnerable
- An Aries life is an open book
- Will give life for the loved one
- Continues action even if others give up

Negative
- Must be the boss
- Brashness
- Blind to his or her effect on others
- Intolerance
- Jealousy
- Doesn't listen
- Selfishness
- Impulsiveness
- Poor judge of character
- Dislikes being told what to do

LISTEN UP, THIS IS IMPORTANT

Aries love to say they will give their life for a loved one, but since they are also poor judges of character, don't listen and dislike being told what to do, they have no loved ones.

Ruling planet and its effect

Mars rules the zodiac sign of Aries, so anyone whose birth chart has a strong Aries influence will tend to look for challenges to overcome. In astrology, Mars is the planet of aggressive energy and creative action. Like Mars, Aries is the knight in shining armor, an inspiration to friends, and a conquering hero to the underdog.

DON'T BE A JERK

If an Aries tells you about their lucky animals, do not make a "ram-and-lamb-a-ding-dong" joke. They will physically hurt you.

THE ARIES LOOK

People who exhibit the physical characteristics distinctive of the sign of Aries are tall and bold. Usually lean, they have strong bodies and may even be quite athletic. They are usually concerned about projecting a physical image of success. They need to be winners and generally do their very best to look the part. Appearances are important to Aries.

THE ARIES MALE

Appearance

The typical Aries man

• has a strong body
• is extremely energetic
• has a dominating sex appeal
• walks with an air of nobility
• dresses in clothes appropriate to the current challenge

Behavior and personality traits

The typical Aries man

- is fiercely competitive
- is honest
- appears to be self-assured
- takes initiative and expects others to follow
- is enterprising
- dreads physical disability
- has very clear goals
- will put his partner on a pedestal
- needs to win
- uses wit and brains to get what he wants

COMMUNICATION

Aries Male = That Bastard Who Beat You Up in High School

THE ARIES FEMALE
Appearance

The typical Aries woman

- is slim and strong
- is very active and glows with energy
- has strong, luxurious hair
- wears sophisticated colors and perfume
- dresses in clothes appropriate to the occasion

Behavior and personality traits

The typical Aries woman

- looks you in the eye and gives a firm handshake

- is enthusiastic and optimistic
- talks back and often gets hurt because of it
- expects loyalty
- is fearless
- has interests outside the home or has a career
- expects to win in any situation
- is direct, open, and honest
- can make miracles happen

SECRET TIP

Aries Female = A Man

YOUNG ARIES
Behavior and personality traits

The typical Aries child
- has a strong, active body and mind
- has a temper when thwarted
- usually walks and talks early
- wants attention and to be in charge
- can be lazy until someone claims to be better
- is generous with toys
- has a vivid, practical imagination
- can achieve much in a short time
- is normally very affectionate
- has an inexhaustible curiosity
- gets over childhood fevers very quickly

Bringing up young Aries

Most Aries children are very direct about their likes and dislikes. They are also very determined to do things their way. Saying "No" doesn't work, nor does persuasion, coaxing, or using other obedient children as examples. Young Aries children of any age respond best to a challenge. Tell him he's probably just slow at organizing his toys or tell her that it isn't her fault that she can't do something very well and young Aries goes into action, to prove he or she is better than anyone else at anything—including doing the things they don't like.

Young Aries needs

Adventure, opportunities to find out, to try things, take charge, solve problems, and be a winner. Above all, Aries needs to know that he or she is loved and valued. Big hugs and reassurance, especially after emotional bumps, are essential, despite the brave face they put on. years of this crap, you will push very hard for an out-of-state college.

 # ARIES AT HOME
Typical behavior and abilities

When at home, an Aries man or woman
- wants to be the top dog
- makes a substantial and secure home
- doesn't like to feel tied down or restricted
- will generously give money, goods, and space to those who need it
- can lend a hand to anything but doesn't enjoy those little jobs needed to run and repair a home

Aries as parent

The typical Aries parent
- won't spoil the children

- will give plenty of hugs and praise
- can create a magical fantasy world for children
- usually insists on strict discipline
- will raise children to be successful
- may try to dictate the future careers of offspring
- will fight to the death if anyone hurts the kids
- will be a devoted dad and an affectionate mom

LISTEN UP, THIS IS IMPORTANT

We might as well apologize to the other eleven signs right now. Clearly, Aries kicks their asses when it comes to being parents.

Two Aries in the same family

Aries can be comfortably married to each other providing they each have separate challenging situations in their lives to confront and win. Two Aries need to converse regularly as neither likes being left out. A parent and child who are both Aries will clash many times, so the parent must recognize that young Aries also hates being told what to do. Families with two or more Aries can be exciting with plenty of affection and challenge to keep them all going.

ARIES AT WORK
Typical behavior and abilities

A typical Aries at work

- is loyal and enthusiastic about the company
- will work all hours and is not a clock-watcher
- will look elsewhere for an opening if bored
- is highly creative and can initiate

- has very strong willpower
- is not suited to political work

Aries as employer

A typical Aries boss (male or female)
- is idealistic and needs the faith of his or her employees and expects their loyalty
- believes he/she can make the future a success
- needs others but will go it alone when necessary
- wants to be recognized as the boss
- can pull a business up from near bankruptcy
- is generous with rewards for hard work
- expects everyone to drop everything to solve a crisis

Aries as employee

A typical Aries employee (male or female)
- works best when answerable only to the boss
- can promote anything
- tends to work late rather than early
- looks for opportunity to learn and progress
- intends to succeed but is careless with details
- knows he or she can do well
- will move to another job if he or she feels the challenges in the current job have run out; security is not a priority, although Aries workers usually make their way under the most difficult circumstances

Working environment

The workplace of a typical Aries man or woman
- will have people and machines to take care of the details
- may be almost anywhere that is exciting

- must be stimulating and allow freedom of movement
- will support an important-seeming image
- must be accessible at all times: days, nights, and weekends

QUICK FIX

You don't have to be a mental giant to glean from all this that Aries are workaholics and probably prefer being at work to being around you. You can counter this behavior by charging for sex. They will see it as a job, and work extra hard to guarantee your satisfaction.

Typical occupations

Aries is associated with work that inspires activity in others—for example, leaders, directors, supervisors, or any job that has authority. Aries must be in command or they will lose interest. Aries works best at the initiation of a project, leaving the consolidation to other people. Typical jobs are in recruitment and training, work in the theater, business enterprises, politics, sports, and the military in any position that has power.

SECRET TIP

In some rare cases, an Aries will agree to take a menial retail position. However, they must be promised that they be allowed to eat all the underperformers.

ARIES AND LOVE

To Aries, love is a conquest. Male Aries love the chase and seem to have little difficulty attracting women, while female Aries also love the challenge of the hunt but go about it a little more subtly. Aries of both sexes are attractive because of their natural energy. Aries in love will have many of the characteristics listed below.

Behavior when in love

The typical Aries
- is very romantic and believes in courtly love
- will insist on doing the chasing and cannot bear to be chased by anyone
- can be extremely possessive of a lover but cannot understand if a lover is possessive
- places the loved one on a pedestal
- will be jealous of any attention the loved one gives to others
- will defend the loved one to the death

Expectations

The typical Aries expects
- total faithfulness from the partner
- the lover to respond as if he or she is the first and best lover ever known
- to be loved exclusively
- never to be criticized

BARE FACTS

Dating an Aries = Faking It

23

The end of an affair

Boredom is the death of most Aries love affairs. Like the knight in a crusade, it is the winning that is the peak of excitement. Once the fair lady (or fair gentleman) is won, there may be nothing left to stimulate the affair further. At this point an Aries will get itchy feet and want to be off to find new conquests. It isn't that love itself is merely a conquest, it is the joy of overcoming obstacles to reach love. The partner of an Aries must always keep a little mystery in reserve and must always believe in every new Aries dream. If all fails—and Aries will try and try before leaving a relationship—then the Aries passion cools and there remains only a lack of interest. A lover who hurts Aries very deeply can expect to be totally frozen out and ignored.

YOU'RE WELCOME FOR THE TIP

Sooner or later, you're going to be frozen out and ignored anyway, so you might as well hurt the Aries as soon as possible and get it over with.

ARIES AND PARTNER

The person who contemplates becoming the marriage or business partner of a typical Aries must realize that Aries will want to be in control of all the major decisions. He or she will be happy to leave the day-to-day details to a partner, but will always expect to be in overall control. Given this, the person who partners Aries can expect an exciting, creative relationship with unexpected surprises and plenty of affection.

Aries man as partner

He will want a partner of whom he can be proud, yet who will never do anything better than he can. A clever partner would be wise to be modest about personal abilities and to put effort into supporting and encouraging the sensitive Aries partner in his own dreams.

In marriage, the Aries husband will regard his wife as the queen of his domain and she must behave accordingly, never failing in her loyalty to him and keeping surprises up her sleeve to stimulate his interest.

BARE FACTS

If science could crossbreed a mouse with an introverted supermodel, the Aries man would be all over that.

Aries woman as partner

Like her male counterpart, the Aries partner must always come first. This makes life difficult for the typical Aries wife in a male-dominant situation. She needs a husband who will recognize and accept her powers. A man must have self-respect and tact to partner an Aries woman.

In return, both male and female Aries will bring bountiful energy, enthusiasm, and loyalty to any partnership.

QUICK FIX

Yes, the partner of an Aries female will do well to keep reserves of tact and self-respect handy. Those big cardboard containers of White Zinfandel really help, too.

Opposite sign

Libra, the scales, is the complementary opposite sign to Aries. Although relationships between Aries and Libra can be difficult, Libra can show Aries how to cooperate, share, and bring people together in harmony. Libra can intervene diplomatically where Aries will bound in and make demands forcibly.

COMMUNICATION

Thank you, Libra, thank you so much for keeping these jerks in line.

Libra

Aries

LISTEN UP, THIS IS IMPORTANT

Get used to the charts and stuff. They're everywhere in books like this.

ARIES AND FRIENDS

In general Aries likes a friend who is special in some particular way and who will regard Aries as his or her best friend (never the second best!).

Positive factors

Aries friends are warm and hospitable, but they are not usually interested in entertaining for its own sake; they usually have a reason for inviting friends around. Many Aries prefer to go out to dinner to find an unusual eating place. Both male and female Aries usually get along better with male friends.

Negative factors

Because Aries are very jealous of other people's abilities and achievements, Aries friendships often don't last very long. However, a person who will admire his or her Aries friend and remain interesting, though not ambitious, can enjoy an enduring friendship with Aries. Aries can become harsh and nasty if his or her fragile ego is under threat. A compatibility chart on page 28 lists those with whom Aries is likely to have the most satisfactory relationships.

SECRET TIP

A review of Aries likes and dislikes finds them really not so different from the rest of us after all. It is worth noting that, although Aries typically dislike anyone who performs better than they do, all those who *have* performed better than Aries have since died under mysterious circumstances.

In general, if people are typical of their zodiac sign, relationships between Aries and other signs (including the complementary opposite sign, Libra) are as shown below:

	Harmonious	Difficult	Turbulent
Aries	•		
Taurus	•		
Gemini	•		
Cancer		•	
Leo	•		
Virgo			•
Libra		•	
Scorpio			•
Sagittarius	•		
Capricorn		•	
Aquarius	•		
Pisces	•		

ARIES LEISURE INTERESTS

Most typical Aries enjoy some physical activity that allows them to display their prowess. Aries may also enjoy board games that give them the opportunity to demonstrate their superior mental and tactical power. On the whole, typical Aries pursue the following leisure interests:

• competitive sports, e.g. football, tennis
• driving a car which has a great image
• racing by car, bicycle, or on foot
• risky physical activities, such as sailing around the world alone or climbing a new peak
• military pastimes
• theatrical activities

ARIES LIKES AND DISLIKES

Likes
- being liked
- the best wines
- a unique license plate on the car
- money to burn
- new clothes
- red roses
- food in bright colors
- personalized gifts
- presents wrapped in intriguing paper
- books
- sparkling gems

Dislikes
- being ignored
- physical restriction
- being placed less than first
- feeling hungry
- anyone who performs better than they do
- old things, second-hand stuff
- having to wait for anything
- lingering after food
- bland food

STRETCHING THE TRUTH

Adventuresome Aries will often combine military pastimes *with* theatrical activities for a truly bizarre evening in the woods.

ARIES HEALTH

Typical Aries are healthy and fight every illness that comes their way, staving off attacks of flu with sheer willpower. When Aries pride is hurt or life teaches a hard lesson, Aries may suffer emotionally and need great comfort. For all their apparent superiority, Aries are extremely softhearted and vulnerable to emotional hurts.

QUICK FIX

Aha! You've found their weakness! Get in there! Attack!

Types of sickness

Fevers and accidents are typical of all fire signs, and especially so with the highly strung Aries character. If ill, Aries will expect constant attention to his or her needs, but recovery is usually very quick. Typical Aries may suffer from acne, epilepsy, neuralgia, headaches, migraines, and baldness. Accidents due to physical activities are common, accompanied by bangs on the tough Aries head. Sinuses, eyes, and ears are also vulnerable.

Aries at rest

Rarely is a typical Aries seen at rest during the day. They seem to have an inexhaustible supply of energy and a considerable willpower. However, when eventually tired, at perhaps three in the morning, the typical Aries will usually sleep well and may either sleep late or take a long time to get started again in the morning. The typical Aries doesn't rest like most other people; both male and female Aries are too busy with some project or other to stop for long. The enthusiasm with which they do things is as good as a rest to them. When enthusiasm wanes, they still don't want to rest but are impatient to be off on a new venture.

WELL LOOK WHO FINALLY MADE THE RODEO

So remember, dealing with the Aries personality can be difficult, but in the end, it is probably not worth it.

2. Taurus: The Bull

April 20 - May 20

The SECOND sign of the zodiac is concerned with:
- beauty, romance, sentimentality, sensuality
- materialistic values, wealth, prosperity
- nature, harmony, love of living things
- possession, control, security, dependability
- habit, organization, tenacity, kindness
- shyness, cautiousness, trustworthiness, calmness
- appreciation of values, talents, abilities

Elemental quality

Taurus is the fixed earth sign of the zodiac. It can be likened to an ancient rainforest full of enduring trees and rare plants that is teeming with the beauty of life, or to a beautiful, old French château that is full of valuable antiques, and which has established vineyards and gardens that offer all manner of delights to the senses. This sign represents an enduring, practical reality.

THE TAUREAN PERSONALITY

CHARACTERISTICS

Positive

- A careful and conservative outlook
- Dependable and offers enduring loyalty
- Calm and patient
- Artistic
- Thorough
- Attentive
- Values the talents of others
- Very loving
- Resourceful
- Gentle and placid
- Excellent cook
- Good sense of time and is orderly

Negative

- A tendency to be self-indulgent
- Can be stubborn, obstinate, and get stuck in a rut
- Materialistic
- Slow-moving
- Little to say
- Delays action by lengthy pondering
- Easily embarrassed
- Boring
- Insensitivity

STRETCHING THE TRUTH

A full ninety-six percent of those involved with Taureans say that they are willing to put up with any amount of self-indulgence, stubbornness or slow-moving, insensitive and boring behavior in exchange for that "excellent cook" part.

Ruling planet and its effect

Venus rules the zodiac sign of Taurus, so anyone whose birth chart has a strong Taurus influence will tend to have a strong set of personal values. In astrology, Venus is the planet of love, affection, values, and sensuality. Like Venus, Taureans can be very affectionate and fond of the good life, as long as it is a peaceful, secure life. Taureans rarely stray from their personal code of what is right. Taurus, like the mythical

Venus, has an idealized concept of beauty, and may, especially in early life, be very self-conscious about his or her body.

<table>
<tr><td colspan="4" align="center">TAUREAN LUCKY CONNECTIONS</td></tr>
<tr><td>Colors</td><td>pastel shades and blues</td><td>Metal</td><td>copper</td></tr>
<tr><td>Plant</td><td>mallow</td><td>Tarot card</td><td>hierophant (High Priest)</td></tr>
<tr><td>Perfume</td><td>storax</td><td>Animal</td><td>bull</td></tr>
<tr><td>Gemstone</td><td>topaz</td><td></td><td></td></tr>
</table>

THE TAUREAN LOOK

People who exhibit the physical characteristics distinctive of the sign of Taurus look as if they are well rooted and in touch with the Earth. They may be plump or slim, but either way they will walk with a slightly ponderous gait, as if each step has been carefully considered. All typical Taureans have a presence that emanates solid reliability.

BARE FACTS

3 out of 5 Taureans are Hobbits.

THE TAURUS MALE
Appearance

The typical Taurus man

- has a stocky body, which is muscular if he does a lot of physical activity
- may be plump
- will bear the discomfort of an injury or disability with extreme stoicism
- has very clear skin
- is likely to have plenty of hair and can grow a substantial beard
- walks with determination

Behavior and personality traits

The typical Taurus man

- rarely changes his point of view
- works hard to build security
- is astute and can evaluate a situation very quickly in financial terms
- is quiet and has a low-key charm
- is unpretentious
- enjoys comfort
- can be defensive and suspicious in a new or unexpected situation
- is wary of others taking advantage of him
- dresses to create an image of respectability
- uses influential connections to get what he wants

COMMUNICATION

Taurus Male = Somewhere between Donald Trump and a paramecium.

THE TAURUS FEMALE
Appearance

The typical Taurus woman

- tends to have a rounded body
- has a beautiful complexion and hair that always looks in excellent condition
- may live by a very strict diet to attain slimness
- has an air of mystery about her because she does not flaunt her sexuality
- wears clothes that give her sensual pleasure
- has a strong body capable of hard work

Behavior and personality traits

The typical Taurus woman

- is an introvert
- has considerable moral and emotional courage
- takes people as they come
- is very loyal to her friends and sticks by them if they are in trouble
- has practical common sense
- is deeply sensual
- prefers the real to the artificial, e.g., real flowers, real silk, and genuine, high-quality antiques

SECRET TIP

Taurus Female = Somewhere between a librarian and a porn star.

 YOUNG TAURUS
Behavior and personality traits

The typical Taurus child

- is usually a quiet baby with rare outbursts
- is stubborn and wants his or her own way
- has a strong little body and can often be found clenching his or her fists when opposed
- is usually calm, pleasant, and a little shy
- is cuddly and affectionate
- dislikes being the center of attention
- responds to common sense and affection
- usually works slowly but steadily at school

Bringing up young Taurus

Never try to force a young Taurus to do something because the Taurean child will turn stubborn and will always hold his or her ground longer than anyone else, except perhaps a Taurean parent. Harsh commands will never discipline the young Taurus, but a loving hug will melt all the resistance out of that obstinate little bull. Both girls and boys are usually competent little people and open to practical, common sense explanations. Both can charm adults, especially of the opposite sex.

Young Taurus's needs

Physical affection given freely and without smothering is essential to the healthy growth of any Taurean child. Young Taurus also needs harmonious surroundings. Colors and sound will affect these children quite deeply. Harmonious blues, shades of pink and rose, and soft sounds will be calming and reassuring.

SNAP OF THE FINGER

So, the good news is, you can keep harmony in the household by constantly playing a CD of the ocean waves and painting your walls in harmonious blues and shades of pink. The bad news is, once word gets around about your hideous house, you will quickly become known as the neighbors no one wants to visit because "that place of theirs gives me a freaking embolism."

TAURUS AT HOME
Typical behavior and abilities

When at home, a Taurus man or woman
- hates anything to be moved around
- enjoys comfort and luxury
- has well-tried habits and likes a well-ordered household
- prefers to own his or her home
- makes his or her home a castle

Taurus as parent

The typical Taurus parent
- is affectionate
- has seemingly endless patience
- can be dominant and possessive
- may find it hard to relax and play with the children
- will support, encourage, nurture, and protect the children with unswerving faith in their own abilities as a parent
- will teach self-respect
- will save for the future
- expects high standards

Two Taureans in the same family

Taureans can get along well together providing they have similar personal values. If they disagree about fundamental issues, their obstinacy could lead to a permanent impasse as neither will give an inch. On the other hand, their mutual serenity and response to physical affection should overcome any serious disagreements.

TAURUS AT WORK
Typical behavior and abilities

A typical Taurus at work
• will work steadily toward achieving what he/she values
• cannot bear interference
• has great respect for institutions
• requires work that gives respectability

Taurus as employer

A typical Taurus boss (male or female)
• patiently tests out the employees
• doggedly sticks to stated principles
• will give everyone more than a fair chance but fire anyone who breaks his or her trust
• is often a self-made person and will make money
• does not make hasty judgments
• wants things done his or her way
• is kind and patient but expects total loyalty
• likes plain facts and hates flattery

Taurus as employee

A typical Taurus employee (male or female)
• needs a regular salary
• is an excellent person to handle money
• is honest and dependable
• is practical, sensible, and down-to-earth
• enjoys sensible routines
• displays foresight
• is rarely thrown off balance
• can handle emergencies

Working environment

The workplace of a typical Taurus man or woman
- must be calm and well ordered
- any noise or color scheme must be low key, if it is an office
- should be at a fixed location—rural or park settings suit Taurus well

Typical occupations

Taurus is associated with banking, farming, floristry, interior design, architecture, food, engineering, construction, general medical practice, executive secretarial positions, stable occupations in established institutions, and any occupation that involves the shrewd acquisition of land, investments, or goods.

TAURUS AND LOVE

To Taurus, love is a physical, sensual romance, which can be expected to last forever. Taureans are attracted by physical beauty and are very sensitive to perfume, color, light, and sound. Taurus in love will have many of the characteristics listed below.

Behavior when in love

The typical Taurus
- is devoted and steadfast
- settles quickly into a stable affair
- loves glamour

- is extremely vulnerable to people who accept his or her affection but only want a flirtation
- will never forgive a betrayal
- the male is generally the strong silent type
- the female is usually an earth mother/Venus

Expectations

The typical Taurus expects
- his woman to be very feminine
- her man to be all male
- a promise to be kept and never broken
- a wholesome, natural approach to physical love
- to be pampered
- to wait for a commitment to be made

The end of an affair

It takes a long time for a Taurean to decide to leave a relationship. Taurus finds it extremely difficult to be convinced that he or she was wrong about a person. However, once the Taurean mind is made up, there is never any turning back. He or she will walk away forever. Being a good judge of character is not one of Taurus's strengths, so some will assume all is well, even when a lover is being deceitful. When a deceit is revealed, Taurus will be very hurt but will still hang on to hope. Some Taurus men can be macho, so when a relationship is ending, the macho Taurus can lose his normally gentle approach, becoming harsh and domineering. This usually indicates the hurt to his ego, which at heart is very trusting and naïve. The lover who walks out on a Taurean will leave behind a bewildered, disbelieving person, who may suffer one vague illness after another as the hurt and rage slowly come to the surface.

TAURUS AND PARTNER

The person who contemplates becoming the marriage or business partner of a typical Taurus must realize that Taurus will expect absolute loyalty through thick and thin and will probably want to establish a routine way of doing things his or her way. Given this, the person who partners Taurus can expect honest devotion, a long-term relationship, and a partner who can keep his or her head in any emergency.

Taurus man as partner

He will want a partner who enjoys his way of doing things. The partner should be prepared to take the responsibility for good public relations while Taurus works quietly away ensuring that money and power come their way. The Taurean husband wants a marriage partner whom he can possess, body, soul and dowry. He needs a woman who enjoys physical love, since to Taureans there is no division between love, sex, and marriage.

Taurus woman as partner

She will want a partner who is attentive and appreciative. Common sense is essential in any partner of a Taurean. She, like her male counterpart, will look for a business partner who will bring prestige to the business. The Taurean wife wants to be given gifts and treated with gentleness. She does not want to be patronized, but she does want her man to remember her birthday and other anniversaries. She needs a husband who will let her organize at least a part of his life and who will never give her cause for jealousy.

BARE FACTS

This thinking that she can get a guy who has prestige, will remember her birthday, never give her cause for jealousy and let her organize his life is typical of the delusional Taurean female.

Opposite sign

Scorpio is the complementary opposite sign to Taurus. Although relations between Taurus and Scorpio can be difficult because they are both stubborn signs, Scorpio can show Taurus how to gain insight into the needs and motives of other people, and thus also into his or her own life. In this way, Taurus can use his or her natural sensitivity to help in the service of others.

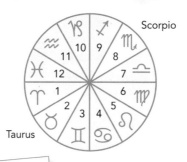

Scorpio

Taurus

QUICK FIX

We don't care how you do it, Scorpio, just whip these Taurean jack balls into shape.

TAURUS AND FRIENDS

In general Taurus likes a friend who is reliable, unchanging, and not given to sudden excitement or changes of plans.

Positive factors

Taureans are very warm and affectionate toward their friends. They enjoy friendship with people who have good taste and with whom they can enjoy a quiet conversation or a concert or a football game. They will enjoy people who have strength of character and qualities of endurance like their own. Toward such friends, Taurus will always be gentle, kind, loving, and totally trustworthy.

Negative factors

Taurus can be jealous of any attention a friend gives to someone else. Taurus does not like signs of weakness, physical or emotional, and can be quite direct about them. Taurus prizes friends who have some power that they can share and enjoy. People who wear cheap perfume, artificial fabrics, and have houses that are built to deceive the eye, e.g., not real stone but faced with stone, are unlikely to attract the friendship of a typical Taurean. A compatibility chart below lists those with whom Taurus is likely to have the most satisfactory relationships.

COMPATIBILITY CHART

In general, if people are typical of their zodiac sign, relationships between Taurus and other signs (including the complementary opposite sign, Scorpio) are as shown below:

	Harmonious	Difficult	Turbulent
Taurus	•		
Gemini	•		
Cancer	•		
Leo		•	
Virgo	•		
Libra			•
Scorpio		•	
Sagittarius			•
Capricorn	•		
Aquarius		•	
Pisces	•		
Aries	•		

 # TAUREAN LEISURE INTERESTS

On the whole, typical Taureans pursue the following leisure interests:

• collecting things of value
• singing or listening to music
• gardening
• painting

- the quieter sports
- activities that give Taurus a chance to enjoy physical pleasure, such as horseback riding

TAUREAN LIKES AND DISLIKES

Likes
- soft, sensual textures
- sensual pleasures
- a good bank balance
- certainty and well-tried routines
- gifts of value, attractively wrapped
- savoring the moments of pleasure at the table
- doing the same thing over and over

Dislikes
- being disturbed
- change
- lending things
- being told to hurry up
- sleeping in strange beds

TAUREAN HEALTH

Typical Taureans are robust people. They may suffer from being a little overweight, but on the whole Taurus is healthy, provided nothing comes along to disturb the status quo. A Taurus who has an unsatisfactory sex life will be rather like a bull with a sore head . . . irritable and prone to grunting and grumbling. The greatest danger for Taurus comes from the ability to hold back anger and to stubbornly hold on to a redundant point of view. That can lead to melancholy and medical depression.

SECRET TIP

The pharmaceutical industry loves Taureans.

Types of sickness

Infections of the throat are said to be linked with Taurus, including laryngitis, swollen glands, and croup. Constipation may also bother a Taurean. When sick or if involved (untypically) in a serious accident, Taurus can withstand any amount of discomfort and pain. The Taurean ability to stubbornly refuse to allow anything to get the better of him or her is a great advantage during times of sickness. Similarly, a Taurean will stand by family and any friend who has a misfortune.

Taurus at rest

Extending the metaphor of the fixed earth sign, Taurus at rest is totally relaxed and lazy. In fact, Taurus can rest with feet up in front of the television or listening to music for days and days. Taureans usually sleep well and wake up slowly. Once they are on the go again, they can keep going for long periods without feeling tired.

WELL LOOK WHO FINALLY MADE THE RODEO

In summary, Taureans are ruled by contradictory forces that churn inside them like a slowly rising torrent of emotional upheaval. Poor bastards.

3. Gemini: The Twins
May 21 – June 20

The THIRD sign of the zodiac is concerned with
- communication, articulation, speech
- dexterity, nimbleness, grace
- wit, instinct, persuasion, change, variety
- movement, curiosity, exploration, short journeys
- education, learning, collecting facts
- attention to details, adaptability
- intellect, intuition, youth, freedom

Elemental quality

Gemini is the mutable air sign of the zodiac. It can be likened to the wind in that it is constantly on the move in all its variety. Air is a metaphor for the invisible thoughts and ideas that motivate Gemini, such as the intellect, the intuition, and the natural instincts.

The quality known as mutable means adaptable, changeable, agreeable. Gemini constantly adjusts ideas in an attempt to create harmony.

THE GEMINIAN PERSONALITY

CHARACTERISTICS

Positive
- Inquisitive
- Entertaining and charming
- Versatile
- Liberal, broad-minded
- Youthful
- Quick
- Stimulating
- Inventive
- Never prejudiced

Negative
- Restless
- Quickly bored
- Impractical
- Impatient and irritable
- Capricious and fickle
- Gossipy
- Nervous
- Manipulative
- Noncommittal
- Dual personality

SECRET TIP

We could have put anything we wanted in the negative column. The Geminian is too restless, impatient and quickly bored to spend time reading some dumb chart. Look, we'll test our theory: "Hey, Gemini, you're not only gossipy and capricious, but I heard your mother is so stupid, it takes her an hour to cook minute rice!" See? They weren't even listening.

Ruling planet and its effect

Mercury rules the zodiac sign of Gemini, so anyone whose birth chart has a strong Gemini influence will tend to be on the go, moving to and fro with many messages like the fleet-footed Mercury of mythology, who was the eloquent messenger of the gods. Mercury wore a winged helmet and carried the caduceus, a stick around which were entwined twin snakes. The snakes represent the libido and the healing powers of the instinctual mind. In astrology, Mercury is the planet of thought and communication, and governs all mental and nervous processes. Mercury is the hermaphrodite of the zodiac, taking the neutral position of mediator between the masculine and feminine viewpoints. Mercury is the planet of duality, the translator, who speaks in two languages that link body and soul.

GEMINIAN LUCKY CONNECTIONS

Color	orange	Metal	quicksilver
Plants	orchid and hybrids	Tarot card	the lovers
Perfume	lavender	Animal	magpie
Gemstone	tourmaline		

THE GEMINIAN LOOK

People who exhibit the physical characteristics distinctive of the sign of Gemini are tall and upright. The youthful look is typical of Gemini. People who always look younger than their actual age, at any stage of life, will have a strong Gemini influence somewhere in their birth chart. Most typical Geminis are light on their feet, regardless of their body size.

BARE FACTS

We can't tell you how many times we've overheard a Gemini at a party trotting out that same lame excuse, "I wish I was thinner, but unfortunately my zodiac neighbors are Taurus and Cancer."

THE GEMINI MALE
Appearance

The typical Gemini man
- is taller than average
- has a pale, rough complexion that will become weather-beaten easily
- is very agile
- has a high forehead and receding hairline
- has quick, darting eyes

Behavior and personality traits

The typical Gemini man
- is eager and always on the move
- is friendly and persuasive
- can sell almost anything to almost anyone
- has a great deal of nervous energy
- can talk himself out of difficulties
- can do two things at once
- likes people
- is adroit, diplomatic, and socially able
- may change his occupation frequently
- is intelligent and witty

COMMUNICATION

Gemini Male = Used Car Salesman on crack.

THE GEMINI FEMALE
Appearance

The typical Gemini woman

• is tall and slender, unless there is a strong Taurus influence causing plumpness
• has very beautiful eyes
• has long arms and legs
• has exquisitely expressive hands
• moves quickly

Behavior and personality traits

The typical Gemini woman

• is a lively conversationalist
• has many interests
• is a composite of many personalities
• is a great friend, taking an interest in any new subject
• will want to have a career
• seeks true romance but finds it hard to settle down
• is a deep thinker and often very intuitive
• will never turn down a cry for help
• is optimistic
• notices every detail
• can be charming and very persuasive

YOU'RE WELCOME FOR THE TIP

Gemini Female = The hottest civil servant you have ever seen.

YOUNG GEMINI

Behavior and personality traits

The typical Gemini child

- can seem to be in two places at once
- loves chattering
- will become irritable if cooped up
- needs lots of space to explore
- is friendly
- is bright and alert
- can be quite precocious
- usually learns to read very quickly
- likes to use his or her hands and fingers
- may be ambidextrous
- can often mimic others

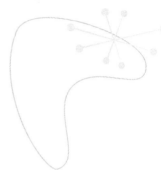

Bringing up young Gemini

Most Geminis have an insatiable inquisitiveness about everything. They like to explore, follow whatever catches their interest, and literally get their fingers into everything. Gemini children tend to live in a world where imagination and reality are so mixed together that it is hard for them to learn where one begins and the other ends. These children will want to be friends with both sexes. As they grow up, they will have a variety of boyfriends or girlfriends. When they actually become emotionally involved with someone they will often pretend they are not interested, because emotional involvement leaves them totally confused. Children of both sexes will be keenly interested in a wide variety of sports.

Young Gemini's needs

The Gemini child needs the freedom to explore, investigate, and learn. Frequent opportunities to change direction, and follow several lines of interest at once, are essential. They need to be understood more than anything. The love that Gemini children need is the attention of those who accept them for what they are and go along with them in their dreams. Confinement and boredom are the worst horrors to a little Gemini.

GEMINI AT HOME
Typical behavior and abilities

When at home, a Gemini man or woman
- likes space to move around in
- will enjoy using gadgets and all the latest technology, especially information technology
- considers a telephone absolutely essential
- will have some form of transport standing by so he or she can take off on the spur of the moment

- will have a bright, cheerful home, surrounded by the evidence of many interests
- enjoys company
- has a deep need for tenderness and emotional warmth, for which he or she finds it very hard to ask

Gemini as parent

The typical Gemini parent
- can get on a child's wavelength very easily
- will enjoy playing with and teaching his or her children
- may find it hard to show his or her real emotions
- uses rational arguments to explain things

Two Geminis in the same family

Unless one or both have planets in the earthy or fixed signs, two Geminis in one family means there will be at least four personalities flitting around. Geminis can get along well, provided both have enough space. They will happily talk with each other, absorbing and discussing all the new facts they can find. However, if two Geminis get into an emotional argument, sparks fly because Geminis can be very confused by and feel threatened by strong emotions, especially their own.

YOU'RE WELCOME FOR THE TIP

The Gemini home is all-too easily disrupted. A Geminian can wake up liking the toilet paper roll coming over the top, and by the time he or she has showered and dressed, will suddenly favor it under the bottom. This is to say nothing of squeezing the toothpaste tube in the middle, or asking for a divorce.

GEMINI AT WORK
Typical behavior and abilities

A typical Gemini at work
- gets things done
- works better with people around
- can deal with emergencies quickly
- will try anything once
- needs variety

Gemini as employer

A typical Gemini boss (male or female)
- is not dogmatic
- delegates astutely and concentrates on schemes to increase profits and cut costs
- makes changes to improve communication and productivity
- is impatient with mundane administration
- will inspect, notice, and question every aspect of every department
- will classify his or her workers' talents
- enjoys building goodwill and increasing client orders by meeting clients in restaurants, on the golf course, or anywhere out on the road in places near or far

Gemini as employee

A typical Gemini employee (male or female)
- can charm his or her way through an interview
- is good at thinking, new ideas, and details
- makes jokes and small talk, and gets things done
- will get bored and fail to carry through an idea if too much red tape holds up a project
- enjoys fast action and quick returns

Working environment

The workplace of a typical Gemini man or woman (if it has to be in a fixed place) must be spacious and stimulating

Typical occupations

Geminis are good in any kind of work that involves public relations, selling, or getting information and ideas across to others such as teaching, writing and work in any of the media. Their quick minds, combined with dexterous abilities, lead some to become surgeons, scientific researchers, artists, or musicians. Because they love words and ideas, they may become politicians or actors.

♡ GEMINI AND LOVE

To Gemini, love is a romantic ideal, which can only be achieved with the soul mate. Consequently, many Geminis may flirt and have frequent affairs, looking for that perfect romantic love. The characteristics of Gemini in love are listed below.

Behavior when in love

The typical Gemini
• is overwhelmed by confusing emotions
• may appear cool and distant
• will think things through rather than act spontaneously

- needs a rational understanding of love
- tends to repress very strong emotions
- is acutely sensitive and open to hurt
- can become emotionally dependent
- feels very deeply but finds it very hard to express love

Expectations

The typical Gemini expects
- to be understood
- their partner to be emotionally telepathic
- sympathy and tenderness
- personal freedom for self and partner
- to enjoy flirting
- faithfulness of partner

BARE FACTS

Guys, if you have a Madonna/whore complex, this Gemini's for you! Gals . . . you're in for a world of hurt. We just don't know how else to put it.

The end of an affair

An affair will end when a Gemini gets bored or when a partner begins to make too many emotional demands or restrict the Gemini's personal freedom. The end may seem like a sudden decision, but it never is; the decision to leave a lover will have been made only after much mental unhappiness. Once the decision has been made, Geminis have no difficulty in communicating that an affair is at an end; they just cool off, freeze the partner out, or vanish. If the partner ends the relationship, Gemini will be deeply hurt and feel insecure and at a loss. The more outward Geminis may hide these feelings behind a sudden outburst of scathing anger, while the quieter ones will probably try to look cool. Either way, Gemini will put on a show of confidence and continue searching for perfect love.

COMMUNICATION

Hey, Geminis, we know break-ups are painful for you, but "getting back on the horse" is just an expression. Boy, you people really are insatiably curious!

GEMINI AND PARTNER

The person who contemplates becoming the marriage or business partner of a typical Gemini must realize that Gemini has probably already had more than one partner and will not stay long with a person who either clings or dominates. Given this, the person who partners a Gemini can expect the talents of at least six people wrapped up in the one Gemini.

Gemini man as partner

He will want a partner who will never attempt to dominate him, nor bore him with endless personal problems. He will be drawn either to someone who will help him climb the professional or social ladder, or a person who will stimulate him with bright ideas. Because he loves to travel, he will be delighted by a partner who will travel with him—or accept his absences without question.

Gemini woman as partner

She will be attracted to a person who can give her emotional security so that she can relax and enjoy expressing her many talents and her "multipersonality." Often the partnership will be short-lived because the restless Gemini nature always wants to be on the move. Many partners fail to understand the need of the mercurial butterfly to have a partner who will fly with her, helping her to find the peace she truly desires.

DON'T BE A JERK

"Don't you see, honey? It's just that I'm a mercurial butterfly." Gee, hard to imagine why anyone would have a problem grasping that concept!

Opposite sign

Sagittarius is the complementary opposite sign to Gemini. From Sagittarius, Geminis can learn to take a broader view of things and to give some structure to the mass of information they collect—and so eventually find the truth.

Sagittarius

Gemini

BARE FACTS

Sagittarius = Glutton for punishment.

GEMINI AND FRIENDS

In general, Gemini likes a friend who is curious about the world and enjoys lively, intelligent conversation.

Positive factors

Geminis generally enjoy people who respond to, or suggest, spontaneous activities. They will run to help you when you are in need. A Gemini friend is full of life, often a Peter Pan, and always eager to be off on a new adventure. They will keep friends amused with endless stories, bits of information, or network gossip.

STRETCHING THE TRUTH

Many Geminis identify so strongly with Peter Pan that they invest in an intricate series of wires that allow them to "fly" around the house. What sucks about being a friend to a Gemini is that whenever you come over you get roped into operating the damn machinery. (NOTE: It is not a coincidence that Peter Pan, a boy, is traditionally played by a woman. We told you this hermaphrodite stuff really screws with a Gemini's head.)

Negative factors

Gemini never wants to miss a thing, and so may be inclined to be early or late for meetings. Stretching or elaborating the truth is not uncommon; Geminis can hardly resist adding extra space to make it more interesting. A compatibility chart on page 62 lists those with whom Gemini is likely to have the most satisfactory relationships.

GEMINIAN LEISURE INTERESTS

SECRET TIP

Excerpt from a typical Geminian personal ad:
"I like candlelight dinners, walks on the beach, and
pseudonyms." Whoa, pseudonyms. Make me hot!
Most typical Geminis like communication, such as
conversation, radio, television, the telephone, letter
writing, sending postcards, and faxes.

On the whole, typical Geminis pursue the following leisure interests:
• "light" sports, e.g., table tennis, archery, darts, pool, bowling
• travel, short or long journeys
• newspapers, magazines, quizzes, crosswords
• public speaking, variety shows, dancing
• discovering and exploring something new
• learning and using languages
• using hands and fingers for crafts, etc.

COMPATIBILITY CHART

In general, if people are typical of their zodiac sign, relationships between Gemini and other signs (including the complementary opposite sign, Sagittarius, are as shown below:

	Harmonious	Difficult	Turbulent
Gemini	•		
Cancer	•		
Leo	•		
Virgo		•	
Libra	•		
Scorpio			•
Sagittarius		•	
Capricorn			•
Aquarius	•		
Pisces		•	
Aries	•		
Taurus	•		

GEMINIAN LIKES AND DISLIKES

Likes

- being free to move around
- knowledge, information
- the excitement of travel
- acting quickly on decisions
- talking
- variety, novelty, change
- telephones, gadgets, instant food
- company, being among people
- acting as devil's advocate
- pseudonyms
- doing several things at once
- getting to the bottom of things

Dislikes

- listening to endless complaints
- making irrevocable commitments
- regimentation
- being defeated
- not knowing what's going on
- fixed ideas
- wasting time
- having to concentrate on only one thing for a long time
- being kept waiting

GEMINIAN HEALTH

Typical Geminis are healthy as long as they have plenty of room to breathe and space to explore. They are liable to collapse from nervous exhaustion if they don't find a personally satisfying way to relax. Geminis are not often heard to complain. On the rare times when sickness strikes them, they may get irritated when well-intentioned people ask how they are.

Types of sickness

Coughs, colds, bronchitis, speech problems, and other chest/lung complaints are most typical of Geminian ill health. Whenever physical misfortune strikes, the person who behaves in the way typical of Gemini is likely to hide the most serious side of things and make even less of the least serious aspect. Geminis usually hate being confined to bed and are restless until they finally exhaust themselves.

Gemini at rest

There is no such animal as a Gemini at rest. Even when apparently relaxed by a winter's fire after playing in the snow with the children all afternoon, the Gemini mind will be at work, inventing a new gadget to make, thinking up a new idea, working over a problem, or rehearsing a conversation to be held with a colleague.

WELL LOOK WHO FINALLY MADE THE RODEO

To sum up, the typical Geminian needs constant stimulation and longs for inner peace. Kind of like the Dalai Lama combined with your dog.

4. Cancer: The Crab
June 21 - July 22

The FOURTH sign of the zodiac is concerned with
- receptivity, sensitivity, defense
- home, protection, comfort, domesticity
- food, nurturing instincts
- nostalgia, sentiment, roots, antiques
- money, business, response to public need
- dreams, the psychic, telepathy
- family, history, memory, patriotism

Elemental quality

Cancer is the cardinal water sign of the zodiac. It can be likened to a safe harbor in which boats can take shelter from the dangers on the sea of life. Water finds its own level—it settles. The metaphorical harbor is the way Cancer provides a safe and organized place for human activity, setting each ship in its allotted place.

THE CANCERIAN PERSONALITY

CHARACTERISTICS

Positive
- Tenacious
- Shrewd and intuitive
- Kind
- Compassionate
- Domesticated
- Good memory
- Helpful
- Caring
- Sensitive to need
- Protective

Negative
- Possessive
- Too easily hurt
- Moody
- Crabby
- Matriarchal
- Holds on to insults
- Selfish
- Manipulative
- Introspective
- Overpowering

LISTEN UP, THIS IS IMPORTANT

Combine "tenacious" from the positive column with any of the qualities in the negative column, and you really have to question whether Cancerians are worth the time.

Ruling planet and its effect

The Moon rules the zodiac sign of Cancer, so anyone whose birth chart has a strong Cancerian influence will absorb and accurately reflect every emotion that is experienced.

In astrology, the Moon's cycle of waxing and waning is a metaphor for the cycle of changing moods of the Cancerian personality, who can experience periods of wondrous elation and of crabby depression. The Moon is also associated with oddities and, when in the mood, Cancerian humor can be quite crazy—almost lunatic. Cancerian humor provides some of the best comedy in the world of entertainment, because it is always based on an accurate observation of human nature.

CANCERIAN LUCKY CONNECTIONS

Colors	yellow, orange, and indigo	Metal	silver
Plants	lotus, moonwort, and almond	Tarot card	the chariot
Perfume	onycha	Animals	crab, turtle,
Gemstones	pearl, amber, and moonstone		and sphinx

THE CANCERIAN LOOK

People who exhibit the physical characteristics distinctive of the sign of Cancer are of three facial types. Whichever type they are, they have very expressive faces. Every mood, emotion, and fleeting response shows in the changing features of the Cancerian face.

♂ THE CANCER MALE
Appearance

The typical Cancer man
- has a fairly bony structure
- may have remarkable teeth, perhaps prominent, irregular, or in some way unusual
- if crab-faced, he will have a prominent lower jaw
- may have broad shoulders
- even if slim, may appear broad or plump
- may be plump or tend to put on weight very easily

Behavior and personality traits

The typical Cancerian man
- is extremely sensitive
- wears clothes with a conservative cut
- does not like to be conspicuous
- has some favorite old casual clothes that he always wears; he would be very cranky if anyone threw out his precious old sweater
- does not push himself into the limelight
- enjoys the limelight if it turns on him for a while
- dislikes discussing his personal life
- loves security, money, food, and children
- uses roundabout tactics to get what he wants
- has an uncanny business sense
- is usually very attached to his mother

COMMUNICATION

Cancer Male = A slightly more dangerous version of the guys who play the dads on TV shows.

THE CANCER FEMALE
Appearance

The typical Cancer woman
• has a face that is typically round and soft but may be a crab type as described on page 67
• may be flat-chested or have a large bust
• has hips that are often slimmer than her bust
• puts on weight easily in middle age
• has a strong bone structure
• has very expressive eyes
• has long arms and legs compared with her body
• has large and long or small and chubby hands and feet

Behavior and personality traits

The typical Cancer woman
• is introspective and emotional
• uses her intuition more often than logic
• will use all her nurturing instincts to care for and protect friends and family
• wants material security and comfort
• never does anything impulsively
• is shy but very sexual
• easily takes offense at minor insults
• is patient, subtle, and often unconsciously manipulative

SECRET TIP

Cancer Female = Nice to have on your arm, but dances like a gibbon having an exorcism.

YOUNG CANCER
Behavior and personality traits

The typical Cancer child
• changes mood frequently
• loves delicious food and drinks but almost always dribbles even when past babyhood
• is fascinated by colors and pictures
• will remember every experience right into adulthood
• longs to be hugged, loved, and encouraged
• withdraws inwardly from any kind of rejection
• can play alone for hours
• often invents invisible playmates
• may cry a lot and use tears to get what he or she wants
• when older, Cancerian children seek any kind of job to earn money and save it

Bringing up young Cancer

Most Cancerians are delightful, fascinating children whose faces show every changing mood. They love to use their imaginations and are easy to manage and discipline when young, providing they are given a lot of warmth, approval, and attention. Parents should laugh and cry with a Cancerian infant and give constant reassurance when he or she is fearful, which is likely to be often. Cancerian children are usually docile and well mannered, but prefer to be the leader rather than the follower.

BARE FACTS

Part of the difficulty in raising a young Cancerian is in trying to explain to them that being constantly fearful, docile and moody tends to put the kibosh on the whole "leader" thing.

Young Cancer's needs

Cancerian children are very sensitive to emotional hurts and rejections and must have parental support at these times. If they feel rejected and unloved they will grow up to be reclusive, withdrawing permanently inside their shell in self-protection.

 ## CANCER AT HOME
Typical behavior and abilities

At home, a Cancerian man or woman
- is capable of most kinds of home improvement jobs
- can cook and will keep a well-stocked kitchen
- feels safe and secure and so can relax
- will tend the garden
- may have collections of antiques
- spoils all visitors
- will hoard anything seen as potentially valuable

Cancer as parent

The typical Cancer parent
- may worry too much about their offspring
- will protect and support the children
- may be over-possessive
- will enjoy looking after and playing with the babies
- will do anything to help and encourage the children's creative development
- remembers every birthday and anniversary

Two Cancerians in the same family

If the mutual need for security and reassurance can be satisfied, two Cancerians can get along well. Their greatest conflicts will arise when they disagree about intuitive matters. Together they can work very well at a moneymaking activity. The Cancerian sensitivity may result in some highly emotional moments, but as long as each person has a creative outlet, all will be well. The Cancerian sense of humor should be encouraged and will relax any stressful moments that arise from Cancerian selfishness.

 # CANCER AT WORK
Typical behavior and abilities

A typical Cancerian at work
- is there to make money
- takes work seriously and works hard
- will take responsibility
- responds to affectionate appreciation
- works steadily and is reliable

Cancer as employer

A typical Cancerian boss (male or female)
- expects his or her people to be neatly dressed
- takes work seriously and does not like frivolity
- has one aim: to make money
- drives a hard bargain but is fair
- rarely forgets anything
- generously rewards hard work

Cancer as employee

A typical Cancerian employee (male or female)
- will work hard for money because a good bank balance makes him or her feel secure
- will accept discipline calmly

- expects the rate of pay to increase steadily in response to increased output and responsibility
- enjoys taking responsibility

Working environment
The workplace of a typical Cancerian man or woman
- must be comfortable and secure
- will have family photos displayed
- will be organized for hard work
- should be furnished with the best quality tools
- a location near water would be an added bonus

BARE FACTS

Actually, a location near water and a very steep cliff would be ideal.

Typical occupations
Occupations that attract typical Cancerians are the food industry, such as baking, candy making, catering, nutrition, hotel or domestic work; animal breeding; horticulture; gardening; anything connected with boats, water, ponds, rivers, fountains, pools, fishing; any kind of trading; counseling; psychotherapy; social work; nursing; obstetrics; political work connected with any of these.

♡ CANCER AND LOVE
For a Cancerian, love thrives when there is a combination of constant affection with a healthy bank balance and substantial assets. A Cancerian in love will have many of the characteristics listed on page 73.

Behavior when in love

The typical Cancerian

- will rarely make the first move
- fears he or she will be rejected
- will retreat, deeply hurt, at the first sign of ridicule or criticism
- will respond to honest warmth and affection
- can become tenaciously attached to the loved one
- is a romantic at heart
- will put the loved one first in all things

Expectations

The typical Cancer expects

- to be loved forever
- to have his or her cooking appreciated
- to work hard for money and security
- the family to come first in all things
- to be needed as a tower of strength and refuge
- unshakable loyalty and devotion

LISTEN UP, THIS IS IMPORTANT

Cancerians need constant reinforcement, and live in constant fear of rejection, ridicule and criticism. That is so hot!

The end of an affair

The confusion between emotional hunger and love can lead to relationship problems. Cancerians often feel they are not loved enough, and so make draining demands on any partner who seems to have become uninterested. The Cancerian will cling more tightly as a relationship deteriorates, making separation very difficult. If the partner has been

unfaithful, the Cancerian will become very jealous and may react aggressively because the hurt is so great. On the other hand, a Cancerian who feels unloved may secretly wander off to find someone else to satisfy their strong emotional needs. Even so, they will resist divorce, no matter how unpleasant the marriage becomes as a consequence.

SECRETS TO MAKE YOU LOOK GOOD

Whoever did that painting of all those bodies writhing in hell had obviously just broken up with a Cancerian.

CANCER AND PARTNER

The person who contemplates becoming the marriage or business partner of a typical Cancerian must realize that Cancer will want to be the dominant partner and will expect total devotion. Given this, the person who partners Cancer can expect consideration, prosperity, and a strong sense of belonging to family or company. The contented Cancerian will never let the partner down.

Cancerian man as partner

He will want a partner who will nurture him and take care of all the domestic details, making sure he has a comfortable nest to return to after a day's work. In marriage or business, he will want others around him. If the marriage proves to be childless, adoption or fostering are likely. A business is itself seen as a family. He will not usually enjoy working freelance.

Cancerian woman as partner

She will seek a partner as soon as she leaves the parental home—someone who will luxuriate in her protective caring. She will devote herself completely to the partner, even taking subtle control of him or her. In business, she will be an excellent manager. A Cancerian woman will want a family, and if denied the joy of children will acquire a household full of animals instead. The Cancer wife is never a dependent when it comes to earning money. She will take a job outside the home to enhance the family's financial security.

Opposite sign

Capricorn is the complementary opposite sign to Cancer, and forms the paternal complement to Cancerian materialism. From Capricorn the Cancerian can learn how to distinguish reality from imagination, thus getting things into the right perspective and consequently making better judgments.

Capricorn

Cancer

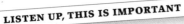

LISTEN UP, THIS IS IMPORTANT

Hey, Cancer! You want a Capricorn? You can't handle a Capricorn!

CANCER AND FRIENDS

In general, Cancer likes friends who will support his or her emotional and financial needs when necessary—and Cancer will reciprocate.

Positive factors

Friends are, in many ways, regarded as family possessions themselves and are treated as such, with loving care, protective hospitality, sensitive consideration, and great tenderness. Although some friends may come and go, friends from younger days are the most precious.

COMMUNICATION

There's no other way to put this: Cancerians' longest-lasting friendships are with co-dependent losers who keep putting up with their crap.

Negative factors

When he or she is hurt by a friend, the Cancerian anger may last for a long time and the friend may be abandoned. However, if the friend is an old friend, then the emotional attachment will finally lead to reconciliation. Cancerians do tend to set their own standards by the progress their friends are making. A compatibility chart on page 78 lists those with whom a Cancerian is likely to have the most satisfactory relationships.

CANCERIAN LEISURE INTERESTS

On the whole, typical Cancerians pursue the following leisure interests:
• boating, sailing, swimming
• water sports that are played in teams
• fishing and gardening
• keeping and breeding animals
• building collections
• keeping in contact with family members

COMPATIBILITY CHART

In general, if people are typical of their zodiac sign, relationships between Cancer and other signs (including the complementary opposite sign, Capricorn) are as shown below:

	Harmonious	Difficult	Turbulent
Cancer	•		
Leo	•		
Virgo	•		
Libra		•	
Scorpio	•		
Sagittarius			•
Capricorn		•	
Aquarius			•
Pisces	•		
Aries		•	
Taurus	•		
Gemini	•		

CANCERIAN LIKES AND DISLIKES

Likes
- anyone who loves his or her mother
- sentimental and family keepsakes
- gourmet food
- shopping trips
- history, especially family genealogy
- any demonstration of affection such as flowers
- a birthday card on the right date
- the company of other people
- a calm working atmosphere
- physical contact

Dislikes
- any tiny criticism of the home
- having to handle a crisis
- pressure to take part in conversation
- anyone who refuses their cooking
- people who forget names and dates (Cancerians have excellent memories themselves)

CANCERIAN HEALTH

Typical Cancerians are calm, docile people able to withstand sickness as long as they have material security, plenty of affection, and are needed by several people. Their greatest problems can arise from worries caused by a lack of these things

Types of sickness

Some Cancerians are complainers when they feel not enough affectionate attention is coming their way, yet when an illness slowly creeps up on them, they are remarkably tough and complain less and less. A melancholy or full depression may then be evident. Typical illnesses often arise from the upper digestive tract, especially the stomach. Indigestion, coughs, anemia, and lowered vitality are common. Cancerians may also suffer from eating disorders.

SECRET TIP

For the Cancerian, a bathroom cabinet well-stocked with antacid, cough syrup and iron supplements is usually better than sex.

Cancer at rest

Extending the metaphor of Cancer as the cardinal water sign, it follows that emotion in action is the key to understanding how Cancerians relax. Although they do enjoy lounging around, preferably on or near water, they are at their most relaxed when their busy emotional sensors are satisfied by being surrounded by the warmth of a contented family atmosphere. When on vacation, Cancerians most enjoy a home away from home, which may mean a luxurious trailer or RV. They can also relax in the peace of a comfortably furnished period house, and generally prefer old buildings to modern styles.

WELL LOOK WHO FINALLY MADE THE RODEO

To sum up, those born under the sign of Cancer live in a somewhat paranoid, unhappy world, and tend to cling to those around them to see them through. They also have a few unattractive qualities.

5. Leo: The Lion
July 23 - August 22

The FIFTH sign of the zodiac is concerned with
- pleasures, fun, playfulness, entertainment
- creativity, recognition, compliments
- romance, love affairs, sex, offspring
- children, childlike activities, childishness
- taking risks, gambling, sports, games
- performance, drama, limelight, applause
- hospitality, appreciation

Elemental quality

Leo is the fixed fire sign of the zodiac. It can be likened to a fire burning in its appropriate place, such as a campfire or a bonfire around which everyone can gather. Leos like transforming things. Leos may be loyal, stubborn, and proud of their achievements.

LEONINE LUCKY CONNECTIONS			
Colors	yellow, orange	Metal	gold
Plants	sunflower, laurel	Tarot card	fortitude
Perfume	olibanum	Animals	lion
Gemstones	cat's eye, olivine		

CHARACTERISTICS

Positive

- Honesty and loyalty
- A sunny disposition
- A sense of dignity
- Pride in the home
- Attractive liveliness
- Friendliness and kindness
- Generosity and hospitality
- Acceptance of people at face value
- A mature sense of responsibility
- Courageousness to the point of self-sacrifice

Negative

- Stubbornness or willfulness
- Contempt or arrogance
- Sulkiness
- Smugness or boasting
- Indifference or an uncaring attitude
- A tendency to take undue credit
- A tendency to cut others down to size
- A tendency to keep up appearances
- Coldhearted when hurt

Ruling planet and its effect

The Sun rules the zodiac sign of Leo, so anyone whose birth chart has a strong Leo influence may expect things in life to orbit around them. In astrology, the Sun is the life giver and the source of creativity. Like the Sun, Leos can be a source of life-enhancing warmth, joy, and pleasure to friends and family.

SECRET TIP

Also much like the Sun, Leos like nothing better than to temporarily blind you, make you sweat and put you at risk for skin cancer. This is all metaphorically speaking, of course.

THE LEONINE LOOK

People who exhibit the physical characteristics distinctive of the sign of Leo look majestic. They may seem tall if (typically) they are proud of their appearance. They are either very particular about their looks or apparently somewhat careless. Either way their appearance catches the attention of others—a usual Leo trait.

SECRETS TO MAKE YOU LOOK GOOD

You have to have a strong voice when you spend most of your time bullsh**ting.

THE LEO MALE
Appearance

The typical Leo man
• has a well-proportioned body
• is slim and athletic if he takes care of himself
• if disabled, will fight to regain prowess in some sports-related aspect
• has sex appeal and may be a playboy when young
• walks tall with a noble bearing
• dresses to impress

Behavior and personality traits

The typical Leo man
• likes to show off
• is trusting
• appears to be in control of himself
• gives and expects loyalty
• likes everything he does to be exciting

- is generous with affection and money
- likes an elegant environment
- is popular
- needs to be adored
- uses charm to get what he wants

 # THE LEO FEMALE
Appearance

The typical Leo woman
- is slim and elegant
- if disabled, will use the disability to her advantage, making it attractive
- has sex appeal
- appears to possess an inner sense of royalty
- is well dressed
- looks attractive even in adverse circumstances
- exudes dignity and class

Behavior and personality traits

The typical Leo woman
- likes to show off in subtle ways
- is trusting and loyal
- is never docile or adoring in affairs of the heart but gives respect, warmth, and real emotional commitment
- likes everything she does to be exciting
- is generous with affection and hospitality

- likes an elegant environment
- is a social leader
- needs to be admired
- uses courtesy to get what she wants

LISTEN UP, THIS IS IMPORTANT

Leo Female = Katharine Hepburn meets one of those chicks from WWF.

YOUNG LEO
Behavior and personality traits

The typical Leo child
- is sunny and friendly
- has a bottomless well of energy
- is more often on the move than still
- loves games and physical play
- when tired often falls fast asleep for a while
- loves to be the center of attention
- is adventurous and sometimes reckless
- likes to be waited on
- dislikes menial tasks
- loves parties
- is generous with whatever is seen as his or hers

Bringing up young Leo

Most Leos enjoy the limelight at school and often take the lead. As they grow up, they will be attracted to the opposite sex and fall in and out of love. Their emotions will be turbulent and often dramatic. To be able to grow and experiment, both sexes need freedom, which they will use well if they have become used to a discipline that is tempered with love. Leo girls are naturally happiest when doing something physical.

Young Leo's needs

Young Leo needs plenty of love and honest compliments. Lies, even flattering ones, are very hurtful to the trusting Leo child. He or she also needs a good balance of affection and discipline: plenty of hugs and praise for their achievements.

STRETCHING THE TRUTH

Seventy-five percent of parents raising Leo children report running out of anything to praise them for after about a year.

LEO AT HOME
Typical behavior and abilities

At home, a Leo man or woman
• is head of the household
• creates an elegant, comfortable home
• offers superb hospitality
• expects others to respect his or her territory
• is able to fix most practical things
• enjoys entertaining
• shows courage and strength in emergencies

Leo as parent

The typical Leo parent

- is conscientious about bringing up children
- wants to be proud of offspring
- may put too much pressure to succeed on children
- expects to be loved and appreciated by offspring
- is capable of giving great warmth
- knows how to play with children
- is generous with pocket money
- insists on honesty
- makes every effort to teach children many things

COMMUNICATION

Yes, it's fun and entertaining to be at home with a Leo. But, once they have a kid, they put all their energies into messing them up with unrealistic expectations. (See also: the other eleven signs of the Zodiac.)

Two Leos in the same family

Leos can be happily married to each other once they realize they both have similar needs for love and adoration. Two Leos in the same family, whether parents or children, can get along well together if they each have a castle of their own on which they can stand and be admired. Each needs to be a leader in his or her own field. If one feels he or she is receiving less praise than the other, there could be some very dramatic quarrels. Otherwise, a home with Leos in it will be a happy, exciting, and relaxing place.

So, basically, as long as each Leo accepts that the other owes them total worship, maintains their own castle-like domain where they can have their ego stroked 24/7, and allows for violent temper tantrums after losing arguments, it's smooth sailing!

LEO AT WORK
Typical behavior and abilities

A typical Leo at work
- gives a good first impression at interviews
- is able to act a part or exaggerate when necessary
- must be in charge of something
- can work very hard
- finds it difficult to apologize

Leo as employer

A typical Leo boss (male or female)
- has huge self-confidence
- can get everyone working hard for him or her
- loses confidence if his or her authority is undermined
- is thoughtful toward workers and their families
- is generous with praise and compliments
- enjoys showing people how to do things
- tends to take the credit for everyone's success
- cannot tolerate failure
- can charm people into working devotedly

Leo as employee

A typical Leo employee (male or female)

- needs to have his or her superiority recognized
- works hard
- is very loyal
- can keep customers happy
- makes a good show person
- responds to genuine praise of his or her efforts

BARE FACTS

Leos traditionally spend very little time as employees, since their ability to snow everyone into working their ass off, their refusal to tolerate failure, and their tendency to take credit for stuff someone else did soon gets them a promotion to boss.

Working environment

The workplace of a typical Leo man or woman

- is convenient and comfortable
- has an air of luxury
- usually has pictures on the wall
- often has status symbols displayed
- is a place that inspires admiration

Typical occupations

Leo is often associated with leadership, promotion and sales, any job, which has a special title, acting, directing, teaching, politics, public relations, management, the law, or a self-employed skill or business. Leo often shows his or her inner strengths when under great pressure or when a crisis occurs.

LEO AND LOVE

To Leo, love is a dramatic ideal. Male Leos seem to have no trouble attracting women, while female Leos attract many men with their natural beauty and liveliness. The typical Leo in love will have many of the characteristics listed below.

Behavior when in love

The typical Leo
- is romantic and proud of it
- becomes more regal and noble
- is very generous to the person who is loved
- is attentive and loyal to the loved one
- is radiant with happiness
- is caring, protective, and supportive
- will make great sacrifices for love
- will fight to the death for the loved one

Expectations

The typical Leo expects
- to be adored by the loved one
- to be the envy of others

- to be treated like royalty
- his or her love to be seen as very special
- total commitment from their loved one
- the partner to be dependent in some way

The end of an affair

If Leo's passions cool, the partner is still needed, but more as a friend than a lover, which may cause problems and lead to parting or divorce if the partner does not like this arrangement. When a Leo wants to end an affair of the heart, pride may make it very difficult for the Leo to say straight out that things are finished. Consequently, some Leos deal with this problem by withdrawing from contact or even by behaving badly toward the partner. If the partner does not confront the Leo and continues to cling, he or she can become quite psychologically cruel, treating the discarded partner with disdain. The partner who is unfaithful to Leo, or who walks out on a serious love affair, will leave behind a very wounded person. It will take Leo months to recover from such a deep hurt and may make him or her very wary of risking serious love again.

LEO AND PARTNER

The person who contemplates becoming the marriage or business partner of a typical Leo must realize that Leo will believe that he or she is superior in some way or other. Given this, the person who partners a Leo can expect warmth, loyalty, support, generosity, and undying devotion. Only lazy, foolish Leos look for a partner who will worship them.

Leo man as partner

He will want a partner who enhances his own image and who enjoys being in the spotlight as much as he does. The partner must be good-looking but should not outshine Leo himself. The Leo man wants a marriage partner who will place him at the head of the table and believe in his dreams. She will be a woman of good manners who will never do anything to tarnish her own, and therefore his, reputation and she will be a devoted mother to their children.

Leo woman as partner

The typical Leo woman looks for a partner who will install her as queen of the whole neighborhood. He must provide her with a house she can make into a welcoming place, where she can entertain with enthusiasm and generous hospitality. With the right partner, a lady Leo will rise in social status due to her boundless strength and persistence. Consequently, her light will shine on her partner too. The Leo woman will take the responsibility of motherhood in her stride and will expect her partner to be as devoted to the children as she is.

DON'T BE A JERK

The man who marries a Leo woman must possess a generous mixture of stupidity, dumbness and idiocy.

Opposite sign

Aquarius, the water-carrier, is the complementary opposite sign to Leo. There may be tough relations between them, but Aquarius can show Leo how to share without needing appreciation, and give the center stage to others. In this way Leos can learn to stand alone and value themselves.

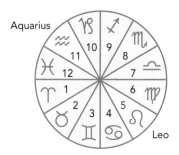

LEO AND FRIENDS

In general, Leos like their friends to be successful, but not so successful as to completely outshine and detract from Leo!

Positive factors

Leos are friendly, warm, and often playful. They enjoy their friends and are proud of them; they are generous to their friends, but the friends are expected to show their gratitude, either in kind or by performance, putting Leo's support to good use.

Negative factors

A friend who in some way fails a Leo, perhaps by seeming to criticize or failing to appreciate something Leo sees as very important, may be dropped without explanation. A friend, partner, or business associate who has personal aspirations may find it increasingly impossible to take second billing to a Leo, and so may end the relationship. A compatibility chart on page 95 illustrates those with whom Leo is likely to have the most satisfactory relationships.

SECRET TIP

It may seem remarkable that so many different signs of the Zodiac have harmonious relationships with Leo, until you consider that most of the harmony was beaten into them.

COMPATIBILITY CHART

In general, if people are typical of their zodiac sign, relationships between Leo and other signs (including the complementary opposite sign, Aquarius) are as shown below:

	Harmonious	Difficult	Turbulent
Leo	•		
Virgo	•		
Libra	•		
Scorpio		•	
Sagittarius	•		
Capricorn			•
Aquarius		•	
Pisces			•
Aries	•		
Taurus		•	
Gemini	•		
Cancer	•		

LEONINE LEISURE INTERESTS

Typical Leos like to follow an exercise routine. Done sensibly, this will strengthen any weak points. As Leos always want to be outstanding in anything they do, they should beware of overdoing exercise—it may make them vulnerable to stress reactions. On the whole, typical Leos pursue the following leisure interests:

• any sport that offers skill with grace
• tennis, diving, running, dancing
• driving, rallying, cycling
• theater and dramatic activities
• family party games
• eating out

COMMUNICATION

One of Leo's favorite family party games is "Pin the Tail on My Social Inferior."

LEONINE HEALTH

Typical Leos are happy, healthy, energetic people as long as they are loved. Only when seriously deprived of affection or appreciation will a Leo tend to look haggard and be heard complaining about life.

Types of sickness

High fevers, sudden illnesses, and accidents are typical of Leonine ill health. Whatever physical misfortune strikes, the person who behaves in a way typical of Leo will enjoy only a brief period of being spoiled in the sickbed before he or she is up again and on the go. To be incapacitated for long is a sign of weakness to a Leo. This desire to get up too soon after an illness may mean that a health problem recurs.

Leo at rest

Extending the metaphor of Leo as the fixed fire sign, it follows that the fire in the grate will sometimes burn brightly and be a center of warmth and delight to everyone who gathers around it. However, fires do go out and have to be relit. So it is with typical Leonine energy. The Leo will sometimes need to rest, relax, and have catnaps. This should not be mistaken for incipient sickness or laziness. Once revitalized, the typical Leo will be on the go again for hours.

WELL LOOK WHO FINALLY MADE THE RODEO

In summation, Leo's are willful, determined people who are better left alone, yet have a seductive energy that can be difficult to resist. Sometimes life is just not fair.

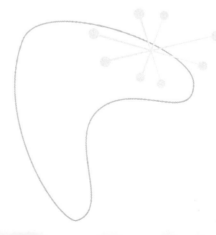

6. Virgo: The Virgin
August 23 – September 22

The SIXTH sign of the zodiac is concerned with
• self-perfection, critical faculties
• altruism, honesty, responsibility
• cleanliness, hygiene, health, healing
• efficiency, daily routines, reliability
• strength of character, veiled sensuality
• service, hard work, passivity, modesty
• incisive communication, shrewd logical thought

Elemental quality

Virgo is the mutable earth sign of the zodiac, indicating adaptable practicality. It can be likened to a semi-shaded patio that has been adapted to make a garden filled with a great variety of plants, climbers, and an arbor. Half hidden, here and there, are garden chaise lounges with rich patchwork covers, bottles of homemade organic wines, and other unexpected practical delights.

THE VIRGOAN PERSONALITY

CHARACTERISTICS

Positive
- Gentleness with the helpless
- Sympathetic
- Humane and helpful
- Organized
- Knowledgeable about good health
- Witty and charming
- Physically sensual
- Painstaking
- Emotionally warm
- Dedicated

Negative
- Scathing criticism of the lazy
- Cranky and irritable
- Dogmatic
- Untidy
- Tendency to be a hypochondriac
- Nervous and worried
- Prudish
- Eccentric
- Undemonstrative
- Overdemanding

LISTEN UP, THIS IS IMPORTANT

There is a fine line between "gentleness with the helpless" and "scathing criticism of the lazy." Pity the person rendered only slightly inactive by a minor leg injury that encounters the cranky and irritable Virgo.

Ruling planet and its effect

Mercury rules the zodiac sign of Virgo, so anyone whose birth chart has a strong Virgo influence will have a good and quick mind.

In astrology, Mercury is the planet of the mind and communication. Being more concerned with practicalities than ideas (Gemini, the ideas sign, is also ruled by Mercury), Virgo is usually interested in acquiring information and in communicating by writing.

The other traditional ruler of Virgo is the mythological Vulcan, the lame god of thunder, who had a confident and brilliant mind.

SECRETS TO MAKE YOU LOOK GOOD

Do we even need to tell you why it's so appropriate that one of Virgo's lucky animals should be a porcupine?

THE VIRGOAN LOOK

People who exhibit the physical characteristics distinctive of the sign of Virgo look neat and fastidious and have a pleasant, often quietly beautiful face. Many Virgos look like loners and are not usually noisy people.

THE VIRGO MALE

Appearance

The typical Virgo man
• has a straight, wedge-shaped nose
• has an extremely large forehead
• has a high hairline
• is upright and has a straight body
• may be quite tall
• often has one foot turned in more than the other

Behavior and personality traits

The typical Virgo man

- is practical and unsentimental
- instinctively has a love of work
- will be devoted to serving those less fortunate than himself
- may relax by working a little less hard than usual
- takes responsibilities seriously
- is subtle and rarely obvious about his intentions
- notices and remembers details

COMMUNICATION

Virgo Male = Frankenstein, but with a strong work ethic.

♀ THE VIRGO FEMALE
Appearance

The typical Virgo woman

- has a pointed chin and a face in repose
- the eyes are often soft and very beautiful
- the hair may be long or short but is normally impeccably groomed
- the mouth and lips are well formed
- is typically clean and very neatly dressed

Behavior and personality traits

The typical Virgo woman

- can analyze situations in detail
- is devoted to her work, usually serving others in some way
- is basically shy
- has incredible strength of purpose

- will pursue happiness wherever it leads
- is pure of mind but not naïve
- thinks of herself as more orderly and efficient than other people
- has a delightful, straightforward personality
- does not express her feelings easily
- can be soothing one moment and critical the next

YOU'RE WELCOME FOR THE TIP

Virgo Female = Can get anything she wants with a pout, except she doesn't want anything.

YOUNG VIRGO
Behavior and personality traits

The typical Virgo child
- is quick, alert, and an excellent mimic, and so can learn many things in a short time
- gets upset if he or she forgets something that has been learned by heart
- rarely questions authority but frequently questions facts
- is honest and reliable
- is usually shy among strangers
- loves to do jobs around the home imitating an adult
- is sometimes a fussy eater
- is usually tidy, with occasional bouts of disorganization
- gets very upset if teased
- is often an early talker and reader

Bringing up young Virgo

Young Virgos will try very hard to please, as long as they know what is expected. As they grow up they will often find close relationships with the opposite sex very difficult. Virgos take a lot of convincing that they are attractive people. Lots of genuine praise and encouragement early in life will help to smooth the path to true love in teenage and early adulthood. Parents should never interfere when their young Virgo begins to notice the opposite sex. Even the slightest hint of criticism or teasing may cause Virgos to withdraw and choose the single life.

BARE FACTS

Don't worry, parents. They say "the single life" is genetic, anyway.

Young Virgo's needs

Young Virgo must have physical affection, in the form of hugs, and sincere compliments every day in order to build the self-confidence that every typical Virgo child lacks.

VIRGO AT HOME
Typical behavior and abilities

When at home, a Virgo man or woman
• enjoys being head of the household
• is domesticated in most areas, such as cooking, managing the household finances, general maintenance, health, hygiene, and gardening
• will always be doing or making something
• is usually at his or her most relaxed
• pursues several hobbies at or from home

Virgo as parent

The typical Virgo parent

- encourages children to ask questions
- supports practical activities during free time
- worries about the children's health
- is helpful, especially about detailed work
- can adapt to almost any practical demand
- may find it hard to express affection warmly
- gets upset by children's dirt and untidiness
- will explain demands he or she makes
- will do anything to help their children

SECRET TIP

Virgos are, more than any other astrological sign, homebodies, getting great enjoyment out of simple, everyday, indoor activities. If that's your cup of tea, by all means hook up with a Virgo.

Two Virgos in the same family

Married to each other, or as members of the same family, Virgos can get along very well. But difficulties will arise if they become too critical of each other and undermine each other's confidence. On the whole, however, Virgos are made of sterner stuff and can adapt their practical arrangements to accommodate any serious differences. Normally their mutual need for cleanliness and tidiness works very well. The Virgo tendency to worry, especially about matters of health, could lead to an air of hypochondria in the home. However, Virgos' quick thinking and wit can usually overcome these disadvantages.

You better pray for quick thinking and wit when you're living under the same roof with two or more Virgos, who spend most of their time having bathroom scum-away competitions and arguing over which one is more susceptible to ringworm.

VIRGO AT WORK
Typical behavior and abilities

A typical Virgo at work

- is best in a supporting role
- is meticulous and self-disciplined
- offers others a sense of stability
- is very helpful to other people
- can enjoy complicated, routine work

Virgo as employer

A typical Virgo boss (male or female)

- is excellent as boss of a small company
- can see the details very clearly
- will call a spade a spade
- expects honesty in all matters
- is kindhearted, honest, and fair
- expects good grooming, good manners, and good habits
- can handle extremely complicated projects
- will reward good work with pay not perks

Virgo as employee

A typical Virgo employee (male or female)

• is good in service work or research, rather than manufacturing
• will become an excellent assistant to the boss
• does good work and expects to be paid well
• is courteous, reliable, and thorough
• is quick-thinking, analytical, and intelligent
• will be cautious, critical, and methodical

Working environment

The workplace of a typical Virgo man or woman

• will not be noisy
• will have the most up-to-date equipment
• is best decorated with subtle, neutral colors
• is organized so that work can have a regular routine

Typical occupations

Any occupation that enables the Virgoan to give service and handle complicated or difficult details will suit most Virgoans.

BARE FACTS

Unfortunately, the profession most associated with "giving service" requires very little skill at complicated or difficult details, so most Virgoans spend long periods of time unemployed. (Unless they have a particular talent, like being able to tie a cherry stem in a knot with their tongue.)

♡ VIRGO AND LOVE

To Virgo, love is not dramatic, emotional, or sentimental. A Virgo's love is devotion and will include love of family, friends, and those less fortunate than he or she. Virgo in love with another person will have many of the characteristics listed below.

Behavior when in love

The typical Virgo
- looks for quality
- is frightened by overt romance
- may wait for years for the right person
- once in love, loves warmly and steadily
- is devoted to the loved one
- will rarely give cause for any jealousy
- will do anything to avoid breaking up

Expectations

The typical Virgo expects
- devotion from the partner
- a sense of decency
- to enjoy platonic flirtation
- to be fussed over when feeling down
- personal matters to be kept private
- feelings to be handled with great care

YOU'RE WELCOME FOR THE TIP

Thinking of getting involved with a Virgo? Call our toll-free number now. Operators are standing by to talk you down.

The end of an affair

Virgos are typically loyal and will avoid ending a marriage or other permanent relationship whenever possible. However, in the long run, Virgos are sensible, practical people. If the Virgoan sense of fair play has been outraged, the Virgo will make a quick and final break, legally and in every other way. It is rare for a typical Virgo to linger in a fading marriage. If sensible, intelligent discussion does not solve the problems, the Virgo soon makes up his or her mind to end it. Reconciliation is not typical of Virgoan behavior. Pleading, tears, sentimentality, or a more aggressive approach will have no effect. Because the Virgoan has good self-discipline, the past is soon put aside. However, if children are involved, the divorced Virgo will want to ensure that the children receive good educations.

LISTEN UP, THIS IS IMPORTANT

In addition to wanting to ensure that the children receive good educations, the divorced Virgo will want to ensure that the ex-spouse receives good drunk-dialing.

SNAP OF THE FINGER

While the Virgoan has a strong sense of what they don't like, their likes are more fluid, and you should pay particular attention to how they manifest themselves. For example, if you catch one grooming himself in the shower with nice soaps *and* tiny animals, you may want to get photographic evidence.

VIRGO AND PARTNER

The person who contemplates becoming the marriage or business partner of a typical Virgo must realize that Virgo will regard the union as permanent, although the finer details can be flexible. Given this, the person who partners Virgo can expect absolute loyalty. Virgos make strong commitments because they combine duty with devotion. The Virgo will approach a proposal with great caution and will analyze the pros and cons thoroughly before getting involved. This is an excellent approach to any long-term partnership but may sound rather cold and clinical in the case of a proposed marriage.

Virgo man as partner

He will be thoughtful, considerate, and honest. He will remember dates, anniversaries, and agreements. He can be a wizard when it comes to the sensible balancing of the budget. He will love, honor, and criticize, but will not expect to be obeyed, waited on, or be dazzled by sexy makeup and clothes. However, he will want cleanliness and a lot of warmth and sincere respect.

YOU'RE WELCOME FOR THE TIP

Wow. This guy's on fire. Well, so much for that minister and charwoman scenario you were going to spring on him.

Virgo woman as partner

She is shy but as tough as nails when the need arises. In business, she will be cool, intelligent, and fully committed. Slow to love, the Virgo woman is not interested in anything less than true love. When it happens, she will love intensely. She will only break a partnership if there has been hypocrisy. She is the most practical romantic in the zodiac.

Start brushing up on your hypocrisy, guys. It's the only way out of this one.

Opposite sign

Pisces is the complementary opposite sign to Virgo. From Pisces, Virgo can learn to let go a little and float with the tide, giving imagination a chance to develop. In this way, Virgo can begin to accept human imperfections, especially his or her own.

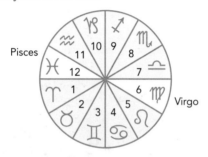

Pisces

Virgo

COMMUNICATION

When you have to learn how to behave better from a fish, you've got problems.

👪 VIRGO AND FRIENDS

In general Virgo likes a friend who is tidy, clean, and intelligent with a broad range of interests. They prefer people who are not given to big shows of emotion and are attracted to those who offer a sense of peace and serenity.

Positive factors

Virgos love any pageantry that gives them an outlet for their tightly controlled emotions. Hence they are delightful companions at these events.

Virgos are discriminating and have a fine artistic taste and a wealth of information on many subjects. They are not coarse and do not waste money. Virgos are loyal to their friends and will be extremely kind, considerate, and helpful.

Negative factors

Virgos are nervous worriers, and a friend who in some way feeds the worries will reduce Virgo to a nervous heap. Virgos can be cold and critical, so a friend who softens the barbed remarks with caring laughter will bring out the Virgo wit. Most Virgos find it almost impossible to admit they are occasionally wrong. A compatibility chart on page 112 lists those with whom Virgo is likely to have the most satisfactory relationships.

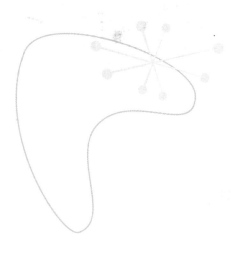

COMPATIBILITY CHART

In general, if people are typical of their zodiac sign, relationships between Virgo and other signs (including the complementary opposite sign, Pisces) are as shown below:

	Harmonious	Difficult	Turbulent
Virgo	•		
Libra	•		
Scorpio	•		
Sagittarius		•	
Capricorn	•		
Aquarius			•
Pisces		•	
Aries			•
Taurus	•		
Gemini		•	
Cancer	•		
Leo	•		

SECRETS TO MAKE YOU LOOK GOOD

The only solution for the friend of a Virgo is to take them to rock concerts for entertainment. The Virgoan gets that outlet for their tightly controlled emotions, and, because it is too loud for you to have a conversation with them, they can't get all pissed off and take anything the wrong way. A win-win if ever there was one.

VIRGOAN LEISURE INTERESTS

Most Virgos enjoy intellectual and practical pursuits. While many will take regular exercise for the sake of their health, they are not natural sportsmen and sportswomen.

VIRGOAN LIKES AND DISLIKES

Likes
- making lists
- a well-stocked medicine cabinet
- self-improvement courses
- punctuality
- mimicking others
- grooming self, taking showers, using nice soaps
- dealing with details
- tiny animals
- helping others
- wearing well-tailored clothes in muted colors and textures

Dislikes
- crowds and noise; brash people
- slang, vulgarity, slovenliness, and dirt
- people who whine and complain a lot
- sitting still for a long time
- disrupted schedules
- lids left off boxes, or tops off toothpaste
- being obligated to others
- people who move Virgo's personal things
- hypocrisy and deceit
- any admission of weakness or failure
- bright, bold, primary colors

On the whole, typical Virgos pursue the following leisure interests:
- theater, concerts, plays, pageants
- books, magazines, dictionaries, encyclopedias
- detailed crafts, especially weaving
- cults, alternative medicines, psychology
- gardening, health foods, flowers
- computers with all the paraphernalia

VIRGOAN HEALTH

Typical Virgos are healthy although, if very worried or unhappy, they may succumb to the Virgoan tendency toward hypochondria.

Types of sickness

Diseases most usually associated with Virgo are disturbances of the lymph system, or the digestive system such as appendicitis, malnutrition, diarrhea, indigestion, hernia, etc. Normally Virgos look after themselves well, so avoid many upsets. When Virgo is sick, he or she needs to have a little fuss made while being encouraged to get well.

Virgo at rest

Extending the metaphor of Virgo as the mutable earth sign, it follows that adaptability (the mutable quality) can sometimes work for Virgo, who finds it easy to change position if the body or mind is under stress. However, a Virgo is also nervously restless, so a Virgo needs plenty of interesting, practical things to keep him or her occupied. Making detailed models or doing needlework can be very soothing and relaxing.

WELL LOOK WHO FINALLY MADE THE RODEO

To wrap up, the Virgo personality is fastidious and particular, with many emotional aspects hiding just under the surface. Why you would want to scratch that surface is beyond us.

7. Libra: The Scales
September 23 - October 22

The SEVENTH sign of the zodiac is concerned with
- partnership, relationships
- ideas, opinions, politics, diplomacy
- music, harmony, balance, romance
- tact, argument, self-control
- good manners, personal appearance
- refinement, sophistication, good taste
- rational thought, ideas for social well-being

Elemental quality

Libra is the cardinal air sign of the zodiac. It can be likened to a finely tuned wind instrument, producing powerful, moving music in perfect harmony.

Air is the breath of life, and cardinal air is a metaphor for ideas put into action. Libras are doers rather than thinkers, although they may spend a long period thinking about a situation before making a decision and acting upon it.

THE LIBRAN PERSONALITY

CHARACTERISTICS

Positive
- Cooperative
- Good companion
- Artistic
- Refined
- Has clear opinions
- Good negotiator
- Very strong beliefs
- Loving and romantic
- Sense of fair play
- Able to lead on behalf of good causes
- Uses intellect when going into action
- Sincere
- Charming
- Communicative
- An excellent mediator

Negative
- Narcissistic
- Indolent or sulky
- Fearful
- Indecisive
- Manipulative
- Overbearing
- Flirtatious

Ruling planet and its effect

Venus rules the zodiac sign of Libra, so anyone whose birth chart has a strong Libran influence will tend to be a gentle, loving peacemaker—until the scales tip too far and need to be adjusted. In astrology, Venus is the planet of values, self, possessions, beauty, and love. Libras tend to express these attributes in words and action.

SECRET TIP

An example of a typical Libra expressing the attributes of their ruling planet might go something like "I love you, now shut up, look pretty and give me something."

Colors	green, purple, pink	Metal	copper
Plants	aloe, myrtle, rose	Tarot card	justice
Perfume	galbanum	Animal	elephant
Gemstone	emerald		

THE LIBRAN LOOK

People who exhibit the physical characteristics distinctive of the sign of Libra are not easy to describe, since there is no typical Libran feature, except for the dimple. It is a Libran habit to spend time deciding what to wear each morning and to change clothes during the day if the occasion demands it.

THE LIBRA MALE

Appearance

The typical Libra man

• is usually handsome, but is never ugly

• has a fine bone structure and balanced features

• has a clear and very charming voice

• dresses with discrimination in subtle colors

• is usually graceful and athletic

• likes to check his appearance in mirrors or as he passes a store window

Behavior and personality traits

The typical Libra man

• wants to make a visual impression that is appropriate to the task at hand, whether it be an international conference, a romantic assignation, or a day on the beach

• gives advice freely

• is interested in the opposite sex, at all ages

- is a master in the art of romance
- is very trustworthy
- can be fickle and change his mind often
- is interested in the facts of a situation so that he can come to a balanced decision
- enjoys art and needs harmony
- can be lavish with money, spending it on things that will bring happiness
- has financial abilities

SECRET TIP

Libra Male = Engaging Playboy age 20–44; creepy old guy age 44–death.

THE LIBRA FEMALE
Appearance

The typical Libra woman
- is usually slim but curvy
- has large eyes
- has delicately flared nostrils
- has a large, well-shaped mouth
- has even teeth, often a gap between the front two

Behavior and personality traits

The typical Libra woman
- is very aware of her looks
- takes care of her body and appearance
- uses her natural attraction to get what she wants

- presents her opinions with diplomacy and tact
- is excellent at partnership and teamwork
- loves luxurious clothes and perfumes
- has excellent powers of analysis
- will create a beautiful home

COMMUNICATION

Libra Female = The love child of Uma Thurman and Henry Kissinger.

YOUNG LIBRA
Behavior and personality traits

The typical Libra child
- is a really beautiful baby
- hates having to decide between two things
- does not like to be hurried
- likes candy
- always seems to know more about things than seems likely for someone of that particular age
- is kindhearted
- likes to be fair and to be treated fairly
- can wheedle almost anything out of adults
- will obey rules if they are seen to be fair
- is usually neat and clean
- teenage Libras are romantics; they love warm water, bubble baths, and lazy days in the sun

Bringing up young Libra

Most young Libras quickly learn how to argue about everything with total conviction. They use this natural ability to make their needs and wants known. It is difficult for a parent to avoid complying with such reasonable, fair-minded demands. To always give in is to risk spoiling young Libra. But to refuse their requests too often may injure the child's developing sensibilities—so the parents of a Libra need to keep their wits about them and aim for a balance in these matters.

Young Libra's needs

A harmonious environment and fair treatment are essential to the developing Libra. Privacy is regarded as sacred. Similarly, Libra will respect the privacy of others and will keep confidences. Affection and, especially, attention are crucial. While Libras can pursue their interests alone, they also need company. It is from close contact with others that they learn who they are.

LIBRA AT HOME
Typical behavior and abilities

When at home, a Libra man or woman

• will spend time just lounging around listening to music or reading pleasant books

• will enjoy arguing about almost everything with all the family—just for the sake of it

• uses good taste to create a place of harmony

• will be a very gracious host, offering good food and wines while making interesting conversation

• will keep the place tidy and clean, unless he or she has become resentful due to unfair treatment

Libra as parent

The typical Libra parent

• is often quite permissive

• may spoil the children

• likes to be proud of the children's appearance and behavior

• will show his or her children much affection

• gives the children the best possible education

• will try to be just and fair

• will probably dominate the family

LISTEN UP, THIS IS IMPORTANT

Home life with a Libra will always feature plenty of good music and fine wine, a party atmosphere. They might also behave this way outside the rearing of their children.

Two Libras in the same family

Two Libras are likely to understand each other's need for a peaceful, pleasant home. Providing they both have similar tastes in music, life will be smooth, although their other interests may be different. If there are children, they may eventually follow very different careers. Two Libras may be quite convinced that they are not at all alike. Anyone listening to them saying this will actually be struck by how similar they are. Libran twins will be extremely attached to each other, although one will usually tend to dominate the other.

LIBRA AT WORK
Typical behavior and abilities

A typical Libra at work

- takes time to get things right
- is usually honest in business
- is more often than not in a partnership
- is a great promoter of ideas
- builds a good network of contacts

Libra as employer

A typical Libra boss (male or female)

- is unhurried but extremely restless
- takes note of everyone's opinion before making decisions
- often suggests unusual answers to problems
- is an expert at the rational analysis of situations
- believes his or her policy is the best
- has strong opinions about finance

Libra as employee

A typical Libra employee (male or female)

- belongs to a union
- expects and gives a fair deal
- never gossips, although he or she talks a lot
- mediates effectively in personality tiffs
- can be moody, but is not rude or mean
- needs periods of rest

Working environment

The workplace of a typical Libra man or woman

• must be harmonious—Libras can get migraines just because the walls are the wrong color

• should be peaceful

• if there is music, it must be classical or refined

• should be free from anything upsetting

• will have a calm but purposeful atmosphere

Typical occupations

Libras are liable to be involved with any aspect of the law, politics, or diplomacy. Their eye for design may lead them into areas such as fashion, art dealership, or graphics. They will also enjoy working in jobs that involve talking and presentation, such as promotional work. Many Libras are good at planning business ventures.

♡ LIBRA AND LOVE

To Libra, love is all. He or she tends to fall in love with love itself and is eager to share life with the partner. The Libran ideal is a life that is filled with the peaceful, rosy glow of romance. Libra in love will have many of the characteristics listed below.

Behavior when in love

The typical Libra

• is emotionally dependent upon the partner

• is casual and easygoing

- enjoys romantic settings
- will ignore the partner's shortcomings in return for love
- does not want a partner who is overly demonstrative
- glows with love for the whole world
- will do anything to avoid hurting the loved one
- gives the loved one complete attention

Expectations

The typical Libra expects
- to be supported and cared for
- faithfulness and loyalty
- to be free to get on with his or her work
- a partner to have his or her own separate interests
- to be amused
- to be admired and even exalted

YOU'RE WELCOME FOR THE TIP

Being involved with a Libra is similar to being in a movie montage sequence, where a happy couple walks on the beach, rows a boat and plays with kids, all to the accompaniment of a Simon & Garfunkel song. Six weeks of this and you won't know whether to puke or throw in the towel.

The end of an affair

If a Libra is rejected, he or she is initially demoralized. However, the Libra quickly takes action to try to redress the balance that has been lost. Often the Libra will do everything to charm the loved one again, courting the partner as if for the first time. If the rejection is final, the hurt Libra will disguise the pain he or she feels by searching once more for true love. A Libra is most likely to reject a partner who makes too many demands on the Libran emotions. If this happens, the break will be as orderly and as well mannered as possible.

SECRETS TO MAKE YOU LOOK GOOD

Libras tend to mope after a break-up. Only the thought that they love themselves more than they could ever love anyone else brings them out of it.

LIBRA AND PARTNER

The person who contemplates becoming the marriage or business partner of a typical Libra must realize that Libra forms partnerships to avoid the terrible sense of loneliness which is always present at the heart of a Libra. Given this, the person who partners Libra can expect the marriage or the business to be happy and successful. Libra is the zodiac sign of partnerships, and typical Libras cannot imagine life without a relationship. The Libra will work hard and thoughtfully to make the partnership a harmonious balance of two personalities.

Libra man as partner

He will want a partner who has some good social or business connections. The young or immature Libra sees himself as the ugly duckling of the fairy tale. He will want his partner to be his personal mirror, reflecting back to him a self-image that is mature and confident. The developed Libra will indeed grow into a swan, but most Libras need plenty of encouragement on the way. In a partnership, Libra will generally take charge of the finances, making sure that there is always a good bank balance. Libras tend to have very strong views about money.

Libra woman as partner

The young, inexperienced Libra female will see a partner as the provider of all that she needs. As she matures, she will want to share herself with her partner. She will have plenty of talent and energy, and her aim is to be successful in every field. She will bring logic and sophistication to any business and a calm beauty to her home—where she will help her loved one to relax and renew.

Opposite sign

Aries is the complementary opposite sign to Libra. Although relations between them can be difficult, they can become entirely complementary to each other as they mature. Aries, the sign of self, can inspire Libra to take the initiative alone sometimes. Libra can thus learn to become self-sufficient and also gain a greater sense of personal identity. In this way, Libra, the sign of partnership, may be able to enjoy a separate identity while in a partnership.

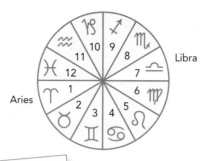

Aries

Libra

SECRET TIP

Plenty of Aries have helped teach a Libra to use their own initiative, only to be thrown over for a younger, more attractive Aries as soon as the Libra makes it big.

👥 LIBRA AND FRIENDS

Libras are usually very social people who like to be on the go. Life for Libras revolves around keeping in touch with other people; this is what makes them happy. Libras will work hard for a friend, giving of themselves tirelessly for days on end. When they become tired, they will need to rest completely. But friends should not mistake the Libra's recuperation periods as a loss of interest.

Positive factors

Libras are loving friends and are unlikely to embarrass anyone with emotional outbursts. A Libran friend is honest and will treat a friend fairly. They make sensitive companions for visits to events concerned with the arts.

Negative factors

Libras can occasionally try the patience of a friend with their indecisiveness. They can be jealous of a friend who is better looking than they are. Friends must also be aware of the periodic depressive moods into which Libras seem to plunge. Such moods can be lightened by a genuine compliment. Friends should never forget that the worst thing for a Libra is to be left alone for too long. If this happens, they can become irritable and sulky, and they can lose their self-esteem. A compatibility chart below lists those with whom Libra is likely to have the most satisfactory relationships.

COMPATIBILITY CHART

In general, if people are typical of their zodiac sign, relationships between Libra and other signs (including the complementary opposite sign, Aries) are as shown below:

	Harmonious	Difficult	Turbulent
Libra	•		
Scorpio	•		
Sagittarius	•		
Capricorn		•	
Aquarius	•		
Pisces			•
Aries		•	
Taurus			•
Gemini	•		
Cancer		•	
Leo	•		
Virgo	•		

Libras are really very sweet and emotional, and can thus inspire great loyalty in their friends. Such loyalty quickly turns into codependence. Which quickly turns into resentment. Which then turns into toxicity. But, what the hell, you had a good ride.

LIBRA'S LEISURE INTERESTS

Most typical Libras are not overly fond of vigorous, sweaty exercise. This offends their preference for a harmony of the senses. Whatever exercise they do, it must enable them to stay relatively neat and unruffled. Many Libras have a lasting interest in the arts. Of these, music is a high priority. On the whole, typical Libras pursue the following leisure interests:

• listening to music, studying music history, playing an instrument in a group, such as a string quartet or a jazz band, listening to poetry
• dancing, especially graceful styles
• dressing with sophistication
• eating out in romantic settings
• the scientific side of cooking
• computers
• any kind of discussion group

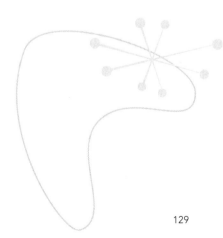

SNAP OF THE FINGER

If you really want to piss off a Libra, schedule a combination discussion group/triathlon.

LIBRA'S HEALTH

Typical Libras have a tendency to become sick if they are obliged to live or work alone for long periods. Otherwise Libras are generally healthy people and recover from any medical problem very quickly when they are in beautiful, calm surroundings.

Types of sickness

Back problems are typical, as are any diseases of the kidneys, liver, and skin. Whatever the physical problem, a Libra puts on a brave face in public and will respond very positively to a lot of fuss and attention from their loved ones and friends.

SECRET TIP

Translation of above: Librans still maintain that charming, attractive appearance even as their intestines are turning to liquid.

The Libra at rest

A typical Libra loves a luxurious bedroom where he or she can lie around in blissful indolence. While at rest, the Libran mind is rarely still, always planning ahead.

WELL LOOK WHO FINALLY MADE THE RODEO

In summation, the Libran personality is graceful and artistic, but vulnerable and irritable, too. Yes, it sucks, but there's a lot of these losers out there, so we'll just have to learn to live with them.

8. Scorpio: The Scorpion

October 23 - November 21

The EIGHTH sign of the zodiac is concerned with
- birth, life, death, sex, sensuality
- passion, pushing boundaries of discovery
- regeneration, transformation, metamorphosis
- finance, investments, wills, inheritance
- hidden matters, secrets, taboos, magic
- collective unconscious, defense systems
- social revolution, reformation, change

Elemental quality

Scorpio is the fixed water sign of the zodiac. It can be likened to still waters that run deep. The relentless power of water to penetrate and transform even the hardest rocks is an excellent metaphor through which to understand the driving passion of the Scorpio personality. Just as stalactites and stalagmites cannot be prevented from growing, once started, Scorpio cannot easily be deflected from his or her purpose.

THE SCORPIO'S PERSONALITY

CHARACTERISTICS

Positive
- Self-critical
- Penetrating
- Investigative
- Passionately caring
- Protective
- Tenacious
- Magnetic
- Dynamic
- Probing
- Emotional
- Sensual
- Compassionate
- Concerned
- Unshockable
- Intense concentration
- Understands failings

Negative
- Self-destructive
- Ruthless
- Overbearing
- Suspicious
- Jealous
- Possessive
- Dangerous
- Quick-tempered
- Obstinate
- Moody
- Sadistic
- Insulting
- Secretive
- Intolerant
- Cunning
- Vindictive

COMMUNICATION

Whoa. These nasty Scorpios have some of the worst negative qualities so far. We can only hope that something from the positive side wins out. ("Self-critical" would be ideal in this case.)

Ruling planet and its effect

Both Mars and Pluto rule the zodiac sign of Scorpio, so anyone whose birth chart has a strong Scorpio influence will tend to have two drives—one influenced by the battling energy of Mars and the other by the hidden depths of Pluto. In astrology, Mars is the planet of aggression, and Pluto is the planet of magnetic forces.

 ## THE SCORPIONIC LOOK

People who exhibit the physical characteristics distinctive of the sign of Scorpio have eyes that look at the world with almost hypnotic intensity. Eye color and shape can vary widely, but if someone looks at you with deep penetration it is a sign of a personality strongly influenced by Scorpio.

 COMMUNICATION

Yes, it is the eyes of the Scorpio that haunt and captivate. This almost hypnotic quality has evolved over many years of trying to get your mind off their thick necks and wide foreheads.

THE SCORPIO MALE
Appearance

The typical Scorpio man
• has strong features
• has penetrating eyes
• has thick eyebrows

134

- has hairy arms and legs
- has a well-proportioned figure
- has an athletic body
- has a tendency to be bowlegged

Behavior and personality traits

The typical Scorpio man

- is never self-effacing
- is possessive of what he believes belongs to him
- has to maintain his dignity
- is a law unto himself and is most courageous in adversity
- will give absolutely honest advice, appraisal, or compliments
- will move mountains to help someone
- is intensely loyal to friends
- never forgets a kindness or an injury
- can be a saint or a sinner, but pursues either course with great zeal

YOU'RE WELCOME FOR THE TIP

Scorpio Male = Bouncer at a Russian nightclub.

THE SCORPIO FEMALE

 Appearance

The typical Scorpio woman

- has a compact and well-proportioned body
- has legs that are often short and thick
- is slender, but has a rather thick waist
- has attractive looks, even when frowning
- inclines her head downward even when looking intensely at a person

Behavior and personality traits

The typical Scorpio woman

- is poised and apparently cool
- never uses flattery
- only smiles when she means it
- wants total freedom of action
- regards flirting and flattery as insulting
- wants to dominate but can accept some restriction in order to win
- has many talents, all used with passion
- is loyal to family and home
- sets and keeps to her own standards

YOU'RE WELCOME FOR THE TIP

Scorpio Female = Bouncer at a Russian Nightclub.

YOUNG SCORPIO

Behavior and personality traits

The typical Scorpio child

- enjoys a good fight and intends to win
- will learn only from a person seen as stronger
- keeps his or her own thoughts secret
- can find out everyone else's secrets easily
- has an instinctive understanding of adult problems
- can often bear pain well
- will be loving and loyal to family and friends
- will take revenge on others who break his/her favorite toys
- knows what he/she wants and attempts to get it
- is suspicious of strangers

Bringing up young Scorpio

Scorpio children are usually active, quick to learn, and intelligent. They have a passionate curiosity, which needs satisfying. They should be tactfully guided away from too much interest in forbidden areas, as they are fascinated by anything that is hidden, mysterious, or a private part of someone else's life! The best way to love a Scorpio child is to always be loyal and to make it possible for him or her to follow an interest in science, medicine, magic, engineering, sports, and literature.

Young Scorpio's needs

A private place is essential for Scorpio's children—somewhere they can be alone and undisturbed. It could be a room of their own or even just a closet. It might be a secret hiding place or a little box with a key. A secret hiding place gives the Scorpio child a sense of security.

SECRET TIP

When encouraging your Scorpio child's love of the mysterious, try to steer them more towards the science, medicine, engineering and sports. Literature and magic will not make them any money, and you don't want these vengeful, argumentative handfuls around any longer than they need to be.

SCORPIO AT HOME
Typical behavior and abilities

When at home, a Scorpio man or woman
- makes the home self-contained
- is protective of children
- is gentle with the sick
- guards home territory jealously
- likes the home kept clean and orderly
- expresses good taste
- enjoys comfort

Scorpio as parent

The typical Scorpio parent
- is strict about rules
- demands high standards
- enjoys the children
- keeps the children busy
- often takes the children out
- finds it hard to change viewpoints and to bridge the generation gap
- cares passionately about the family
- remains his or her child's friend throughout life

YOU'RE WELCOME FOR THE TIP

A Scorpio's home is their castle. Do not be alarmed at the moat with the alligators.

Two Scorpios in the same family

They will understand each other only too well. Two Scorpios mean double the passion, and it is essential that both have the facilities to follow their own passionate interests, so that no jealousies arise. Two Scorpios can get along well, provided each has a space of his or her own that is private. The greatest problems could arise from sexual jealousy if the two are of the same sex and age group. However, in the final analysis, the Scorpionic loyalty to family will overcome all other problems.

STRETCHING THE TRUTH

Putting two Scorpios together in a room is much like putting two actual scorpions together in a glass case. Except the scorpions may eventually need a break from constantly trying to poison each other.

SCORPIO AT WORK
Typical behavior and abilities

A typical Scorpio at work
• will eventually know everyone's secrets
• will sense the moods of other people
• is indefatigable
• will excel as a team leader
• will appear to be calm in all situations

Scorpio as employer

A typical Scorpio boss (male or female)
• will demand total loyalty
• will do anything to help someone he/she likes
• will solve even the most difficult problems
• will never reveal the depth of his or her competitiveness
• confronts problems directly

• will be concerned and compassionate toward the workers' families, regarding them as part of the team

Scorpio as employee

A typical Scorpio employee (male or female)

• is self-motivated
• knows what he/she wants to achieve
• will take any amount of criticism from someone who has something he/she wants
• will accept failure as inevitable only when the odds are overwhelming
• is tenacious, intense, and career minded
• does not waste time and is not a clock-watcher

LISTEN UP, THIS IS IMPORTANT

The person at the Monday morning meeting who suggests employees should lose a finger for every minute they are late coming back from lunch? That's the Scorpio.

Working environment

The workplace of a typical Scorpio man or woman

• suggests an air of quiet confidence
• is usually tidy, or at least orderly
• contains nothing superfluous to the job
• contains equipment that helps Scorpio increase knowledge and undertake shrewd analysis

Typical occupations

Scorpios enjoy solving mysteries and penetrating the secrets of life. They love to get to the heart of any problem, human or mechanical.

They may be detectives, pathologists, surgeons, scientists, researchers, undertakers, sewage workers, insurers, market analysts, butchers, members of the armed services, or pharmacists. Any occupation that Scorpios feel is important and offers the opportunity to investigate and analyze complex problems will satisfy them. Scorpios can run a big business or a small enterprise as long as they feel that they are achieving something.

♡ SCORPIO AND LOVE

To Scorpio, love is an intensely passionate and enduring emotion that may be directed at one person only. Love is central to the life of typical Scorpios and inspires many of their ambitions and actions. Scorpio in love will have many of the following characteristics.

Behavior when in love
The typical Scorpio
- is deeply attached to the loved one
- attracts the loved one like a magnet
- is possessive
- hides emotions in public
- keeps dependence on the loved one hidden
- is faithful when in love
- dominates the loved one
- remains true to his/her own feelings

Expectations
The typical Scorpio expects
- absolute faithfulness and loyalty
- demonstrative love
- no great emphasis on romance

- genuine tenderness
- acknowledgment of how lucky the loved one is to be party to Scorpio's secrets

BARE FACTS

The scorpion is known for its sting, and sooner or later those who date Scorpios will be stung by them. Of course, after putting up with being dominated, and asked to acknowledge how lucky you are to be part of their lives, a nice sting could be downright refreshing.

The end of an affair

If a Scorpio has an affair, it is often because the sexual life within the marriage has serious problems. Scorpios seem able to attract partners without much effort, and they will take the upper hand from the start, so that ending an affair is an easy matter. However, the Scorpio who is rejected is always very wounded and may want to take revenge. Some Scorpios immediately attempt to hurt their ex-partner. Others take their revenge in more subtle ways over a period of time. A rejected Scorpio is unlikely to forgive and will never forget the hurt.

SCORPIO AND PARTNER

The person who contemplates becoming the marriage or business partner of a typical Scorpio must realize that Scorpio will expect to dominate the partnership. Given this, the person who partners Scorpio can expect unwavering loyalty, hard work, and a passionate drive to succeed—whether in business or marriage.

Scorpio man as partner

In business, the Scorpio man will inevitably be in charge of the partnership and is most likely to have initiated the terms of agreement. A Scorpio who accepts orders from a partner is doing so for a particular reason. For example, if money or future progress is the reward, Scorpio will appear to accept even a subordinate position for as long as it takes to achieve the results he wants. Scorpio will be proud of his partner and his partner's skills, and he will go out of his way to enable the partner to achieve ambitions, too.

YOU'RE WELCOME FOR THE TIP

Scorpio men are known for their compelling PowerPoint presentation "Why You Will Submit To A Relationship With Me."

Scorpio woman as partner

A Scorpio woman is often even more subtle than her male counterpart. She happily accepts the subordinate role and plays this part well. Again, however, this is only so that she can achieve her ambition in the end. Like her male counterpart, she will be loyal to the partner and do everything to help the partner. Scorpios can work very hard, and they often provide the dynamic quality in a business. It is unlikely that Scorpio and her partner will have an equal footing. The Scorpio will, in reality, have the edge on the partner—but only in ways that the Scorpio sees will be helpful to the joint venture. Scorpio shrewdness is a vital asset in any partnership.

Opposite sign

Taurus is the complementary opposite sign to Scorpio. From Taurus, Scorpio can learn to recognize the talents of other people and appreciate their value. In this way, Scorpio can learn to value his or her own talents more realistically, because Scorpio is more self-critical than critical of others, and often reproaches him or herself.

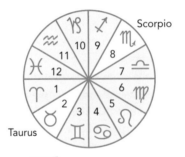

SCORPIO AND FRIENDS

In general, Scorpio likes a friend who recognizes Scorpio's magnetic superiority without fear or undue compliments. Scorpio chooses only a few friends and expects loyalty from them. Scorpio is not a natural socializer, but will keep close friends for many years.

Positive factors

Scorpios have good memories and enjoy telling jokes. They are generous and hospitable toward friends, and also make strangers welcome when they call for help or advice. Friends of Scorpios will be treated like family and given every help and consideration. Whenever Scorpio gives a friend advice it will be reliable. A friend can also trust Scorpio never to gossip.

Negative factors

Scorpios are unlikely to visit friends without making arrangements and having a good reason. Scorpios like others to do the visiting. If they are out when a friend comes to visit, their attitude is that it is the friend's loss and that the friend will have to visit again. Scorpios have an almost psychic insight into the motives and secrets of their friends. Anyone who dislikes someone knowing their secrets should stay away from Scorpios. A compatibility chart on page 146 lists those with whom Scorpio is likely to have the most satisfactory relationships.

Compatibility chart

In general, if people are typical of their zodiac sign, relationships between Scorpio and other signs (including the complementary opposite sign, Taurus) are as shown below:

	Harmonious	Difficult	Turbulent
Scorpio	•		
Sagittarius	•		
Capricorn	•		
Aquarius		•	
Pisces	•		
Aries			•
Taurus		•	
Gemini			•
Cancer	•		
Leo		•	
Virgo	•		
Libra	•		

COMMUNICATION

It's simple algebra. If anyone who dislikes people knowing their secrets should stay away from Scorpios, and everyone dislikes people knowing their secrets, therefore everyone should stay away from Scorpios.

SCORPIONIC LEISURE INTERESTS

Finding out how things work, taking something apart and reconstructing it, or delving into the mysteries of the human mind are all of interest to Scorpios, who also enjoy a variety of sports. Winning is important to them.

On the whole, typical Scorpios pursue the following leisure interests:

- any sport that demands shrewd tactics
- competitive driving, flying, or cycling
- scientific hobbies
- archeology, anthropology, psychology
- detective novels, treasure hunts, caving
- breeding animals or plants

STRETCHING THE TRUTH

The Scorpio engaged in a demanding sport should be extra careful, as a serious injury could require that very intrusive, expensive and painful procedure, the Scorpionic.

SCORPIONIC LIKES AND DISLIKES

Likes	Dislikes
• activity	• being analyzed
• mysteries	• being asked personal questions
• secrets	• people who know more than they do
• winning	• too many compliments
• sex	• having to trust a stranger
• being acknowledged	
• home	

✛ SCORPIONIC HEALTH

Typical Scorpios are rarely sick. When they do become ill it is generally serious, but they have the willpower to get well. Scorpios can destroy their own health by allowing themselves to get depressed or by doing too much hard work.

Types of sickness

Some Scorpios are prone to accidents due to their burning desire to finish a job or get somewhere more quickly than anyone else. Nose and throat problems, hernias, piles, bladder disorders, and problems with the reproductive organs are the most common Scorpio illnesses. The phoenix symbolizes Scorpio's activities, and in matters of health, it seems that Scorpio has a tremendous ability to rise from the metaphoric ashes of sickness and fly again.

Scorpio at rest

Scorpios often find it hard to relax. Some Scorpios will even avoid situations where they can relax.

When on vacation, they often seem to have a small accident or minor illness in the first days. Many Scorpios try to relax by continuing to work because of the intense pressure they put on themselves to finish everything before leaving for that much-needed rest. Their best policy is to have an alternative interest or hobby that they can pursue with passion, thus giving them relaxation from their main work. This especially applies to Scorpios who are homemakers and parents caring for children, as they may find it difficult to take even a short break.

WELL LOOK WHO FINALLY MADE THE RODEO

So, to sum up. Scorpios will do anything to get their way, and, having gotten it, like to gloat about it. If that isn't marriage material, we don't know what is.

9. Sagittarius: The Archer
November 22 - December 21

The NINTH sign of the zodiac is concerned with
- philosophy, idealism, religion, spiritual growth
- optimism, positive outlook, forward planning
- travel, freedom of movement, the outdoors
- honesty, justice, morality
- imagination, aspirations, open-mindedness
- wit, intellect, flashes of intuition
- generosity, pleasure, romance

Elemental quality

Sagittarius is the mutable fire sign of the zodiac. It can be likened to stars, a thousand lighted candles, the sparks rising from a rapidly spreading grass fire, or the reflectors marking the route along the center of a major road. Fire changes substances and Sagittarians have a knack of transforming negative situations with their optimism. Mutable means adaptable. Sagittarians can adapt to almost any situation, whether earthly or spiritual.

2 | THE SAGITTARIAN PERSONALITY

CHARACTERISTICS

Positive
- Frank and open
- Optimistic
- Sees the best in people
- Honest and fair-minded
- Spiritual
- Enthusiastic
- Inspiring
- Disarmingly happy
- Stimulating
- Happy-go-lucky
- Holds no grudges
- Sensual

Negative
- Argumentative
- Impatient to be moving
- Critical of those who deny their talents
- A gambler at heart
- Can be a fanatic
- Hotheaded
- Fails to plan adequately
- Tends to preach
- Denies sadness
- Uncommitted
- Fears any responsibility that curtails freedom
- Blundering and inept
- Indulgent

Ruling planet and its effect

Jupiter rules the zodiac sign of Sagittarius, so anyone whose birth chart has a strong Sagittarius influence will tend to be expansive, pleasure-loving, benevolent, and have a strong sense of justice. In astrology, Jupiter is the planet of beneficence. Psychologically, Jupiter is linked with wisdom and is the guide to the psyche.

SAGITTARIAN LUCKY CONNECTIONS

Colors	blue, royal blue, purple, white	Metal	tin
Plants	rush, oak, fig, hyssop	Tarot card	temperance
Perfume	lignaloes	Animals	horse, dog
Gemstones	jacinth, lapis lazuli		

DON'T BE A JERK

Hey, Sagittarius, is that a lapis lazuli in your pocket, or are you just glad to see me?

THE SAGITTARIAN LOOK

People who exhibit the physical characteristics distinctive of the sign of Sagittarius look strong and active. They are often taller than average and have handsome faces. Since a typical Sagittarius is an optimist, the face often appears about to break into a smile—and regularly does.

THE SAGITTARIUS MALE

Appearance

The typical Sagittarius man

• can be likened to a lively horse and often has a mane of hair that falls over the forehead and has to be tossed away. In later life, the Sagittarius may become bald, yet still retain a youthful look

• is physically noticeable because of his strong sense of confidence

• will retain his physical faculties to a very old age

Behavior and personality traits

The typical Sagittarius man

• is a risk taker

• says exactly what is on his mind

• enjoys physical danger

• has an unerringly accurate wit

• has a good memory for facts, but often forgets where he has left everyday objects such as keys

• is trusting until let down

• can tell really funny jokes, but often fluffs the punch line—which makes the joke even funnier
• may be tactless but is never deliberately cruel
• likes learning, study, and creative interpretation

QUICK FIX

Sagittarius Male = Fabio with an MBA.

♀ THE SAGITTARIUS FEMALE
Appearance

The typical Sagittarius woman
• has an oval face, a high forehead, and a pointed chin
• has a tall and slender body
• has eyes that are steady, bright, open, and honest
• has movement that is purposeful and even graceful

Behavior and personality traits

The typical Sagittarius woman
• is honest
• enjoys freedom of thought and travel
• will laugh about her misfortunes and mistakes, even while she is upset or in pain
• is angry if her integrity is questioned
• is kindhearted, though sometimes tactless
• can be deceived in romance, but is rarely misled in other areas of life
• enjoys taking risks, both physical and intellectual
• is often unconventional in relationships
• sticks by her own very clear moral standards

- can be cuttingly sarcastic when hurt
- regards herself and all others as equals

YOUNG SAGITTARIUS
Behavior and personality traits

The typical Sagittarius child
- is a happy, playful little clown
- greets everyone and is despondent if others don't say "Hello"
- acts on impulse
- is active, interested in many things, and usually adores animals
- tends to get more bumps, bruises, and cuts than many children because he or she is so adventurous and rarely sits still
- gives and expects total honesty
- enjoys company
- when left on his or her own, will hug a teddy bear or a blanket
- asks endless questions
- expects to be trusted

Bringing up young Sagittarius

Most young Sagittarians enjoy learning but dislike being held back by what they see as needless rules. They are capable of setting their own standards and should be encouraged to do so. A frustrated Sagittarian child can turn from being a happy-go-lucky optimist into an angry, sarcastic adult; therefore, it is important that the child be allowed to take any opportunities for learning and socializing. Sagittarian children question adult values and poke fun at adult hypocrisy. The best thing that the parents of a Sagittarian can do is to be totally honest.

SNAP OF THE FINGER

Parents being totally honest with the moody Sagittarian may want to draw the line at "you were adopted."

Young Sagittarius's needs

Love is essential to all children, but the way it is given varies. In the case of young Sagittarius, there should be no pressure or possessiveness, but love should be given by way of encouragement and by showing pleasure. Young Sagittarians hide their hurts, disappointments, and sorrows behind a spirited belief that everything must get better. The clown who laughs while his or her heart is breaking is behaving in a very Sagittarian way.

 # SAGITTARIUS AT HOME
Typical behavior and abilities

When at home, a Sagittarius man or woman
• could be almost anywhere; Sagittarians make their home wherever they happen to be; some have, or would like, several homes, while others may be permanent travelers. It is not unusual for Sagittarians to spend time living abroad, or to divide their time between two different countries
• is usually planning for the next journey
• is not naturally domesticated
• enjoys making and receiving social visits
• does not enjoy formality, but loves informal gatherings where he/she is free to roam

Sagittarius as parent

The typical Sagittarius parent

- has very clear moral standards
- has faith in the children
- may expect too much intellectually
- will provide a very stimulating home
- will be eager to play with children, talk with them, and take them on travels
- enjoys the children and is great fun as a parent
- will always answer questions honestly
- will encourage the children to leave home when grown up

STRETCHING THE TRUTH

Jovial and carefree Sagittarians may indeed have several different homes, as well as several different children by several different spouses, and several different overdrawn bank accounts bled dry trying to support their wanderlust. When challenged, they can always blame books like this, which make their B.S. sound almost palatable in list form.

Two Sagittarians in the same family

Sagittarians are not usually very good at family relationships because they are natural wanderers and resume contact sporadically. Hence, two typical Sagittarians in the same family should get along perfectly well; each will understand the other's need for freedom of thought and action. Two Sagittarian children are apt to get into more physical scrapes, since they are both risk takers.

SAGITTARIUS AT WORK
Typical behavior and abilities

A typical Sagittarian at work
• needs a challenge, so even in the dullest, most routine job, he or she will seek intellectual stimulation
• is versatile
• needs to do several things at once
• may have two jobs
• needs intellectual and physical exercise
• gets tired only when bored

Sagittarius as employer

A typical Sagittarian boss (male or female)
• is rarely naturally tactful and may be quite blunt
• has a sense of overall planning, although they may overlook details
• expects people to be straightforward
• can be erratic and hard to tie down
• can promote anything extremely well
• can boost morale and will fight for what he/she believes is right
• is generally cheerful
• is kind and understanding

156

Sagittarius as employee

A typical Sagittarian employee (male or female)

• works best when allowed to get on with the job at his or her own speed—which is usually fast

• is cheerful and does not complain

• is enthusiastic, willing, and generally ahead of everyone else

• enjoys praise and will promise almost anything

• is interested in current pay but not in long-term career plans

• will boost everyone's spirits when they are depressed

LISTEN UP, THIS IS IMPORTANT

The Sagittarians' need for movement and variety make them people who rush through jobs in order to get where they want to go next. Paradoxically, the quality of their work does not suffer. Which is really irritating, because you want to fire these flighty twits so damn badly it hurts.

Working environment

The workplace of a typical Sagittarian man or woman

• is wherever they are—they take their tools with them

• will be open and airy

• may be decorated imaginatively

Typical occupations

Anything in sales and promotion that involves travel and knowledge of foreign languages; anything that allows Sagittarius to perform; and any career that involves learning and the use of the intellect such as teacher, lawyer, or writer. A Sagittarius will be attracted to work that combines intellect and physical activity, such as veterinary practice, or indeed any kind of work with animals.

♡ SAGITTARIUS AND LOVE

To Sagittarius, love is a romantic adventure. Sagittarius in love will have many of the characteristics listed below.

Behavior when in love

The typical Sagittarius

- enjoys love on the move in foreign places
- is inventive
- needs good intellectual compatibility
- is totally honest with the loved one
- enjoys the physical pleasures of love
- is happy when he or she is loved
- is very generous and good-natured

Expectations

The typical Sagittarius expects

- not to be tied down
- to feel secure in love
- the loved one to be honest
- to retain freedom of movement
- never to be falsely accused of philandering
- to stimulate, amuse, and be enjoyed by the loved one

The end of an affair

If a partner is possessive or jealous of Sagittarius, the relationship will begin to crack. Eventually, these pressures will cause Sagittarius to simply pack up and move on. Sagittarians enjoy meeting people and may indulge in the occasional affair. On the whole, the attraction of the affair will be its excitement, rather than true romance. Sagittarius is prone to look elsewhere if an existing relationship becomes routine.

SAGITTARIUS AND PARTNER

The person who contemplates becoming the marriage or business partner of a typical Sagittarius must realize that Sagittarius will value his or her freedom above everything. Given this, the person who partners Sagittarius can expect honesty and plenty of creative ideas.

Sagittarian man as partner

He will want a partner who enjoys spontaneity and who will appreciate his grand gestures and courageous outbursts of enthusiasm. He will also want a partner who will not try to control him. In business, a person who has a sound understanding of financial matters would make the perfect partner.

LISTEN UP, THIS IS IMPORTANT

The Sagittarian man likes nothing more than a quiet evening three thousand miles from home. (Your presence optional.)

Sagittarian woman as partner

Frank and friendly, she wants a partner who can love her for her outspoken charm, not wilt under it. Her words and actions will always show what she is thinking and feeling, so a potential partner should be quite clear about his own feelings. Sagittarian women are neither coy nor evasive, and will want a partner who does not play silly games. In marriage or in business, a partner must always ask her to do something, never tell her. However, she will respond to hints.

YOU'RE WELCOME FOR THE TIP

The Sagittarian woman is strong and independent. Guys with mother issues should go find some pansy-ass Libra or something.

Opposite sign

Gemini is the complementary opposite sign to Sagittarius. Although relationships between the two may have some difficulties, Sagittarius can learn from Gemini how to notice and take account of details. In this way, Sagittarians can become inspiring guides, lighting the way for others, rather than leading them by preaching what the route should be.

Sagittarius

Gemini

SAGITTARIUS AND FRIENDS

In general, Sagittarius likes a friend who is open-minded, ready for an adventure, and trusting.

Positive factors

Sagittarians are friendly, gregarious people who accept any friend who matches up to their personal standards. They will defend a friend with great loyalty, but they will also say exactly what they think. Sagittarians have friends from many walks of life. Among those are likely to be both men and women, straight and gay people, a range of ages, and a mixture of ethnic groups; they will all be treated as equals. Sagittarians respond to all calls for help. They will lend a friend money without expecting it to be repaid; they take in stray animals and stray people and will support any cause in the name of friendship.

Negative factors

Close friendship with just one or two people is not the Sagittarian norm. In fact, anyone who tries to get too familiar with, or who takes advantage of the Sagittarian natural friendliness, may be struck by the fiery rocket of Sagittarian temper. They generally fight with words, as sharp as darts, but some may also use their fists. Sagittarians can be eccentric and may find it difficult to keep a secret. A compatibility chart on page 163 lists those with whom Sagittarius is likely to have the most satisfactory relationships.

COMMUNICATION

The fact that a Sagittarian will lend you money and not expect to get paid back is awesome, but it gets old after you've been struck by that freakin' fiery rocket of Sagittarian temper enough times.

SAGITTARIAN LEISURE INTERESTS

Sagittarians are versatile and like to kick against authority, so their leisure interests may be both varied and radical. Sports are natural activities for Sagittarians, who enjoy them for the social contact as much as for the competition. A Sagittarian who has not traveled is unusual. Long-distance travel to foreign places is one of the main Sagittarian interests. Some may prefer to "travel" in the world of literature or religion, but their travels will also be far and wide. On the whole, typical Sagittarians pursue the following interests:

• gambling, gaming, racing cars, skydiving, and other risk-taking sports
• travel, exploration, cracking codes, tracking down mysteries, solving problems, speaking foreign languages, breeding animals, keeping pets
• religions, belief systems, new ways of being

COMPATIBILITY CHART

In general, if people are typical of their zodiac sign, relationships between Sagittarius and other signs (including the complementary opposite sign, Gemini) are as shown below:

	Harmonious	Difficult	Turbulent
Sagittarius	•		
Capricorn	•		
Aquarius	•		
Pisces		•	
Aries	•		
Taurus			•
Gemini		•	
Cancer			•
Leo	•		
Virgo		•	
Libra	•		
Scorpio	•		

Likes
- freedom of action
- alternative ideas
- being on the move
- food and drink
- perfumes and beauty aids
- raffles and lotteries
- parties, flirting

Dislikes
- disapproval from others
- making promises
- being too safe, secure, or confined
- administration
- tight clothes
- having their honesty doubted

SAGITTARIAN HEALTH

Typical Sagittarians are healthy, energetic, and able to keep going in adversity. They hate to be confined to bed, unless it is to dream a little; any kind of routine will tax the Sagittarian optimism. However, their positive outlook helps them to overcome illnesses quickly and keeps them going if serious illness strikes.

Types of sickness

Diseases often linked with a Sagittarian influence in the chart are the whole range of arthritic and rheumatic problems, diseases that attack the hips and legs, and problems arising from the Sagittarian tendency to fall over, trip over, or collide with things. Asthma is linked with Sagittarius, as are sicknesses caught from animals—Sagittarians are very fond of animals and like to be closely involved with them. Sagittarians tend to take physical risks, so accidents arising from dangerous sports can be expected from time to time. The jovial Jupiter influence is said to lead many a Sagittarian into indulgence in food or drink. And this may lead to health problems.

Sagittarius at rest

A typical Sagittarian never rests. A Sagittarius who lounges around looking bored is one who feels restricted and needs to break free again. The way that typical Sagittarians rest is by sleeping, thinking, and dreaming—and then moving off somewhere new.

WELL LOOK WHO FINALLY MADE THE RODEO

In review, Sagittarians need to be free, love movement and tend to flee relationships where they are not given room to roam. Why this concept is represented by a minotaur with a bow and arrow is beyond us.

10. Capricorn: The Goat
December 22 - January 19

The TENTH sign of the zodiac is concerned with
- practicality, realism, hard work, accomplishment
- planning, determination, persistence, success
- high status, good quality, reputation
- responsibility, difficulties, problems
- paternalism, authority, discipline
- money, wealth, long-term projects
- wisdom, loyalty, sensitivity to beauty

Elemental quality

Capricorn is the cardinal earth sign of the zodiac. It can be likened to the oldest and most valuable tree in the forest. Surefooted and thoroughly practical, in the end the Capricorn goat always reaches the heights, beating others who are faster but less determined. The cardinal signs must put their resources to good use. Earth resources represent practical skills: material, financial, and social resources that can be used to further an ambition.

THE CAPRICORNEAN PERSONALITY

CHARACTERISTICS

Positive
- Good organizing skills
- Cautious and realistic
- Hard working
- Scrupulous
- Fearless
- Calculates risks but takes them when necessary
- Is an admiring spectator
- Conventional
- Concerned
- Gives sound advice
- Loyal to tradition
- Respects authority

Negative
- Tendency to believe their way is always the best
- Egotistical
- A slave driver
- Unforgiving
- Anxious, allows inner fears to dominate decisions
- Takes a very critical view
- A perfectionist who is never satisfied
- Fatalistic
- Status seeking

COMMUNICATION

"Good organizing skills." That's the type of thing you put on a resume when you spent most of college being in charge of ordering the keg.

Ruling planet and its effect

Saturn rules the zodiac sign of Capricorn, so anyone whose birth chart has a strong Capricorn influence will tend to take life seriously. In astrology, Saturn is the planet of fate, time, sorrow, caution, and wisdom. It is often called the great teacher, because Saturn is associated with the lifelong task of gently working out our fears and overcoming them. Saturn is also the most beautiful of the planets.

Colors	green, black, gray, indigo, violet	Metal	lead
Plants	yew, ash, hemp, weeping willow	Tarot card	the devil
Perfume	musk	Animals	goat, ass
Gemstones	jet, black diamond, onyx, ruby		

THE CAPRICORNEAN LOOK

People who exhibit the physical characteristics distinctive of the sign of Capricorn generally have a small skeletal structure. The shape of the body will depend on how well the musculature has been developed. If physical training is part of Capricorn's routine, then it will be done with determination and discipline, resulting in a well-developed musculature, which may make a Capricorn, look heavier than he or she really is. A typical Capricorn has a serious look, and young Capricorns often look older than their years. It is also typical that aging Capricorns eventually tend to become more relaxed and so look younger than their years.

THE CAPRICORN MALE

Appearance

The typical Capricorn man

- is stocky
- has sharp, penetrating eyes
- rarely smiles
- has very strong white teeth
- is conscious of his appearance
- dislikes removing his clothes in public—for example, he will still be wearing a shirt during a heat wave when other men are bare-chested

Behavior and personality traits

The typical Capricorn man

- is dignified in his manner and very polite
- seems unapproachable and self-protective
- is totally reliable in pursuit of an aim
- takes his time sizing up other people before he will relax enough to share his inner warmth
- seeks honors but is not interested in becoming famous; on the contrary, he avoids publicity
- has strong opinions but is not at all vain

YOU'RE WELCOME FOR THE TIP

Capricorn Male = That one Chippendale dancer that no one ever told to try another line of work.

♀ THE CAPRICORN FEMALE
Appearance

The typical Capricorn woman

- has a small and well-shaped body with slender neck
- has deep, serious eyes
- has an "earthy" beauty
- has a full mouth and very white teeth
- has shapely legs, slim ankles, small feet

Behavior and personality traits

The typical Capricorn woman

- is very self-conscious
- behaves in a ladylike manner in public

- dresses according to what she intends to achieve that day
- needs to gain recognition for her work
- appears as steady as a rock, but is quite moody inside herself
- runs a well-kept home, although she finds domesticity tedious
- is totally loyal to close family and distant relatives
- cannot bear to be teased
- smiles little, but when she does it is a very beautiful smile

COMMUNICATION

Capricorn Female = An enticing combination of hippie chick and drywall installer.

YOUNG CAPRICORN
Behavior and personality traits

The typical Capricorn child
- tends to prefer older company
- often looks very old when still a baby
- is self-contained and strong willed
- is usually even-tempered
- gets what he or she wants by slowly wearing down parental resistance
- likes the security of routine and orderliness
- has just one or two close friends
- enjoys pretending to be grown up
- usually loves reading
- likes to make things that have a practical use

Bringing up young Capricorn

Young Capricorns are not particularly enthusiastic about sports or the outdoors, so they need to be encouraged to spend time outside in the fresh air getting some exercise. Trips to museums, archeological sites, or even rock climbing are likely to satisfy them. Usually, Capricorns work doggedly at school subjects and aim to get good grades and gain honors. It may be that they need to be encouraged to relax and play. They may seem very serious children, but they have a sense of humor; this needs to be encouraged—but not by teasing.

Young Capricorn's needs

A secure, warm home with a regular routine and reliable, appreciative parents are essential to Capricorns. In spite of all their capable maturity, young Capricorns can lose self-confidence very easily.

CAPRICORN AT HOME
Typical behavior and abilities

When at home, a Capricorn man or woman
- really enjoys providing for the family and having visits from relatives
- likes having a routine and an organized household
- wants quality furniture and fixtures
- is basically loyal to home and family
- needs home as a safe haven for personal pleasure and business entertaining

SECRET TIP

It may not escape your notice that "quality furniture and fixtures" ranks above loyalty to home and family. People involved with Capricorns must find industrious ways to ensure their needs get prioritized. For example, when selecting a new house with your Capricorn, make sure it's far, far away from the nearest Ikea.

Capricorn as parent

The typical Capricorn parent

- is strict but always fair
- takes parenthood seriously
- has an ironic sense of humor
- provides the very best for the children
- is tender and sensitive
- has difficulty relating to young children, but will find it easier as they get older
- will teach the children good manners
- provides plenty of educational stimulation

Two Capricorns in the same family

Since the need for public recognition is basic to Capricorn's well-being, two Capricorns in the same family will get along quite well, provided they each have an area of endeavor in which they can succeed and achieve some adulation from others. On the whole, Capricorns are not jealous people; nor are they quarrelsome, unless someone is trying to give them orders. So Capricorn siblings or spouses should remember never to try to make the other one conform to his or her ideas of how things should be done.

Great, so you can't even make someone conform to your ideas about how things should be done? That's half the fun of living together!

CAPRICORN AT WORK
Typical behavior and abilities

A typical Capricorn at work

• works hard and for long hours

• likes to have some home comforts in the workplace so he or she can change and go on to another appointment, or stay all night if necessary

Capricorn as employer

A typical Capricorn boss (male or female)

• does not neglect family life for business, and family members may visit him or her at work

• is kind but expects obedience to the rules

• has a strong sense of duty and works very hard

• is not a good mixer, but others trust him or her

• does not give perks but responds when people are in need

• takes responsibilities to others very seriously, but may neglect personal needs

• dresses conservatively and is well organized

• can keep complex operations moving smoothly

Capricorn as employee

A typical Capricorn employee (male or female)

• arrives a little early and leaves late

• is dependable and can carry huge workloads

- minds his or her own business
- works steadily and quietly, staying with the same company a long time
- occasionally reveals a wry sense of humor
- is conscientious and aims high (for power not glory)
- will expect a salary in keeping with the work done
- has respect for superiors, elders, and those more experienced
- enjoys common-sense procedures

YOU'RE WELCOME FOR THE TIP

Industrious Capricorn is known for going the extra mile. In fact, many Capricorns have instituted their own version of "Take Your Daughter to Work Day." It's called "*Put* Your Daughter to Work Day."

Working environment

The workplace of a typical Capricorn man or woman
- must be comfortable, like a home away from home
- must be tidy and well organized
- will probably have a framed photo of the family on the desk
- must not have money wasted on it unnecessarily

Typical occupations

Any occupation that requires good organization and smart management, but which does not require the Capricorn to be the front person. Capricorns prefer to work in private. They generally make good bankers, systems analysts, accountants, researchers, dentists, architects, engineers, manufacturers, and politicians. Many Capricorns are jewelers, funeral directors, art dealers, anthropologists, and managers of musicians and other entertainers. They are also to be found on radio and television interview programs; their quiet, unflappable natures are perfect for serious work under pressure.

LISTEN UP, THIS IS IMPORTANT

"Quiet and unflappable" = huge porn collection.

♡ CAPRICORN AND LOVE

To Capricorn, love is the source of all inspiration. Shy, awkward with the opposite sex, and very much private people, Capricorns are, nevertheless, deeply interested in love and are reputed to be the most capable and loyal of lovers. Capricorn in love will have many of the characteristics listed below.

Behavior when in love
The typical Capricorn
• is slow to make approaches and never flirts for fun
• only says "I love you" when it is meant and does not see any reason to keep repeating it
• may worry about the emotional aspects of the relationship
• must feel financially secure to enjoy love
• is caring, considerate, and committed to the loved one

Expectations
The typical Capricorn expects
• to be taken seriously
• to make a long-term commitment
• faithfulness
• privacy

- to make a home and family
- to be admired by the loved one

The end of an affair

Typical Capricorns do not have casual affairs. If the relationship begins to fail, it often takes Capricorns a long time to take action, as they have a strong sense of duty to the partner and the family. In general, they dislike divorce. However, once a Capricorn realizes he or she has made a mistake in choosing a mate, then the parting will be abrupt and final. If a partner betrays a Capricorn, he or she will try first to organize things so that the partner can be reunited with the family, but if the betrayal continues, Capricorns can turn vengeful.

SECRET TIP

Of course, the shy and reserved Capricorn's version of being vengeful is to go Dutch at the break-up dinner.

CAPRICORN AND PARTNER

The person who contemplates becoming the marriage or business partner of a typical Capricorn must realize that Capricorn will take over the organization of the partner's working life. Given this, the person who partners Capricorn can expect stability, security, and success.

Capricorn man as partner

He will want a partner who can help him to achieve his ambitions. He will want to organize the business and will expect absolute loyalty and a disciplined routine. He may assume that the partner is dependent on him.

YOU'RE WELCOME FOR THE TIP

Are you the woman who can help a Capricorn man achieve his ambitions? Probably, since his ambition is to be your damn husband.

Capricorn woman as partner

She seeks a partner who has a good, secure position in life already. She is more likely to make a bad choice of partner than the male Capricorn, but she will soon recognize her mistake. In business, Capricorn women do not often choose other women as partners. If the partner, in marriage or business, is lost through death or similar misfortune, Capricorns of both sexes find it hard to replace the partner and will tend to withdraw into themselves.

BARE FACTS

A Capricorn woman is great for a guy's ego. Just knowing she'll probably never boff anybody again after you're dead is a real comfort.

Opposite sign

Cancer is the complementary opposite sign to Capricorn. Both are strong willed and may battle for supremacy concerning organization. However, Cancer can teach Capricorn how to sense other people's needs and feelings, and how to express his or her own emotions.

Capricorn

Cancer

Now if Cancer could just get these people to tap their feet to some halfway decent music.

CAPRICORN AND FRIENDS

In general, Capricorn likes a friend who is well-bred, good-mannered, and not too extroverted.

Positive factors

Capricorns are loyal, kind, and often very generous to friends. They try to prove their sincerity by showing total devotion to the friendship, but this can go wrong if the choice of friend has been a bad one in the first place. They will continue to love a friend who is old or disabled. They will not desert or neglect a loyal friend, no matter how bad the circumstances.

Negative factors

Capricorns are not very good judges of character. If a friendship goes wrong, because of bad judgment in the first place, Capricorn may turn hateful. If a Capricorn suspects a friend of deception, he or she will start to suspect all friends. A Capricorn may test the trustworthiness of friends several times. Capricorns have an irritating habit of organizing things that they think will be good for a friend, which the friend does not want. At their very worst, Capricorns may use a friend to further an ambition without a word of thanks. A compatibility chart below lists those with whom Capricorn is likely to have the most satisfactory relationships.

LISTEN UP, THIS IS IMPORTANT

While it is indeed noble of Capricorn to remain loyal to friends who become disabled, once the friend has become disabled it makes it tougher for them to get away.

COMPATIBILITY CHART

In general, if people are typical of their zodiac sign, relationships between Capricorn and other signs (including the complementary opposite sign, Cancer) are as shown below:

	Harmonious	Difficult	Turbulent
Capricorn	•		
Aquarius	•		
Pisces	•		
Aries		•	
Taurus	•		
Gemini			•
Cancer		•	
Leo			•
Virgo	•		
Libra		•	
Scorpio	•		
Sagittarius	•		

CAPRICORNEAN LEISURE INTERESTS

Most typical Capricorns are not much interested in team sports. They will work hard at a hobby and want to make a success of it. Whatever they choose to do, it must be respectable and increase their chances of being admired or honored. Capricorns are so aware of their duties and responsibilities that they often find it very difficult to allow themselves to enjoy anything for its own sake. As they get older and become grandparents, they tend to let loose a little and enjoy playing with their grandchildren. On the whole, typical Capricorns pursue the following leisure interests:

• music, listening or playing
• golf, walking, playing chess, tactical games
• visiting museums, galleries, and the theater
• reading, gardening, improving the home

CAPRICORNEAN LIKES AND DISLIKES

Likes
- hot, simple food
- antiques, history
- duties and responsibilities
- not being pressured by others, having plenty of time
- sexual love
- privacy
- what is regarded as the best, such as a Rolls Royce
- membership of an exclusive club
- home and family
- personalized gifts
- new books
- expensive gemstones

Dislikes
- untidiness
- being teased
- familiarity
- surprises
- new ideas
- loneliness
- being made to feel useless
- being embarrassed in public

✚ CAPRICORNEAN HEALTH

Typical Capricorns are likely to be less robust than most when they are young, but their resistance to disease increases with age. They are usually sober and temperate, so they often live to a ripe old age. Worry, heavy responsibilities, gloomy moods, and general pessimism tend to take their toll on Capricornean health, so Capricorns need brightening up sometimes and should learn to relax.

Types of sickness

Many Capricorns seem to have some difficulty thrust upon them. Sometimes that problem may be a chronic illness but, if this is the case, they bear it with great fortitude. Other sicknesses linked to Capricorn are rheumatism, bone diseases, sterility, damage to leg and knees, skin problems, and depression.

Capricorn at rest

A typical Capricorn likes to be doing something, even when relaxing. Many are to be found doing needlework or knitting while watching TV.

11. Aquarius: The Water Carrier
January 20 - February 18

The ELEVENTH sign of the zodiac is concerned with
- scientific analysis, experimentation, detachment
- friendship, courtesy, kindness, tranquility
- mystery, intrigues, magic, genius, originality
- eccentricity, independence, humanitarian issues
- fame, recognition, politics, creative arts
- electricity, magnetism, telecommunications

Elemental quality

Aquarius is the fixed air sign of the zodiac. It can be likened to a paraglider, jumping off the earth to explore a rainbow, yet aware of the practicalities of thermals and how to ensure a safe landing. Air represents the mind and the ability to think; Aquarian ideas may be unusual or even original, but once formed, they tend to remain fixed. Fixed air, in brief, is a metaphor for fixed opinions.

THE AQUARIAN PERSONALITY

CHARACTERISTICS

Positive
- Communicative
- Thoughtful and caring
- Cooperative and dependable
- Scientific
- Strong belief in humane reforms
- Independence of thought and action
- Intense interest in people
- Loyal friendship
- Inventive

Negative
- Unwilling to share ideas
- Tactless and rude
- Perverse and eccentric individuality
- Self-interested
- Unwillingness to fight for beliefs
- Uncertainty and lack of confidence
- Voyeuristic curiosity about people

BARE FACTS

Yeah, we know, we'd like to latch onto that "perverse and eccentric individuality" thing too, but unfortunately these books go by category and we're nowhere near the sex part yet.

Ruling planet and its effect

Uranus and Saturn both rule the zodiac sign of Aquarius, so anyone whose birth chart has a strongly developed Aquarius influence will tend to have original, unexpected ideas. In astrology, Uranus is the planet of the unusual and the unexpected, and Saturn is the planet of applied wisdom and forward planning.

THE AQUARIAN LOOK

People who exhibit the physical characteristics distinctive of the sign of Aquarius often look like nonconformists.

 ### SECRETS TO MAKE YOU LOOK GOOD

You would be confused about your inner identity too if you were as proud as an eagle, but still had to splash on half a bottle of galbanum before every party.

THE AQUARIUS MALE

Appearance
The typical Aquarius man
- is usually taller than average
- has long bones
- may have broad hips
- is strongly built
- has a distinctive facial profile
- has a high, broad forehead

Behavior and personality traits
The typical Aquarius man
- is unwilling to reveal his feelings

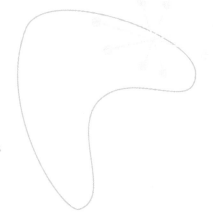

184

- is friendly toward everyone
- is a group person
- is fair minded and has his own very strong, but personal, moral code
- has wide interests
- is attracted to the mysterious and the secret
- is an intuitive thinker with a very practical streak
- does not usually aim to become rich but to develop his ideas and communicate them

LISTEN UP, THIS IS IMPORTANT

Aquarius Male = Abraham Lincoln getting a lap dance.

 # THE AQUARIUS FEMALE
Appearance
The typical Aquarius woman
- may have broad shoulders
- has a large bone structure
- has a long neck
- ignores feminine conventions, but always dresses in such a way that she looks stunning

Behavior and personality traits
The typical Aquarius woman
- has a wide circle of friends from all walks of life
- is concerned about and deeply involved in the community
- is adept at getting people to settle feuds
- can be totally unpredictable
- has a wide variety of interests and a mind of her own

- will have a basic lack of self-confidence
- can be easygoing and accepts the many differences among people

COMMUNICATION

Aquarius Female = Part Amazonian, part Zoning Board Commissioner.

YOUNG AQUARIUS
Behavior and personality traits

The typical Aquarius child
- is a quick thinker
- is sensitive and intuitive
- is outwardly calm, relaxed, and delightful
- is unpredictable and full of amazing ideas
- wants to analyze everything and everyone
- does not like emotional demands
- rebels against commands and rules but comes to sensible conclusions when allowed to think things through for him or herself
- is generous to friends
- has a huge number of friends of all kinds
- tends to be absentminded

Bringing up young Aquarius

Young Aquarius has an enquiring and analytical mind and is constantly on the go. He or she needs plenty of opportunity to make discoveries, try out inventions and communicate ideas to others. Young Aquarius tends to be detached and dispassionate, finding close relationships difficult.

Young Aquarius's needs

A peaceful, calm, and harmonious environment is essential to young Aquarius, because he or she is so sensitive to underlying tensions. Young Aquarius often looks more confident than he or she is, so parental understanding and genuine encouragement are needed. Like any child, Aquarius needs love, especially in the form of respect, listening, appreciation, and friendship.

AQUARIUS AT HOME
Typical behavior and abilities

When at home, a suave Aquarius man or woman
- lives in a spacious, elegant apartment filled with interesting items.
- eats unusual menus of gourmet food
- enjoys having houseguests from all walks of life

When at home, a messy Aquarian man or woman
- lives in a tiny, untidy condo filled with oddities
- eats strange mixtures of plain food
- enjoys a wide variety of friends dropping in who feel at home in a creative mess

- leaves inventions lying around
- only washes up when in the right frame of mind

YOU'RE WELCOME FOR THE TIP

Gee whiz, none of the other zodiac signs get to decide whether they want to be "suave," or "messy." Judging from the above criteria, the suave Aquarian is the one in the turtleneck that you just want to drop with a swift right, and the messy Aquarian's tiny, untidy condo is most likely notable for its padded walls.

Aquarius as parent

The typical Aquarius parent

- is a friend for life
- encourages independence of thought
- does not concentrate on discipline
- is prepared to discuss even adult problems
- is kind, relaxed, and makes rational judgments
- does not like or encourage emotional arguments
- will want the best of modern education for the children

Two Aquarians in the same family

When married, they usually enjoy a peaceful, friendly relationship. Aquarius parents and children can also get on well, although serious personal problems may be ignored in favor of taking a broad view of humanitarian ideas. Aquarians can be quite crazy together on occasion, as they all have bright minds and are intuitive.

The real fun starts when a "messy" hooks up with a "suave." Keep plenty of bleach on hand to thoroughly eradicate the bloodstains.

AQUARIUS AT WORK
Behavior and abilities

A typical Aquarius at work
- enjoys working within a group
- usually likes to use his or her mind
- dislikes routine and decision-making
- enjoys variety

Aquarius as employer

A typical Aquarius boss (male or female)
- is fair and will pay employees exactly what the job deserves
- will be generous to anyone doing extra special work beyond the terms of a contract
- although not a natural executive, he or she will carry out the role of boss using all the Aquarian skills of quick thinking and shrewd analysis
- will expect a day's work for a day's pay
- dislikes any form of dishonesty
- is unshockable
- will not forgive lies or broken promises
- will give employees all the rope they need (even to hang themselves)

LISTEN UP, THIS IS IMPORTANT

Those of you too young to remember the last days of the Nixon administration will, unfortunately, have no accurate frame of reference for what it's like to work for an Aquarian.

Aquarius as employee

A typical Aquarius employee (male or female)

• is aloof but gathers a large circle of friends

• will regularly go off into a mental exploration of future possibilities—and return with some very creative ideas

• brings a fresh approach to any task

• will frequently change his or her job or type of occupation in the early years; later he or she will settle down and stay with one company

• is conscientious, courteous, and has a knack for sensing what's wrong with machinery

Working environment

The workplace of a typical Aquarius man or woman

• could be almost anywhere in the world

• will have the latest communication technology

• changes frequently

• should be free from emotional tensions and noise

DON'T BE A JERK

The jerk sitting naked with the laptop, Bluetooth and BlackBerry while you're trying to relax on that secluded strip of Thailand beach? He was born between January 20th and February 18th. Guaranteed.

Typical occupations

Anything that involves experimentation, ideas, investigation, analysis, and innovation attracts Aquarius. For example: dancer, scientist, photographer, astrologer, singer, TV or radio presenter, writer, charity worker, inventor, archeologist, radiographer, electronics engineer, humanitarian aid worker.

SECRET TIP

Don't worry, even though they would make good astrologers, we wouldn't have let their type near this book.

♡ AQUARIUS AND LOVE

To Aquarius, love is an attitude of caring for all humanity. Aquarius in love will have many of the characteristics listed below.

Behavior when in love

The typical Aquarius

- attracts the opposite sex in the first place by their friendly, open manner
- may try to seem glamorously aloof
- is afraid of a deeply emotional involvement
- genuinely wants friendship with the loved one
- will guard his or her independence jealously
- enjoys a living-apart relationship

Expectations

The typical Aquarius expects

- his wife to stay at home
- her husband to share or take over the running of the home
- personal freedom of movement and action

- loyalty and faithfulness, which Aquarius will give in full once happily married
- understanding and tolerance of his or her oddities
- the partner to enjoy frequent visits from a wide variety of friends from every walk of life

BARE FACTS

As noted above, the Aquarian will give loyalty and faithfulness in full once happily married. Your job, however, is to find someone to get them out of the hot tub full of hotties an hour before they're supposed to marry you.

The end of an affair

The typical Aquarius has only one love affair at a time and is devoted to that partner until curiosity leads them elsewhere. Aquarius, male or female, likes to dominate the relationship (as a way of controlling the feared emotions). A partner who makes too many demands, becomes jealous, or tries to put limitations on Aquarius's freedom is usually dropped quite suddenly and may be treated like a total stranger. If the partner does not take the hint, Aquarius is quite capable of doing something to make the partner end the affair. Once Aquarius has settled into a marriage, he or she does not like the idea of divorce and will often want to remain friends with a past partner.

YOU'RE WELCOME FOR THE TIP

Here are some of the things you could do that would make an Aquarian want to end the relationship: 1) speak, 2) have an opinion, and 3) talk.

AQUARIUS AND PARTNER

The person who contemplates becoming the marriage or business partner of a typical Aquarius must realize that Aquarius will need to have unlimited freedom. Aquarius will also want to dominate the partnership in order to ensure his or her interests in the wider world are not restricted. Given this, the person who partners Aquarius can expect loyalty, a fair share of the work, and never to have the business taken away from them. Although Aquarius has no great driving ambition, the typical Aquarius has a very fine mind (one of the best in the zodiac) and can be an asset to any venture. If fame comes their way, the Aquarius partner will happily lap it up.

Aquarius man as partner

He will want a partner who recognizes the ideas and inventiveness that he can bring to the business and who will allow him the freedom to introduce new concepts. Business partners contemplating asking an Aquarius to join them should first ensure that he has enough knowledge about the business. Aquarius man wants a marriage partner who will run the home and children and be a loyal, lifelong friend. He wants a woman who is capable of looking after herself and who will not need to lean on him. A woman who wants a good income from a steady breadwinner should look elsewhere.

LISTEN UP, THIS IS IMPORTANT

What do you call an Aquarian man without a girlfriend? Homeless.

Aquarius woman as partner

So long as she is left to circulate freely among her many friends and pursue her dozens of outside interests, Aquarius woman will be a faithful partner. Although she can be tender and caring, she inhabits a world of ideas. She needs a partner who recognizes her brilliant mind. In business or marriage, Aquarius woman will be concerned that her partner is recognized for his intellectual achievements; she is far less interested in making money. She will enjoy physical closeness, but will also be happy with long periods when the relationship remains relatively platonic.

SECRETS TO MAKE YOU LOOK GOOD

Translation: the Aquarian woman needs a bunch of friends outside the relationship to keep her mind from settling on how much she hates your guts.

Opposite sign

Leo is the complementary opposite sign to Aquarius. Although relations between them can be difficult, Leo can show Aquarius how to make choices to please the self, rather than for an ideal. In this way, Aquarius can build emotional self-confidence.

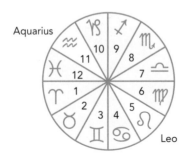

AQUARIUS AND FRIENDS

Aquarius makes many friends but has very few confidants. In general, Aquarius likes a friend who has intellectual interests and enjoys the unusual and the radical. Aquarius will be friendly toward anyone and will tend to regard any relationship as platonic.

Positive factors

Aquarius rarely passes judgment upon the ethical codes of friends—but will expect them to live by their codes. Aquarius will put a lot of effort into his or her friendships and make friends with anyone: rich and poor, black and white, good and bad. An Aquarian friend is a constant source of mental stimulation, information, and practical help.

Negative factors

An Aquarius will take a great interest in his or her friend's ideas, and may eventually adopt some of them as his or her own, using them whenever it is convenient. Aquarius tends to take over a friendship, slowly but surely, and put the friend in a subordinate role. Aquarius also pours out troubles to friends, expecting their concerns to be regarded as more important than anything else. However, when friends need help with their own problems, Aquarius tends to draw back and tell them to ignore the problem and it will go away. A compatibility chart on page 196 lists those with whom Aquarius is likely to have the most satisfactory relationships.

Basically, an Aquarius will manipulate, disappoint, and negate you no matter if you're rich or poor, male or female, or good or bad. They're generous that way.

COMPATIBILITY CHART

In general, if people are typical of their zodiac sign, relationships between Aquarius and other signs (including the complementary opposite sign, Leo) are as shown below:

	Harmonious	Difficult	Turbulent
Aquarius	•		
Pisces	•		
Aries	•		
Taurus		•	
Gemini	•		
Cancer			•
Leo		•	
Virgo			•
Libra	•		
Scorpio		•	
Sagittarius	•		
Capricorn	•		

AQUARIAN LEISURE INTERESTS

On the whole, a typical Aquarius pursues the following leisure interests:

• radical arts and theater
• music, rhythm, dance, controlled exercise
• clowning, juggling, witty comedy

- flying, parachuting, gliding
- writing his or her autobiography or a personal diary
- scientific or creative hobbies
- local politics

SNAP OF THE FINGER

If you have any say in the matter, steer them away from the damn juggling.

AQUARIAN LIKES AND DISLIKES

Likes
- fame or recognition
- thinking about self
- privacy
- rainbows, dreams, magic
- change, eccentricity, surprises
- credit cards
- telling others what needs to be done—then watching them do it
- get on with it
- weird friends
- living within their means

Dislikes
- emotion and intimacy
- people who show off
- being taken for granted
- being pinned down in any way
- any kind of hard sell
- violence and fighting
- making loans or borrowing
- conventional authority
- revealing own motives
- extravagance

AQUARIAN HEALTH

A typical Aquarius needs lots of fresh air, plenty of sleep, and regular exercise to stay healthy—alas, they often do not give themselves enough of any of these. Young Aquarius is usually very healthy, except for the odd complaint, which seems undiagnosable and goes away of

197

its own accord. When mature, Aquarius may suffer from nervous complaints due to their intense mental activity. They may also acquire a series of phobias. Aquarians may respond to hypnosis.

Types of sickness

They have a tendency to suffer according to the weather—which is always too hot, too cold, too humid, or too dry for their comfort. Circulatory problems are linked with Aquarius. Diseases of the blood and nervous system are common, as are varicose veins and accidents to the calves and ankles. Aquarius is linked with the extraordinary in every way and that includes sicknesses. Sudden, inexplicable illness can overtake Aquarius and may then clear up equally mysteriously.

YOU'RE WELCOME FOR THE TIP

Aquarians: not only prone to illness, but a pain in the ass about it, too!

Aquarius at rest

Any opportunity to lie in a hammock in the garden and dream the day away is wonderful for Aquarius's well-being.

WELL LOOK WHO FINALLY MADE THE RODEO

Let's review: Aquarians are controlling, independent to a fault, but also somewhat airheaded and unreliable. Whatever you do, do not fall asleep, or you may wake up and find that your body has been snatched by an Aquarian. Now, more than ever, they must be stopped.

12. Pisces: The Fishes
February 19 - March 20

The TWELFTH sign of the zodiac is concerned with
- compassion, sympathy, love, altruism
- dreams, the psychic, clairvoyance, sixth sense
- illusions, magic, film, fantasy, make-believe
- art, drama, music, poetry, prose, dance
- unusual talent, memory, wisdom, versatility
- sensitivity, intuition, humor, satire
- secrets, fulfillment of life, eternity

Elemental quality

Pisces is the mutable water sign of the zodiac. It can be likened to a warm, turquoise lagoon, twinkling in the sunshine, or to a strong ocean current rising from the depths to break over a rocky shore, smoothing the pebbles for all time. Mutable means changeable, and water can change its form in many ways: rain, hail, snow, mist, frost, clouds, rainbows, warm pools, and puddles; thus, Piscean feelings can change a dozen times a day.

THE PISCEAN PERSONALITY

CHARACTERISTICS

Positive
- Loving and caring
- Trusting, hospitable, and will help all in distress
- Shy
- Helpful
- Romantic
- Creative
- Mystical
- Gentle and kind
- Compassionate
- Understanding of others

Negative
- Self-pitying
- Gullible and will give all in a lost cause
- Temperamental
- Dependent
- Escapist
- Sensationalist
- Depressive
- Can lose touch with reality
- Too emotionally involved with the problems of others
- Tends to blame self for everything

COMMUNICATION

If one of these altruistic souls ends up being your paramedic after the accident, try to focus on their positive qualities.

Ruling planet and its effect

Jupiter and Neptune rule the zodiac sign of Pisces, so anyone whose birth chart has a strong Piscean influence will tend to bring benefit to others through their sensitivity. In astrology, Jupiter is the planet of expansion, optimism, and generosity. Neptune is the planet of dreams, sensitivity, the unconscious, and the world of unreality.

SECRETS TO MAKE YOU LOOK GOOD

Don't worry, environmentalists: Pisces are dolphin-safe!

THE PISCEAN LOOK

People who exhibit physical characteristics of Pisces look more clumsy than they actually are. They give off a feeling of otherworldliness, and usually have very sensitive, caring eyes. They may have a trusting, eager look or a quality of empathy and nonjudgment exclusive to those who truly understand human sorrows and failings.

STRETCHING THE TRUTH

Ninety-eight percent of people at the open casting call for "Angry Russian Mob" are Pisces.

THE PISCES MALE
Appearance

The typical Pisces man
• may be tall but is not physically distinctive
• has a somewhat clumsy appearance

- has rather heavy jowls
- has broad or thick shoulders

Behavior and personality traits

The typical Piscean man
- has few prejudices
- is not ambitious for status, fame, or fortune, although he can make good use of opportunities if they come his way
- is very romantic
- cannot easily be fooled
- has few material needs, but needs his dreams
- talks slowly and is knowledgeable on many subjects
- is rarely jealous, but gets hurt all the same
- is emotionally involved in whatever he does, although he may never show it

SECRET TIP

Pisces Male = A Navy Seal with self-esteem issues.

THE PISCES FEMALE
Appearance

The typical Pisces woman
- is normally slim, but tends to put on weight easily in later years
- has large eyes and an oval face
- has a clear, soft skin, whatever her color
- has an air of feminine mystery
- has a very warm, charming smile

Behavior and personality traits

The typical Pisces woman

- does not try to dominate her partner in any way
- often appears vague and dreamy
- is subtle and, while appearing to be helpless or incapable, gets things organized and manages the finances extremely well
- protects her vulnerability with humor or a sophisticated exterior
- needs to belong to someone
- has a warm, sympathetic heart

LISTEN UP, THIS IS IMPORTANT

Pisces Female = Betty Boop on Prozac.

 # YOUNG PISCES
Behavior and personality traits

The typical Pisces child

- has the sweetest, dimpled smiles and the most winning ways of all babies
- lives in a world of make-believe
- dislikes orderliness and routines
- has an amazing imagination
- holds secret conversations with invisible (and sometimes long dead) people
- has a very active sixth sense
- believes in magic, fairies, and Santa Claus, and may reinvent myths
- enjoys the company of adults more than that of other children
- rarely loses his or her temper, and instead just happily goes his or her own way

Bringing up young Pisces

At school, young Pisces avoids the limelight and does not take leadership positions, so he or she should never be pushed to take such roles. However, Piscean children are the source of wonderful ideas for play and adventure in which Pisces will be happy to let other children take the lead. Parents would be wise to gently help young Pisces to distinguish between fantasy and reality, without destroying his or her rich imagination. Because of their passive, nonaggressive natures, Piscean children may sometimes be the victims of bullies, so it would be useful to teach them strategies for dealing with such situations.

Young Pisces's needs

Young Pisces needs to feel he or she belongs to someone or several someones. Emotional connections with people are absolutely essential to Piscean happiness. He or she is less concerned about places and things, although attachments to animals are often sought as well. Consequently, a Pisces child should be helped to believe in him or herself and prevented from becoming too clinging. Parents who cling to their Pisces child are doing him or her no good at all.

PISCES AT HOME
Typical behavior and abilities

When at home, a Pisces man or woman

• will often enter a fantasy world
• will feel safe to freely explore his or her imagination
• will probably have no fixed routine
• is likely to be untidy, although he or she may have a sudden urge to tidy everything to avoid confusion: this can happen at any time
• should keep a large, clear clock
• will need a space for personal privacy
• will make the home itself into a wonderful world of art, music, design, and good food and wine

Pisces as parent

The typical Pisces parent

• can happily accommodate all the fantasies of childhood
• will allow a child plenty of imaginative freedom
• may lack discipline
• listens with understanding
• encourages personal development
• may have to teach the children punctuality
• is warm and loving and rarely uses harsh words
• may tend to spoil the children
• will probably have a very personal and unusual set of rules to which the children must adhere

Two Pisces in the same family

Pisces in the same family should get along very well, providing they have an outlet for their vivid, unworldly imaginations. For example, Piscean siblings may build an imaginative world together; or a Piscean parent who makes fictional films will find inspiration in the ideas of his or her offspring.

PISCES AT WORK
Typical behavior and abilities

A typical Pisces at work

• is rarely in an executive position, nor does he or she enjoy being tied to working in a team that has a strict routine

• enjoys work that offers freedom of expression, which usually means working alone or in a self-directed position

• if working in a team, Pisces prefers an occupation that allows for frequent changes and adaptations

Pisces as employer

A typical Pisces boss (male or female)

• is more likely to be found in organizations as a director rather than as the boss

• will serve people rather than accumulate power

• uses his or her gifts to make the correct move

• is a shrewd judge of character

• is unconventional and creative

• values those who are conventional and well organized, because they are needed to back up his or her ideas

• will never refuse help to someone in need

• may act tough to hide a deep belief in the mystical

SECRETS TO MAKE YOU LOOK GOOD

If, at your periodic employee reviews, you are asked to "visualize" and/or "manifest" a raise, you probably have a Pisces boss.

Pisces as employee

A typical Pisces employee (male or female)

• needs work where there is plenty of outlet for either human understanding or creative imagination

• will be depressed, lazy, and useless if neither of these needs is satisfied

• will be very affected by surroundings

• when happy is a loyal worker

• will get the job done, although nobody seems to understand how he or she operates

Working environment

The workplace of a typical Pisces man or woman

- must feel comfortable
- will have a pleasant atmosphere
- should be a large and flexible space
- may be brightly colored

Typical occupations

All kinds of jobs in film, theater, TV, radio, ballet, music, and art will attract Pisces, who is often a good actor. A job that allows travel will be attractive. Advertising, public relations, and any job that is part of the service industry. Helping people to solve their problems and charitable and church work are also very attractive to Pisces.

♡ PISCES AND LOVE

To Pisces, there is no difference between love, affection, and romance. A Pisces needs all three. A Pisces who feels unloved is an unhappy person to whom life seems very gray. Love revitalizes Pisces.

Behavior when in love

The typical Pisces

- is romantic
- eager to please

- adapts to the demands of the relationship
- appears to be helpless, delicate, and vulnerable, but being loved enables Pisces to cope very well with a range of difficulties, problems, and tragedies
- is emotionally involved, to the point of not recognizing when he or she is being deceived or treated badly

Expectations

The typical Pisces expects

- to have his or her dreams valued and to be protected from harsh criticism
- to be cared for romantically
- to have children (Pisces love children)
- to be frequently reassured that they are loved
- all birthdays and anniversaries to be remembered

LISTEN UP, THIS IS IMPORTANT

Dating a Pisces is like being involved with an extremely needy Hobbit.

The end of an affair

Some Pisces tend to drift into another relationship almost without noticing, yet are surprised when they are accused of unfaithfulness. The self-doubt, which haunts many Pisces, can only be dispelled by repeated reassurance that they are lovable. Consequently, Pisces may sometimes just leave a relationship for no clear reason and with no regrets. It is not that Pisces does not love the abandoned partner anymore. On the contrary, Pisces will often show much sympathetic understanding and will try to retain a friendly relationship with the one he or she has left. The worst possible event for a Pisces is to be rejected by the one who loved them. A partner who wants to end a relationship with a typical Pisces will find this a very difficult thing to do. Pisces will cling, convinced that if they reform in some way, everything will be all right again. The ex-partner of a Pisces may have to go to extremes to extricate him or herself from the emotional mess that a hurt Pisces can produce.

BARE FACTS

So basically, they think nothing of dumping you, but if you dump them all hell breaks loose? Ladies, you may have to face the uncanny possibility that every man you've dated since high school is a Pisces.

PISCES AND PARTNER

The person who contemplates becoming the marriage or business partner of a typical Pisces must realize that Pisces will expect to be supported—emotionally or financially. Given this, the person who partners Pisces can expect loyalty and sensitive understanding.

Pisces man as partner

He will want a partner who will work for him: someone to run the household efficiently and who will entertain his friends and business colleagues. In return, the married Pisces will bring great joy to a household with his wonderful imagination. Marriage gives male Pisces more self-assurance, so he will become more decisive. Potential business partners should be prepared to undertake the practical, administrative side of the business, leaving the Piscean partner free to exercise their creativity and understanding.

Pisces woman as partner

She will want a marriage partner who will support her in every respect. To many men, Pisces is the perfectly feminine woman. She may appear to be a helpless, fluffy person but, once married, she will feel secure, and her reserve of talents and abilities will pour out in every direction. In business, a Pisces woman will be best in creative positions and in public relations, but should not be expected to do the routine office jobs.

BARE FACTS

The lucky fellow who commits to a life together with Mrs. Pisces will soon discover that she is like the perfect sitcom mother. That is, if June Cleaver was wearing crotchless panties underneath that apron.

Opposite sign

Virgo is the complementary opposite sign to Pisces. While Pisces adapts himself or herself to the emotional needs of others, Virgo works hard to serve others by responding to the needs of the moment with practical solutions. From Virgo, Pisces can learn how to translate Piscean sensitivity and understanding into practical action—thus dispelling self-doubt and building confidence in his or her Piscean abilities.

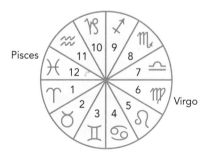

YOU'RE WELCOME FOR THE TIP

Hey, Pisces, these Virgos are just trying to make you behave like normal people, so don't give them so much aggravation, all right?

PISCES AND FRIENDS

In general, Pisces likes a friend who is useful and reassuring. In return, they will give unprejudiced understanding and loyalty to their friends.

Positive factors

Pisces are emotionally attached to their friends and will rarely notice if the friend is taking advantage of this involvement. Pisces are friendly, humorous, and caring friends, even if there are long periods of time between meetings. Pisces will always think up something interesting to do and will enjoy any kind of artistic ventures.

Negative factors

Pisces can be a confusing person, so arrangements may be difficult to make. Pisces can sometimes seem to be cool and offhand. This is usually temporary and due to a moment of insecurity. Pisces needs a hero or heroine to identify with. If a friend happens to be the chosen one, this can be pleasant enough but may become a nuisance when Pisces gives the friend talents he or she hasn't got and expects them to be demonstrated! Pisces does not find it easy to conform; friends with conservative attitudes may find this a difficulty. A compatibility chart on page 213 lists those with whom Pisces is likely to have the most satisfactory relationships.

It's great that Pisceans are easily taken advantage of, but they don't really have anything you can use, so where's the fun in that?

COMPATIBILITY CHART

In general, if people are typical of their zodiac sign, relationships between Pisces and other signs (including the complementary opposite sign, Virgo) are as shown below:

	Harmonious	Difficult	Turbulent
Pisces	•		
Aries	•		
Taurus	•		
Gemini		•	
Cancer	•		
Leo			•
Virgo		•	
Libra			•
Scorpio	•		
Sagittarius		•	
Capricorn	•		
Aquarius	•		

PISCES LEISURE INTERESTS

Most typical Pisces love artistic pursuits and anything that has an element of mystery, fantasy, and imagination. Pisceans love films, theater, traveling entertainers, pantomimes, witches, monsters, elves, gypsies, and mythical creatures. Team sports are not a natural Piscean activity, but Pisceans often love gentle water sports, noncompetitive skiing, and

213

skydiving. Dangerous sports, such as racing cars, can also appeal to the Pisces because they have an unerring instinct in such situations.

STRETCHING THE TRUTH

Pisces unerring instincts when racing cars come from all the witches, monsters, and elves in their pit crew.

PISCEAN LIKES AND DISLIKES

Likes
- seafood, champagne and organic foods
- romantic places, sunsets over the sea, mountain vistas, waterfalls, ponds and water lilies
- background music, poetry
- people who need their understanding
- mystical settings, candles, incense
- being loved
- freedom to drift along from time to time
- privacy
- colorful food
- personalized gifts
- presents wrapped in magical paper
- new books
- diamonds

Dislikes
- bright, noisy, crowded places
- dirty, ugly objects
- being told to get a grip on things
- stiff clothing
- authorities
- people knowing too much about him or her

✚ PISCES HEALTH

Typical Pisces are healthy people so long as they feel loved and have an outlet for their dreams. Unhappy Pisces are vulnerable to problems arising from turning to drink, drugs, or other ways of getting relief from what may seem unbearable emotional insecurities. Pisces often has to work hard to swim against the current that would pull him or her under. The constant effort of avoiding being sucked into oblivion is the cause of much distress to many Pisces, who, consequently, may suffer depression and other emotional problems.

Types of sickness

Troubles with the feet and toes are common among Pisces: bunions, corns, boils and foot deformities may occur. Pisces may become forgetful when illness is about to strike. They may also suffer from the effects of too much wine or too many drugs. The sensitive Piscean psyche suffers greatly in times of stress and has little to draw on by way of personal resources.

LISTEN UP, THIS IS IMPORTANT

Like many of us, Pisceans can turn to drugs and alcohol to cope with their inner turmoil. However, most of us would not classify bunions as inner turmoil.

Pisces at rest

A relaxed Pisces is the happiest person on earth. A chance to lie back, sip wine, listen to music and let the imagination wander is perfect bliss to Pisces.

WELL LOOK WHO FINALLY MADE THE RODEO

In summation, Pisceans are loving and helpful, but tend to live in an imaginary world of their own devising. And, just so you know, they are usually more loving and helpful to the people in *that* world than they are to you.

Part II:
Chinese
Astrology

Introduction

History

Astrology is one of the most ancient of the Chinese philosophies. It is at least 2,000 years old. Originally, astrology was inseparable from astronomy. The two were considered to be one discipline. China has one of the oldest civilizations in the world, and from very early on practitioners of astronomy/astrology were always present as officials of the imperial court.

In ancient China, astrology was used to reveal what was expected to happen to a nation. It was not until the beginning of the Christian era that astrology began to be used to give individual readings. By the time of the Tang dynasty (618–907 A.D.), a whole encyclopedia had been written about the art of giving personal astrological readings.

Legends

The origin of the twelve animal signs of Chinese astrology is unclear. Chinese legend attributes the creation of the signs to the Yellow Emperor in 2637 B.C. The Yellow Emperor is a semimythical figure in Chinese history. Other legends credit Buddha (c. 563–c. 483 B.C.) with the creation of the twelve-animal cycle. Apparently, he invited all the animals to visit him, but, for some reason, only twelve animals showed up. To thank them, Buddha gave each animal a year which would be dedicated to that animal alone throughout history. The years were allocated in the order in which the animals had arrived.

A Depiction of Buddha

The Twelve Animals
1 Rat
2 Ox
3 Tiger
4 Rabbit
5 Dragon
6 Snake
7 Horse
8 Goat
9 Monkey
10 Rooster
11 Dog
12 Pig

How to use this section

In this section, we have considered five different aspects of the Chinese astrological chart. These are:

- the animal sign
- the natural element

- the dominant element
- Yin and Yang
- companion in life

Also, at the end of each animal chapter is a brief look at how the Western and Chinese zodiacs can be combined to give even more-detailed readings.

All you need to know to access information about all these aspects is:
- year of birth
- date of birth
- hour of birth (the nearest hour or two is enough)

For example, if you were born on July 30, 1970 between the hours of 3 P.M. and 5 P.M.

1. First, using your year of birth, find out your animal sign from the tables on pages 220–227. In this instance, the person is a dog.

2. We know that the natural element of all dogs is metal and that they are Yang people (this information is included at the start of each animal chapter and is also shown by the chart on page 228).

3. Also from the year of birth, we know that the person's dominant element is metal (see the sections on elements in the relevant animal chapter). In this case, the dominant and the natural element are both metal—but they are not always the same.

4. From the hour of birth, we know that the person's companion in life is the monkey (see the chart on page 232 to calculate your inner companion).

5. From the date of birth, we can calculate that the person is a Leo (see chart on page 233 to work this out).

In this example, the person should read the chapters on the dog and the monkey to get a full Chinese astrological reading. Further information on the elements and Yin and Yang forces can be obtained by reading the relevant parts of this introduction.

Animal Signs

The animal signs are the most basic aspect of Chinese astrology. The signs are not based on the position of the stars as in Western astrology, but instead on the person's year of birth. Each animal is allocated its own years. There are twelve animals and they always appear in the same order (rat, ox, tiger, rabbit, dragon, snake, horse, goat, monkey, rooster, dog and pig). The cycle of animals, therefore, repeats itself every twelve years.

The Chinese calendar is based on the lunar year (orbits of the Moon around the Earth). The Western calendar is based on the solar year (orbit of the Earth around the Sun). The two do not correspond exactly. Each lunar year, therefore, begins on a slightly different date of the solar year.

To find your animal sign, look up the year of your birth in the first column of the following tables. If you were born in January or February of that year, however, remember to check the dates that the Chinese lunar year begins on, as you may find that you actually belong to the previous animal year. Once you have identified your animal sign, read the chapter devoted to that animal.

JAN. 31, 1900 – FEB. 17, 1912

1900	Jan. 31, 1900–Feb. 18, 1901	Rat
1901	Feb. 19, 1901–Feb. 7, 1902	Ox
1902	Feb. 8, 1902–Jan. 28, 1903	Tiger
1903	Jan. 29, 1903–Feb. 15, 1904	Rabbit
1904	Feb. 16, 1904–Feb. 3, 1905	Dragon
1905	Feb. 4, 1905–Jan. 24, 1906	Snake
1906	Jan. 25, 1906–Feb. 12, 1907	Horse
1907	Feb. 13, 1907–Feb. 1, 1908	Goat
1908	Feb. 2, 1908–Jan. 21, 1909	Monkey
1909	Jan. 22, 1909–Feb. 9, 1910	Rooster
1910	Feb. 10, 1910–Jan. 29, 1911	Dog
1911	Jan. 30, 1911–Feb. 17, 1912	Pig

FEB. 18, 1912 – FEB. 4, 1924

1912	Feb. 18, 1912–Feb. 5, 1913	Rat
1913	Feb. 6, 1913–Jan. 25, 1914	Ox
1914	Jan. 26, 1914–Feb. 13, 1915	Tiger
1915	Feb. 14, 1915–Feb. 2, 1916	Rabbit
1916	Feb. 3, 1916–Jan. 22, 1917	Dragon
1917	Jan. 23, 1917–Feb. 10, 1918	Snake
1918	Feb. 11, 1918–Jan. 31, 1919	Horse
1919	Feb. 1, 1919–Feb. 19, 1920	Goat
1920	Feb. 20, 1920–Feb. 7, 1921	Monkey
1921	Feb. 8, 1921–Jan. 27, 1922	Rooster
1922	Jan. 28, 1922–Feb. 15, 1923	Dog
1923	Feb. 16, 1923–Feb. 4, 1924	Pig

FEB. 5, 1924 – JAN. 23, 1936

1924	Feb. 5, 1924–Jan. 24, 1925	Rat
1925	Jan. 25, 1925–Feb. 12, 1926	Ox
1926	Feb. 13, 1926–Feb. 1, 1927	Tiger
1927	Feb. 2, 1927–Jan. 22, 1928	Rabbit
1928	Jan. 23, 1928–Feb. 9, 1929	Dragon
1929	Feb. 10, 1929–Jan. 29, 1930	Snake
1930	Jan. 30, 1930–Feb. 16, 1931	Horse
1931	Feb. 17, 1931–Feb. 5, 1932	Goat
1932	Feb. 6, 1932–Jan. 25, 1933	Monkey
1933	Jan. 26, 1933–Feb. 13, 1934	Rooster
1934	Feb. 14, 1934–Feb. 3, 1935	Dog
1935	Feb. 4, 1935–Jan. 23, 1936	Pig

Jan. 24, 1936 – Feb. 9, 1948

1936	Jan. 24, 1936–Feb. 10, 1937	Rat
1937	Feb. 11, 1937–Jan. 30, 1938	Ox
1938	Jan. 31, 1938–Feb. 18, 1939	Tiger
1939	Feb. 19, 1939–Feb. 7, 1940	Rabbit
1940	Feb. 8, 1940–Jan. 26, 1941	Dragon
1941	Jan. 27, 1941–Feb. 14, 1942	Snake
1942	Feb. 15, 1942–Feb. 4, 1943	Horse
1943	Feb. 5, 1943–Jan. 24, 1944	Goat
1944	Jan. 25, 1944–Feb. 12, 1945	Monkey
1945	Feb. 13, 1945–Feb. 1, 1946	Rooster
1946	Feb. 2, 1946–Jan. 21, 1947	Dog
1947	Jan. 22, 1947–Feb. 9, 1948	Pig

Feb. 10, 1948 – Jan. 27, 1960

1948	Feb. 10, 1948–Jan. 28, 1949	Rat
1949	Jan. 29, 1949–Feb. 16, 1950	Ox
1950	Feb. 17, 1050–Feb. 5, 1951	Tiger
1951	Feb. 6, 1951–Jan. 26, 1952	Rabbit
1952	Jan. 27, 1952–Feb. 13, 1953	Dragon
1953	Feb. 14, 1953–Feb. 2, 1954	Snake
1954	Feb. 3, 1954–Jan. 23, 1955	Horse
1955	Jan. 24, 1955–Feb. 11, 1956	Goat
1956	Feb. 12, 1956–Jan. 30, 1957	Monkey
1957	Jan. 31, 1957–Feb. 17, 1958	Rooster
1958	Feb. 18, 1958–Feb. 7, 1959	Dog
1959	Feb. 8, 1959–Jan. 27, 1960	Pig

JAN. 28, 1960 – FEB. 14, 1972

1960	Jan. 28, 1960–Feb. 14, 1961	Rat
1961	Feb. 15, 1961–Feb. 4, 1962	Ox
1962	Feb. 5, 1962–Jan. 24, 1963	Tiger
1963	Jan. 25, 1963–Feb. 12, 1964	Rabbit
1964	Feb. 13, 1964–Feb. 1, 1965	Dragon
1965	Feb. 2, 1965–Jan. 20, 1966	Snake
1966	Jan. 21, 1966–Feb. 8, 1967	Horse
1967	Feb. 9, 1967–Jan. 29, 1968	Goat
1968	Jan. 30, 1968–Feb. 16, 1969	Monkey
1969	Feb. 17, 1969–Feb. 5, 1970	Rooster
1970	Feb. 6, 1970–Jan. 26, 1971	Dog
1971	Jan. 27, 1971–Feb. 14, 1972	Pig

FEB. 15, 1972 – FEB. 1, 1984

1972	Feb. 15, 1972–Feb. 2, 1973	Rat
1973	Feb. 3, 1973–Jan. 22, 1974	Ox
1974	Jan. 23, 1974–Feb. 10, 1975	Tiger
1975	Feb. 11, 1975–Jan. 30, 1976	Rabbit
1976	Jan. 31, 1976–Feb. 17, 1977	Dragon
1977	Feb. 18, 1977–Feb. 6, 1978	Snake
1978	Feb. 7, 1978–Jan. 27, 1979	Horse
1979	Jan. 28, 1979–Feb. 15, 1980	Goat
1980	Feb. 16, 1980–Feb. 4, 1981	Monkey
1981	Feb. 5, 1981–Jan. 24, 1982	Rooster
1982	Jan. 25, 1982–Feb. 12, 1983	Dog
1983	Feb. 13, 1983–Feb. 1, 1984	Pig

Feb. 2, 1984 – Feb. 18, 1996

1984	Feb. 2, 1984–Feb. 19, 1985	Rat
1985	Feb. 20, 1985–Feb. 8, 1986	Ox
1986	Feb. 9, 1986–Jan. 28, 1987	Tiger
1987	Jan. 29, 1987–Feb. 16, 1988	Rabbit
1988	Feb. 17, 1988–Feb. 5, 1989	Dragon
1989	Feb. 6, 1989–Jan. 26, 1990	Snake
1990	Jan. 27, 1990–Feb. 14, 1991	Horse
1991	Feb. 15, 1991–Feb. 3, 1992	Goat
1992	Feb. 4, 1992–Jan. 22, 1993	Monkey
1993	Jan. 23, 1993–Feb. 9, 1994	Rooster
1994	Feb. 10, 1994–Jan. 30, 1995	Dog
1995	Jan. 31, 1995–Feb. 18, 1996	Pig

Feb. 19, 1996 – Feb. 6, 2008

1996	Feb. 19, 1996–Feb. 7, 1997	Rat
1997	Feb. 8, 1997–Jan. 27, 1998	Ox
1998	Jan. 28, 1998–Feb. 5, 1999	Tiger
1999	Feb. 6, 1999–Feb. 4, 2000	Rabbit
2000	Feb. 5, 2000–Jan. 23, 2001	Dragon
2001	Jan. 24, 2001–Feb. 11, 2002	Snake
2002	Feb. 12, 2002–Jan. 31, 2003	Horse
2003	Feb. 1, 2003–Jan. 21, 2004	Goat
2004	Jan. 22, 2004–Feb. 8, 2005	Monkey
2005	Feb. 9, 2005–Jan. 28, 2006	Rooster
2006	Jan. 29, 2006–Feb. 17, 2007	Dog
2007	Feb. 18, 2007–Feb. 6, 2008	Pig

The Five Elements

Unlike Western astrology, Chinese astrology has five, not four, elements. These are based on the five planets that were visible to the ancient Chinese astronomers. The elements are:

• water (ruled by Mercury)
• metal (ruled by Venus)
• fire (ruled by Mars)
• wood (ruled by Jupiter)
• earth (ruled by Saturn)

Each of these elements can manifest itself either positively or negatively. In the following tables, the negative and positive characteristics that each of the elements can bestow on a person are listed.

WATER

Positive	Negative
• artistic	• illogical
• expressive	• fearful
• nurturing	• stressed
• sensitive	• nervous
• understanding	• overly sensitive
• sympathetic	• subjective
• gentle	• manipulative
• caring	• fickle
• flexible	• passive
• nonconfrontational	• dependent
• persuasive	• overimaginative

Metal

Positive
- protective
- visionary
- prosperous
- resolute
- inspirational
- controlled
- determined
- romantic
- conviction
- strength

Negative
- inflexible
- harsh
- longing
- homesick
- self-righteous
- single-minded
- competitive
- solitary
- cantankerous
- melancholic
- opinionated

Fire

Positive
- cheerful
- passionate
- honorable
- loving
- charismatic
- dynamic
- exciting
- courageous
- decisive
- inventive
- optimistic

Negative
- destructive
- cruel
- impatient
- tempestuous
- excessive
- reckless
- demanding
- radical
- headstrong
- exploitative
- ambitious

WOOD

Positive
- compassionate
- resourceful
- community minded
- cooperative
- expansive
- inspired
- sociable
- extroverted
- problem solving
- ethical
- practical

Negative
- frustrated
- bad tempered
- impatient
- dissipated
- unexpressive
- excessive
- violent
- angry
- pessimistic
- temperamental
- susceptible

EARTH

Positive
- peaceful
- methodical
- stable
- patient
- enduring
- just
- receptive
- supportive
- practical
- objective
- conservative
- logical

Negative
- smothering
- confining
- anxious
- pessimistic
- slow
- narrow-minded
- rigid
- overly cautious
- stubborn
- conservative

Dominant Element

Each year is ruled by a different element. The element that rules a person's year of birth is called the dominant element. When you consider that every year is also ruled by one of the twelve animal signs, you can calculate that each combination of animal and element occurs only once every sixty years (12 x 5 = 60). For instance, the year 1901 was an ox/metal year. The next ox/metal year was 1961 and the next one will be in 2021. This is referred to as the sixty-year cycle. According to the Chinese calendar, we are currently in the seventy-eighth cycle.

Natural Element

In addition, each animal sign is considered to have its own, natural element. This is always the same, regardless of a person's year of birth. The wheel below shows the natural element of each animal, as well as whether the animal is Yin or Yang. Yin and Yang are discussed on the next page. You will notice that only four (water, wood, metal, and fire) of the five elements are natural elements.

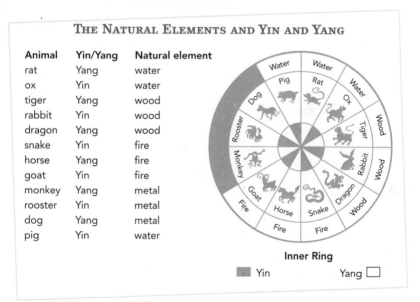

THE NATURAL ELEMENTS AND YIN AND YANG

Animal	Yin/Yang	Natural element
rat	Yang	water
ox	Yin	water
tiger	Yang	wood
rabbit	Yin	wood
dragon	Yang	wood
snake	Yin	fire
horse	Yang	fire
goat	Yin	fire
monkey	Yang	metal
rooster	Yin	metal
dog	Yang	metal
pig	Yin	water

Inner Ring

■ Yin   Yang □

YIN AND YANG

According to Chinese philosophy, the whole universe is controlled by two primal forces. These are Yin and Yang. Everything can be categorized according to this system: from people to furniture, and even countries. The balance of the universe, the Earth, a nation, and even the health and moods of individuals are determined by the balance or imbalance of Yin and Yang.

YIN AND YANG SYMBOL

The ideal balance of Yin and Yang is depicted by the symbol shown above. As the Yang part (white) decreases, the Yin part (black) increases; when one is at its height, the other is at its lowest ebb. Often people assume that Yang is male and Yin female. This is not quite true. Although they are associated with opposite genders, each contains within itself the seed of the other. So, even though Yang is a masculine force, women can possess it. In such ways, Yin and Yang are opposing yet complementary principles. Neither is more important than the other and only together do they make a whole. In the tables on page 230 are listed some examples of Yin and Yang manifestations that show the opposing natures of these forces.

Everyone has his or her own balance of Yin and Yang. To help you understand what makes you an individual and your compatibility with other people, the tastes, colors, foods, flowers, and plants associated with each animal sign are listed, together with the most auspicious seasons, time of birth, and climate.

YIN

- Moon
- dark
- feminine
- water
- black
- passive
- negative
- night
- empty
- cold
- no
- left
- south

YANG

- Sun
- light
- masculine
- fire
- white
- active
- positive
- day
- full
- hot
- yes
- right
- north

Yin and Yang and the Five Elements

Each of the five elements has a positive and a negative side. Which of these is expressed in people depends on whether their animal sign is Yin or Yang. To work out if your animal sign is Yin or Yang, see the chart on page 228. For example, the rat is a Yang water animal. So, for rat people, the qualities of the element water are expressed positively. Pigs, on the other hand, are Yin water people. Therefore, the qualities of the element water express themselves negatively in pig people. In the tables on page 231 are some of the qualities that are commonly attributed to people of either the Yin or Yang tendency.

YIN PEOPLE

- average weight or slender
- often tall
- smiling face
- like strong colors
- delicate health
- individualist
- introspective
- responsive
- psychic
- meditative
- intelligent
- independent
- solitary
- spiritual
- rebellious
- nonmaterialistic
- introverted

YANG PEOPLE

- corpulent
- medium height
- healthy
- serious features
- self-preoccupied
- susceptible
- unstable emotionally
- fear failure
- confident
- conservative
- sociable
- hospitable
- optimistic
- active
- pragmatic
- efficient
- community orientated
- distrustful
- materialistic
- passionate

Companion in Life

The Chinese concept of the companion in life does not refer to another person, but rather to an inner person within an individual. This inner companion acts as a guide, guardian, or devil's advocate. Your companion in life is determined by your hour of birth. Every two-hour slot of the day is governed by one of the twelve animal signs.

Identify your inner companion by referring to the table below. Once you have established which of the animal signs is your inner companion, read the chapter devoted to that animal. Do not assume, however, that this means that you have the attributes of both the animal signs. Instead, your companion in life modifies the traits of your animal sign. For example, tigers are usually reckless and unpredictable people. A tiger whose inner companion is the ox, however, will be more stable than would otherwise be expected. If a person has the same animal sign and inner companion, then they have the potential to balance the negative and positive aspects of their character.

COMPANION IN LIFE

The twenty-four–hour cycle of the animals is shown in the table and the diagrams. The hours given refer to local standard time. If you were born in a month when daylight saving or summer time were in use, you will need to deduct an hour (sometimes two) from your birth time before looking up the sign of your companion.

Time of birth	Sign of companion
11 P.M. – 1 A.M.	Rat
1 A.M. – 3 A.M.	Ox
3 A.M. – 5 A.M.	Tiger
5 A.M. – 7 A.M.	Rabbit
7 A.M. – 9 A.M.	Dragon
9 A.M. – 11 A.M.	Snake
11 A.M. – 1 P.M.	Horse
1 P.M. – 3 P.M.	Goat
3 P.M. – 5 P.M.	Monkey
5 P.M. – 7 P.M.	Rooster
7 P.M. – 9 P.M.	Dog
9 P.M. – 11 P.M.	Pig

The companion in life and compatibility

The compatibility of different animals can be radically altered by their respective companions in life. For example, horse and rat are naturally antagonistic toward each other. If the rat's companion in life is the horse and the horse's companion in life is the rat, however, then the reverse can be true.

Western astrology

To add an extra dimension to your Chinese astrological reading, you can consider it in conjunction with your Western zodiac sign. Use the chart below to determine your Western star sign. There is a brief analysis of the effect of each star sign on an animal sign toward the end of each of the animal chapters. More detailed information on Western astrology can be found in part 1, Zodiac Types, which has a chapter devoted to each zodiac sign.

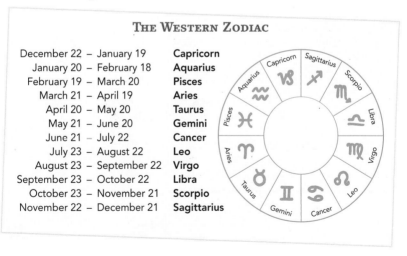

THE WESTERN ZODIAC

December 22 – January 19	**Capricorn**
January 20 – February 18	**Aquarius**
February 19 – March 20	**Pisces**
March 21 – April 19	**Aries**
April 20 – May 20	**Taurus**
May 21 – June 20	**Gemini**
June 21 – July 22	**Cancer**
July 23 – August 22	**Leo**
August 23 – September 22	**Virgo**
September 23 – October 22	**Libra**
October 23 – November 21	**Scorpio**
November 22 – December 21	**Sagittarius**

13. The Rat:
The Yang Water Animal

The rat was welcomed in ancient times as a protector and a bringer of material prosperity.

COMMUNICATION

The disease-carrying vermin bit came later.

LUNAR YEARS RULED BY THE RAT

1900	Jan. 31, 1900–Feb. 18, 1901
1912	Feb. 18, 1912–Feb. 5, 1913
1924	Feb. 5, 1924–Jan. 24, 1925
1936	Jan. 24, 1936–Feb. 10, 1937
1948	Feb. 10, 1948–Jan. 28, 1949
1960	Jan. 28, 1960–Feb. 14, 1961
1972	Feb. 15, 1972–Feb. 2, 1973
1984	Feb. 2, 1984–Feb. 19, 1985
1996	Feb. 19, 1996–Feb. 7, 1997

THE RAT PERSONALITY

Anxious not to be a failure, the affable, elegant, and generous rat lives for today. When rat is being a charming socialite or a lighthearted gossip, this animal should never be underestimated. Attracted to whatever is clandestine, secretive, or a potential bargain, the rat is a very clever animal who enjoys taking the best possible advantage of all situations.

CHARACTERISTICS

Positive
- intelligent
- charming
- imaginative
- placid
- opportunistic
- passionate
- elegant
- sentimental
- affectionate
- constructive critic
- alert
- honest
- practical
- materialistic
- quickly learns from experience

Negative
- calculating
- mean
- secretive
- restless
- has ulterior motives
- quick-tempered
- a critical nitpicker
- a grumbler
- a gossip and a scandalmonger
- an obsessive hoarder
- overambitious
- busybody

STRETCHING THE TRUTH

A quick overview of the negative qualities reveals that ninety-six percent of *Enquirer* writers are rats.

Element

Rat is linked to the ancient Chinese element of water. Water endows rat with qualities of quiet restraint, persistence, diplomacy, and the ability to predict future trends, especially in business and the material world. Water rats can influence others but need to turn their inner restlessness into active leadership.

Balance

The rat itself is Yang, but it is associated with the element water, which is Yin, so rat people have a built-in potential for good balance. The Yin tendency of water, linked with night, darkness, and introversion, can make good use of the resources of Yang, which is linked with day, light, and extrovert initiative. For example, Yin has a natural inclination to respond to opportunities as they occur. Therefore, to thrive, rats have to work hard in response to situations not immediately under their control. This is stressful for rats, but their innate Yang tendency enables rats also to create opportunities for themselves, thus removing the stress and keeping labors to a minimum. Rats do not enjoy very hard work, especially that which is thrust upon them.

BARE FACTS

It was an unhappy, overworked rat who first used the phrase "up the yin-yang."

Best associations

Traditionally, the following are said to be associated with rats:

Taste	salt	Plants	savory, wormwood
Season	winter	Flowers	orchid, thistle
Birth	anytime in the summer	Food	peas, pork
Colors	white, black, blue	Climate	cold

THE MALE RAT

If a man has a typical rat personality, he will generally display the behavior listed below:

- attempts to profit from everyone
- has an alert eye for the best opportunities
- thrives on the rat race in his line of work
- lives by his wits
- has business acumen
- saves for his old age
- takes gambles
- enjoys spending money
- has a wide circle of acquaintances
- picks up gossip easily and hoards it
- is quick to calculate the odds in any situation
- is sentimental about his family
- has a very active imagination
- is suspicious of the ulterior motives of others
- is basically honest

SECRET TIP

Male Rat = Ebeneezer Scrooge, somewhere between the visit from the Ghost of Christmas Present and the visit from the Ghost of Christmas Yet To Be.

THE FEMALE RAT

If a woman has a typical rat personality, she will generally display the behavior listed below:

- rules the nest
- appears placid
- profits from her many acquaintances
- is a very resourceful businesswoman
- communicates well
- is an inveterate gossip
- is quick-witted
- never misses a sale or a special offer
- keeps plenty of things in stock
- is fashionable but always elegant
- is a superb homemaker
- rarely denies herself anything
- is passionate
- is direct and honest to a fault
- is intellectually creative
- is very good at getting other people working
- is generous to those she loves

YOU'RE WELCOME FOR THE TIP

Female Rat = An enticing combination of nonthreatening bookstore clerk and nonthreatening gift shop clerk.

THE RAT CHILD

If a child has a typical rat personality, he or she will generally display the behavior listed below:

• is adventurous
• always takes things apart
• can't bear to be left out of anything
• will often be in trouble
• gets into fights
• will be able to get wants fulfilled
• is constantly busy
• embarrasses parents
• is into everything
• is happy and carefree
• loves exploring

SECRETS TO MAKE YOU LOOK GOOD

Because the young rat gets into everything, the best its parents can hope for is that the meddlesome little tyke will raid the liquor cabinet and drink enough to pass out for a while.

RAT AT HOME

Rats are not domestic people. They do, however, like to have somewhere that they can use rather like a retreat. The typical rat home is comfortable, well protected and well furnished. On special occasions, rats like to invite guests around. So a rat home will be a place fit for entertaining. Rats are good hosts and enjoy cooking for and entertaining guests. They are generous and have a flair for lighthearted pleasures. Rats like to enjoy the profits from their labors and are often sentimental at special times such as birthdays and anniversaries. Rats keep their homes tidy and are organized about chores. If they live in a shared house, rats will be the ones to introduce a cleaning rotation and a household kitty.

COMMUNICATION

In very ancient Chinese, the word "rat" means "roommate from hell."

RAT AT WORK

Rats have an aggressive drive that needs direction; they can be troublemakers if there is not enough to do. Although self-contained, rats can become neurotic about things at work. Rats need comfort and may seem lazy—they prefer others to be doing the really hard work. No matter how much a rat earns, the money is often soon spent. Some rats get a reputation for being a bit of a crook, but this is only because they have an uncanny knack of making a profit out of any situation. Rats prefer to use their minds and their wits, rather than take part in any kind of physical labor.

SOME TYPICAL RAT OCCUPATIONS

- critic
- financial advisor
- broker
- pawnbroker
- lawyer
- detective
- antique dealer
- auctioneer
- connoisseur
- confidential situations
- songwriter
- pathologist
- underground work

RAT PREFERENCES

Likes
- entertaining
- oddities and the unusual
- being the first to explore new places
- underground passages
- mysteries
- unearthing solutions
- money
- taking a gamble
- company
- good-quality worldly possessions
- pleasure

Dislikes
- mundane everyday life
- alarm clocks
- rigid timetables
- agendas
- red tape
- bureaucracy
- having nothing to do
- any kind of failure
- being isolated

LISTEN UP, THIS IS IMPORTANT

Note the snobbery inherent in the disdain for "mundane everyday life." You'd think a rat would be the last thing to think the sun shines out of its butt.

GOOD FRIENDS FOR RATS

The diagram on page 242 shows the compatibility of the rat with other animals. There is no fixed ruling, however, because there are other influences on both the rat person and any potential friend. These influences are:

- the companion in life (see page 231)
- the dominant element (from the year of birth)

COMPATIBILITY OF RAT WITH OTHER ANIMALS

		Key
■ Rat	▲ Horse	▲ Highly compatible
▲ Ox	● Goat	● Amicable
■ Tiger	▲ Monkey	■ No conflict, but needs some effort
● Rabbit	● Rooster	● Lack of sympathy
▲ Dragon	● Dog	▲ Antagonistic
● Snake	● Pig	

♡ RAT IN LOVE

All is romance and passion when a typical rat falls in love. Rat will be as sentimental about little things shared together as about anniversaries. The love partner of a rat can expect rat to be cautious and nervous at first until the relationship is better established, then rat's generosity will know no bounds. Rats are sensual people who will do much to please their partners. Unfortunately, once rats feel secure in a relationship, they have a tendency to be selfish and demanding. Unless they are strong-minded, rat partners may get depressed by this side of rat's nature.

SNAP OF THE FINGER

There are ways to make rat's selfish and demanding side work for you. For example, let your resentment against them build until it becomes a toxic, festering ball of hate inside you. Sure, you might get cancer, but God it's satisfying.

HEALTH

Rat's element, water, is associated in ancient Chinese acupuncture with the kidneys and bladder, so it is these organs that should be kept in good balance. The rat's tendency to hide anxieties could lead to an imbalance. The more rats learn to talk about their problems, the better for their general health.

LEISURE INTERESTS

Rat people are most likely to enjoy puzzles and games of chance. Following the stock market, keeping up with fashions and bargain hunting for all kinds of antiques will please rat. Sports are not really rat's forte, except exploratory activities such as caving. Rats usually like to be associated with the current in-groups and enjoy all kinds of lighthearted socializing.

SECRET TIP

Rat Leisure-Time Heaven: Bargain-hunting in a cave.

THE RAT YEARS AND THEIR ELEMENTS

The rat is a Yang water animal. Each of the rat years, however, is associated with an element which is said to have its own influence. These elements are wood, fire, earth, metal, and water. They influence rat in a regular sequence, which is repeated every sixty years. In the table on page 244, for example, the rat year 1900 is a metal year. The next metal year is sixty years later in 1960, and the next will be 2020.

Rat's natural element is water. When the year is a metal year, the influences of water and metal are said to be combined. Those born in the year of the rat 1960 are Rat Water–Metal people. The possible effects of the year elements are listed on pages 244–245.

LUNAR YEARS RULED BY THE RAT AND THEIR ELEMENTS

1900	Jan. 31, 1900–Feb. 18, 1901	metal
1912	Feb. 18, 1912–Feb. 5, 1913	water
1924	Feb. 5, 1924–Jan. 24, 1925	wood
1936	Jan. 24, 1936–Feb. 10, 1937	fire
1948	Feb. 10, 1948–Jan. 28, 1949	earth
1960	Jan. 28, 1960–Feb. 14, 1961	metal
1972	Feb. 15, 1972–Feb. 2, 1973	water
1984	Feb. 2, 1984–Feb. 19, 1985	wood
1996	Feb. 19, 1996–Feb. 7, 1997	fire

Rat Water–Metal (1900, 1960)

This rat is endowed with integrity, ambition, and the ability to make a sustained effort to carry a project through to its conclusion. On the negative side, metal can be too inflexible, leading to rigid attitudes which threaten to stifle creative thought. This rat should try to be more malleable and open to compromise, although water does help to soften this tendency of metal.

LISTEN UP, THIS IS IMPORTANT

Although a tendency to be rigid has never led to any complaints with the ladies.

Rat Water–Water (1912, 1972)

Rats born in water years are in their natural element. They are, therefore, doubly endowed with the ability to persuade diplomatically and have very acute awareness of future trends. On the negative side, the double water rat may become swamped with too much information and keep too much hidden in their watery depths. Atypically, water rats are very sensitive and are too concerned about the opinions of others. This rat should try to be more forthcoming and take the lead occasionally.

Rat Water–Wood (1924, 1984)

Wood is a creative element, so rats born in these years may be artistic in some way. They are also endowed with self-confidence, a strong moral sense, and an ability to grow, expanding their activities widely. On the negative side, wood can create too many options, leading to a complexity that is unmanageable. Combined with indecisive water, this can mean trouble. These rats should try to control their inclination to bite off more than they can chew and, instead, concentrate their resources.

Rat Water–Fire (1936, 1996)

This rat is endowed with decisiveness, wisdom, and a capacity for innovation that leads to success. They can tolerate periods of rapid change and adjustment. On the negative side, they sometimes become too enthusiastic and passionate, which can lead to destruction of the very thing that they were about to achieve. This rat should try to control a sharp tongue and keep energies flowing in a positive direction.

Rat Water–Earth (1948, 2008)

Earth combined with water is a balancing combination for the rat. Earth rats are endowed with practicality, prudence, self-discipline, and the ability to work hard. On the negative side, they may move too slowly, losing the initiative and delaying making crucial decisions. This rat should use self-discipline to keep to a rigorously paced schedule, allowing the imagination more freedom.

 # RAT AND THE ZODIAC OF WESTERN ASTROLOGY

To work out your zodiac sign see page 233. General character traits of rats of the twelve zodiac signs are given on pages 246–248. Bear in mind that the Western zodiac sign modifies the basic rat nature—especially in the area of personal relationships.

Aries rat
Independent, enthusiastic and original, this combination has great potential unless there is opposition, in which case Aries rat can be extremely aggressive. Aries' lack of stamina is balanced by rat's staying power.

Taurus rat
Conservative, resourceful, and artistically inclined, Taurean rats have great charm, love the good life but can be excessively indulgent. Taurus, however, will help rat to appreciate more fully the talents of others.

Gemini rat
Social, great communicators, and collectors of interesting ideas, these rats have a touch of magic and are quick-change artists. Having nothing to do is a disaster for Gemini rats and can lead to depression. Their quick wits will help them to achieve their ambitions.

Cancer rat
These rats are very emotional, sensitive to the needs of others, and protective. This combination can be overpowering, and care should be exercised to keep things in perspective. Cancer rats, however, are great dreamers but have a good business sense.

Leo rat
Dignified, optimistic, and generous to a fault, Leo rats need to be in the limelight. This will have to be balanced with rat's preference for dark, secret places. These rats are great creative leaders, especially in the literary field.

Virgo rat

Virgoan rats are meticulous, sensual, and logical. This combination is excellent at painstaking research. The Virgo attention to detail and the rat desire to hoard can be put to excellent use in building reserves, but these will never seem adequate.

SNAP OF THE FINGER

Meticulous, sensual and logical, the Virgo rat can be a challenge in the bedroom. If you've never used a T-square as a marital aid, it may be worth experiencing at least once.

Libra rat

These rats are so charming, peaceable, and refined that aggression almost never occurs. They are well-balanced, diplomatic, and value loyalty in personal relationships and in business. Libra rats seek companionship so are very romantic and must have music.

Scorpio rat

Penetrative, investigative, and passionate, Scorpio rats have accurate instincts and are aware of the darker side of human nature. These rats can become great criminologists or criminals. Others should be wary since these rats like to work alone.

Sagittarius rat

Energetic, bluntly honest, and disarmingly happy with life, these rats keep their sorrows and disappointments hidden. This combination can be successful in almost any project, provided variety and constant change are involved.

Capricorn rat

Rats born under this sign are ambitious, controlling, and difficult to change. The rat personality, however, helps them to loosen up and enjoy a little fun from time to time.

Aquarius rat

Energetic Aquarius combines to make this rat very intellectual and an authority in several areas of research. A tendency to eccentricity can work wonders or lead to neuroticism, but it will ensure that life will never be dull for Aquarius rat.

Pisces rat

An intuitive, well-intentioned, and versatile combination, Pisces and rat can lead to confusion or the tendency to live in an illusory world. The rat's ability to gain from most situations, however, can result in success.

14. The Ox:

The Yin Water Animal

In China, many people do not eat beef as the ox is respected for the help it gives in working the land. The ox is associated with water, and figures of oxen were once thrown into rivers to prevent flooding.

LUNAR YEARS RULED BY THE OX	
1901	Feb. 19, 1901–Feb. 7, 1902
1913	Feb. 6, 1913–Jan. 25, 1914
1925	Jan. 25, 1925–Feb. 12, 1926
1937	Feb. 11, 1937–Jan. 30, 1938
1949	Jan. 29, 1949–Feb. 16, 1950
1961	Feb. 15, 1961–Feb. 4, 1962
1973	Feb. 3, 1973–Jan. 22, 1974
1985	Feb. 20, 1985–Feb. 8, 1986
1997	Feb. 8, 1997–Jan. 27, 1998

THE OX PERSONALITY

Basically, oxen are honest, straightforward, kindhearted people—often described as down-to-earth. Oxen have great reserves of strength to call on and are very hardworking. They are normally easy to get along with because they have no duplicity in them. Oxen do exactly what they say, and mean what they say. Despite being respectable and conventional, oxen are very independent minded and not easily swayed by the opinions of others. They cannot take advice very well and can be intolerant and scathing to those they disagree with.

BARE FACTS

Oh, sure, having no duplicity in you looks good on paper, but it takes all the fun out of stuff like back-stabbing, manipulation and adultery. What a rip.

CHARACTERISTICS

Positive
- conscientious
- patient
- hardworking
- reliable
- serious
- gentle
- strong
- careful
- persistent
- determined
- clear-thinking
- capable
- practical

Negative
- slow
- stubborn
- intolerant
- biased
- hot tempered
- dogmatic
- conservative
- materialistic
- complacent
- conformist
- gloomy
- dull

Fun! Combine any two qualities from the positive and negative columns to create a zany, schizophrenic oxen pal! (Our favorite is "persistent gloomy clear-thinking conformist.")

Element

Ox is linked to the ancient Chinese element of water. Water is linked to the arts and expressiveness. In oxen, however, water is more likely to be stagnant and passively, rather than actively, expressed. Bear in mind, water can be both as nurturing as rain or as destructive as a hurricane.

Balance

Oxen highly value their privacy. They very rarely confide their feelings to anyone. Oxen go to great lengths to keep their innermost secrets, and the barriers they build to protect themselves can become a prison. Unless people born in the year of the ox learn to balance this need for privacy with a more open and relaxed attitude to their emotions, they will become neurotic and suffer from self-delusion, as too much repression can direct the ox's quite formidable energies inward.

Best associations

Traditionally, the following are said to be associated with oxen:

Taste	sweet	Plant	hemp
Season	winter	Flower	orchid
Birth	summer night	Food	ginger
Colors	yellow, blue	Climate	cold, wet

THE MALE OX

If a man has a typical ox personality, he will generally display the behavior listed below:

• is difficult to understand
• keeps doubts to himself
• appears to be a pessimist
• values his family life
• plans ahead for the future
• is not particularly quick-witted
• is disciplined and dutiful
• has a tendency to be authoritarian
• loves good food and drink
• will be lazy at home
• is likely to be a chauvinist

YOU'RE WELCOME FOR THE TIP

Male Ox = Equal parts snotty hotel concierge and regional head of the dockworkers' union.

THE FEMALE OX

If a woman has a typical ox personality, she will generally display the behavior listed below and on page 253:

• can be outspoken

- is lacking in the social graces
- is very good at organizing things
- is reticent but not shy
- will never forgive those who betray her
- is very industrious
- enjoys her home comforts
- is loyal to her family
- will always repay a debt
- is always dignified
- is a very private person
- is less inhibited than male oxen

COMMUNICATION

Female Ox = A regional head of the dockworkers' union who shows up at meetings in a teddy.

THE OX CHILD

If a child has a typical ox personality, he or she will generally display the behavior listed below:

- is best left alone when in a bad mood
- enjoys collecting things
- is serious and thoughtful
- has few close friends
- likes to make and build things
- is often a bookworm
- needs encouragement to relax
- enjoys own company
- will organize himself or herself

OX AT HOME

Oxen enjoy the material things in life. An ox home will be comfortable, but not necessarily luxurious, as Oxen are practical people. They prefer to live in a rural area rather than a large city, and the best location for an ox home is near water such as a river. If an ox is unable to live in the country, a garden is essential. It will be well maintained as oxen like to work with the earth and grow plants. If none of these options are possible, you are guaranteed to find many flourishing houseplants in an ox's home. An ox is likely to have a study or some area devoted to work in their house. It will be cluttered with old letters, photos, mementos and knickknacks collected over the years. There will, of course, be some organizing system—but only the ox will understand it.

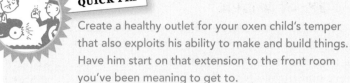

OX AT WORK

Oxen can achieve something in most professions, as they will apply themselves and succeed through hard work and diligence. Before embarking on a project, they have to first be interested and convinced of its worth, then they will explore all facets of the situation, and finally decide on the best plan of action. In this calm and methodical way, logical oxen achieve a lot. They are, however, not suited to jobs that require negotiating skills. Working with food or in agriculture is often advantageous for an ox. Surprisingly, their ability to bring a carefully thought out and often highly unique solution to a problem makes oxen good candidates for the arts. Oxen are suited to musical careers, as they can apply themselves to the necessary practice as well as employ their creative capacities. As employers, oxen will be fair bosses and pay good wages but will expect loyalty to the company. As workers, oxen tend to blame others for their own mistakes. They are always punctual, though.

SOME TYPICAL OX OCCUPATIONS

- composer
- landlord
- doctor
- religious leader
- estate management

- cook or chef
- farmer
- police or military officer
- soldier
- teacher

- philosopher
- judge
- banker
- insurance broker
- gardener

STRETCHING THE TRUTH

Many forward-thinking oxen have attempted to combine the professions of insurance broker and religious leader, thereby offering some small glimmer of meaning in an uncaring universe with a low-deductible and manageable premiums.

? OX PREFERENCES

Likes
- to save money
- home-cooked food
- the familiar
- to be appreciated
- sensible clothes
- traditional festivals such as Shrove Tuesday
- handmade crafts
- sober or earthy color schemes
- to plan ahead

Dislikes
- stressful occupations or pursuits
- fads and fashions
- change, especially if not voluntary
- novelties and gimmicks
- being taken for granted
- modern art
- heart-to-heart chats
- garish colors
- foolish or frivolous behavior
- washing dirty linen in public

GOOD FRIENDS FOR OXEN

The diagram below shows the compatibility of ox with other animals. There is no fixed rule, however, because there are other influences on both the ox and any potential friend. These influences are:
- the companion in life (see page 231)
- the dominant element (for the year of birth)

COMPATIBILITY OF OX WITH OTHER ANIMALS

▲ Rat
■ Ox
▲ Tiger
▲ Rabbit
▲ Dragon
● Snake

● Horse
● Goat
■ Monkey
▲ Rooster
● Dog
■ Pig

Key
▲ Highly compatible
● Amicable
■ No conflict, but needs some effort
● Lack of sympathy
▲ Antagonistic

♡ OX IN LOVE

Oxen are wary about falling in love. They know that it destroys routines and brings new and unfamiliar experiences. Oxen rarely lose their heads, let alone their hearts, over another. They appear to be dispassionate and unromantic because their forthright natures do not understand the subtleties and game playing of romantic entrapments. But do not be deceived, oxen are still capable of deep feelings and will be faithful, loving, and devoted to their partners. Loyalty is very important to ox. Once betrayed, they will find it hard to enter a new relationship. Ox will probably neglect anniversaries, as ox is not particularly sentimental. Although oxen try not to be hurtful, they do need to learn how to respect their partner.

STRETCHING THE TRUTH

Former partners of oxen have likened the relationship to being in one of those slowly moving lines for a theme-park ride, which shuffles along in excruciating one-inch increments and makes an hour feel like three days. Then, when you get on the ride, it's a total letdown. Yet, millions of people suffer through these circumstances each and every year. This capacity for punishment bodes well for you, ox.

✚ HEALTH

Ox's element, water, is associated with the kidneys, so ox should pay particular attention to keeping these organs in working order. Water is also associated with the ears and bladder. Drink plenty of water and do not allow your body to get lazy. Oxen should also guard against neuroses by learning to express their emotions.

LEISURE INTERESTS

Oxen enjoy exercise and like to keep themselves in shape. They prefer traditional sports—rugby, football, or hockey, for example. Fighting sports are good for oxen as they allow them to vent their aggression in a controlled environment. Oxen are well suited to activities such as martial arts, that require patience, practice, and hard work to become skilled at. For holidays, oxen do not like to travel more than they have to and definitely not alone. They are happier to go in a group. Nevertheless, oxen are capable of extremes and may decide to sail single-handedly around the world.

SECRET TIP

Those in long-term relationships with ox partners have wished long and hard that they would hurry up and sail single-handedly around the world already.

THE OX YEARS AND THEIR ELEMENTS

The ox is a Yin water animal. Each of the ox years, however, is associated with an element which is said to have its own influence. These elements are water, fire, earth, metal, and wood. They influence ox in a regular sequence, which is repeated every sixty years. In the table on page 259, for example, the ox year 1901 is a metal year. The next ox metal year is sixty years later in 1961, and the next will be 2021. Ox's natural element is water; the influence of this combines with those of the element of the year of birth. The possible effects of the year elements are listed on pages 259–261.

Ox Water–Metal (1901, 1961)

Metal strengthens some of the ox's qualities, so metal oxen are even more stubborn and hardworking. They are also incredibly self-sufficient and resourceful. Conversely, metal also makes the ox less objective and more intuitive, while the ox's own strong character makes them the warmest of all metal people. Metal oxen are artistic and eloquent, and they have both logic and vision. This produces charismatic people who inspire others with their inevitable achievements. These oxen can be domineering, however, and are prone to taking themselves too seriously.

YOU'RE WELCOME FOR THE TIP

It is highly likely that Water-Metal oxen born in 1901 are all dead. So anything nasty you want to say about them, feel free.

Ox Water–Water (1913, 1973)

Water ox is in his natural element. Water brings sensitivity to this ox who is more likely to listen and help others. Atypically, this ox is almost diplomatic. Water helps oxen focus and channel their energies, and water oxen find it easier to express their emotions. Therefore, they are less prone to neuroses. Although double water slows the ox down, it also allows them to be more flexible. Despite being very patient, they are intolerant of weakness or self-pity in others.

Ox Water–Wood (1925, 1985)

The ox's natural water element allows the wood to flower. Wood oxen have physical strength combined with natural energy. They are the most innovative, creative, and eloquent of all the oxen. These oxen have a better developed sense of humor and, at times, are even witty. Good learners, oxen born in a wood year are exceptional as they are not afraid to try new things. Wood makes this ox more sociable but due to its flammable nature also more quick-tempered.

COMMUNICATION

The difficulty here is that while the Water-Wood ox is the most desirable because of its more developed sense of humor, the most viable option for getting anything going here would be with one born in 1985. This could well mean that funny to them means Adam Sandler, so it's up to you whether or not it's worth the risk.

Ox Water–Fire (1937, 1997)

Fire conflicts with water to produce an impatient ox who lacks the typical ox's placid approach to life. Fire oxen are combative and forceful characters. Although they often offend people, fire oxen do try not to cause unnecessary conflict. All oxen consider themselves superior to others, but they usually conceal this with modesty. Fire oxen, however, lack the ox's normal self-effacing manner and can appear proud and arrogant. In fact, they are basically kind and honest but lack the skills of tact and diplomacy.

Ox Water–Earth (1949, 2009)

The element earth is associated with many of the ox's innate qualities: reliability, resourcefulness, practicality, steadfastness, and patience, for example. So these people are stereotypical oxen. Earth oxen are hugely materialistic but will always earn their wealth. They have a high sense of justice and are generous to those who need help. Earth allows the ox to be relatively at ease in expressing love physically. Earth oxen are the least creative of all oxen, and they never take risks or shortcuts. These people are very homey and pleasant but perhaps a little dull.

OX AND THE ZODIAC OF WESTERN ASTROLOGY

To work out your zodiac sign see page 233. General character traits of oxen of the twelve zodiac signs are given below and on pages 262–264. Bear in mind that the Western zodiac sign modifies the basic ox nature—especially in the area of personal relationships.

Aries ox

The combination of steadfast ox and volatile Aries makes these oxen both imaginative and persistent. They are interesting people who are both capable and spontaneous.

Taurus ox

The bull and ox combine to accentuate the ox's character, good points and bad. They are very stable, reliable, and down-to-earth, yet more tender. But these oxen must learn to be flexible.

Gemini ox

These oxen are less serious then their counterparts. Relatively quick-witted, they are lively conversationalists, but they can be too opinionated. Gemini oxen are very good company.

SECRETS TO MAKE YOU LOOK GOOD

Well, Gemini oxen are good company relative to other oxen. Compared to a Gemini rat, or a Gemini monkey, for example, they kind of suck.

Cancer ox

Cancer diminishes some of the ox's assets, such as reliability and determination. If they are not careful, Cancer oxen may never achieve their goals. Cancer can make the ox touchy but, deep down, they are very sensitive. These oxen are generally careful with money.

Leo ox

Leo allows these people to get out of the traditional ox rut. They are more easygoing and fun-loving, unless opposed—Leonine oxen can be aggressive. Mostly, however, they are caring people who have great style.

Virgo ox

Virgo brings precision to the patient ox, although others can find their perfectionism irritating and their manner too critical. Virgo oxen are often eccentrically conservative.

Libra ox

Charming and popular, Libra oxen are at ease in social situations. They are sensual and love to indulge themselves. Atypically, these oxen don't mind talking about themselves; in fact, they feel a need to be understood.

SECRET TIP

After an hour of meaningful post-coital conversation with Libra ox, you will be kicking yourself for leaving the old, dull, non-communicative ox you used to sleep with.

Scorpio ox

Ox determination combined with Scorpio depth make formidable characters who are still emotional and sensitive at heart. Dangerous when angry, however, they can be stubborn and are even violent at times. Scorpio oxen never compromise on anything.

Sagittarius ox

Sagittarius bring balance to the ox. These oxen are the most open-minded of the breed. All oxen are given to reflection, but Sagittarian oxen go to lengths philosophizing.

Capricorn ox

These people seek status, power, and recognition. Eventually they will achieve them through perseverance. The most serious of all oxen, Capricornean ones do not suffer jokers.

Aquarius ox

Ox born under this sign is more flexible than others. Aquarian oxen are very talkative but nervous, and they find it hard to say what they really mean. Still powerful, they disguise their strength with subtlety.

Pisces ox

An unlikely combination of flighty Pisces with steady ox produces a relatively happy person. They are difficult to understand but are basically kind and loving. Piscean oxen should try a career in the arts.

WELL LOOK WHO FINALLY MADE THE RODEO

To wrap up, Oxen are quite, methodical folks who can acheive great success over time through perserverance. Although once you're past, like, 35, perserverance is a huge pain in the ass.

15. The Tiger:

The Yang Wood Animal

Associated with good fortune, power, and royalty, tigers are viewed with both fear and respect. Their protection and wisdom is sought after. The Chinese see the tiger, and not the lion, as the king of animals.

LUNAR YEARS RULED BY THE TIGER

1902	Feb. 8, 1902–Jan. 28, 1903
1914	Jan. 26, 1914–Feb. 13, 1915
1926	Feb. 13, 1926–Feb. 1, 1927
1938	Jan. 31, 1938–Feb. 18, 1939
1950	Feb. 17, 1950–Feb. 5, 1951
1962	Feb. 5, 1962–Jan. 24, 1963
1974	Jan. 23, 1974–Feb. 10, 1975
1986	Feb. 9, 1986–Jan. 28, 1987
1998	Jan. 28, 1998–Feb. 5, 1999

☺ THE TIGER PERSONALITY

Tigers are contrary creatures. The striped coat reflects tiger's ambivalent nature. Tigers are creatures of great strength and ability; but how this is used can very greatly. They are born leaders or rebels, and they are instinctively protective, though prone to taking risks, so it may not always be wise to follow one. Often critical, tigers make fine revolutionaries. Once involved in battle, they usually come out on top, though their impetuosity can be their downfall.

CHARACTERISTICS

Positive
- loyal
- honorable
- wise
- protective
- generous
- ambitious
- charismatic
- daring
- fortunate
- idealistic
- courageous
- determined
- sensitive
- benevolent

Negative
- impetuous
- disobedient
- arrogant
- impatient
- critical
- imprudent
- domineering
- aggressive
- selfish
- demanding
- vain
- stubborn
- quarrelsome

SECRET TIP

Aggressive, selfish and domineering, the charismatic tiger will screw with your head until you admit that being aggresssive, selfish and domineering are actually good things.

Element

Tiger is linked to the ancient Chinese element of wood. The symbolism of wood is as ambivalent as that of the tiger. As a tree, wood's branches reach for the sky while its roots anchor it in the earth. This endows tiger with the ability (not necessarily used) to moderate his impulsive behavior. Yet wood also gives the tiger passion, which can either lend gentleness to their behavior or may make them violent and destructive.

Balance

The tiger itself is Yang; its striped coat, however, represents the union of both Yin and Yang forces—the balance of which confers great power. It is this contradiction that is at the heart of understanding the nature of tigers. So, while tigers have huge potential, it is a potential for both success or failure. Although usually fortunate, tigers are predisposed to dangerous situations. If they act wisely, tigers can take advantage of this and become very successful. Otherwise, they may fail on a grand scale. Whether a tiger is calm and wise or impetuous and hotheaded in the use of power depends on the individual's ability to learn from experience, heed advice, and channel their energy constructively.

STRETCHING THE TRUTH

Indeed, balance is an uphill battle for tigers. Below are the top three examples of how independently-tested tiger personalities defined "channeling their energy constructively."

1. Tailgating
2. Yelling at waiter and waitresses
3. Tailgating waiters and waitresses

Best associations

Traditionally, the following are said to be associated with tigers:

Taste	acid	Plant	bamboo
Seasons	winter/spring	Flower	heliotrope
Birth	night	Food	bread, poultry
Colors	orange, dark gold	Climate	windy

THE MALE TIGER

If a man has a typical tiger personality, he will generally display the behavior listed below:

- is good-natured
- is peaceful in appearance
- is confident of his good fortune
- possesses a very strong will
- needs to achieve power and recognition
- gives good advice
- seeks attention
- is quick to take the lead
- is usually well mannered
- is a smart and elegant dresser
- takes risks
- is outspoken against authority
- often champions good causes
- is protective toward those weaker than himself
- is a passionate lover

THE FEMALE TIGER

If a woman has a typical tiger personality, she will generally display the behavior listed below:

- is attracted to unusual places, things, and people
- tries to be honest
- dislikes authority
- hates, and will fight against, injustice
- is intense in her feelings of love
- lives an adventurous life
- is not easily impressed by the fashionable
- is very good with children
- likes to be independent
- does not feel remorse or guilt easily
- is often a daring dresser
- will try to avoid the mundane in life
- is a good storyteller
- may be easy to offend
- is strong-spirited and intelligent
- can be demanding if she feels she is not valued
- is frank in her opinion of others
- tends to be authoritarian
- if bored, she will become aggressive and quarrelsome

THE TIGER CHILD

If a child has a typical tiger personality, he or she will generally display the behavior listed below:

- is prone to accidents and injuries
- will not be a sneaky child
- likes school
- needs to experience a feeling of danger
- is difficult to discipline
- acts before thinking
- will probably be a constant source of worry
- likes to be the center of attention
- is impatient and demanding
- will often get into scrapes
- is very energetic and playful
- likes to be treated maturely

SECRET TIP

The parents of tiger children are often those with a bumper sticker that reads: "My Child Is An Honor Student And We Couldn't Have Done It Without Ritalin."

TIGER AT HOME

A typical tiger home will be very comfortable. Probably expensive, the furnishings will be tasteful and deceptively simple in design. Having a taste for the unusual, tiger's home may be decorated in a unique, though still elegant, fashion, perhaps decorated with mementos from travels abroad, for tigers like to roam and are not happy in one place for long. Tigers are not fond of housework, but, anxious to keep up appearances, they will do their chores quickly with a minimum of fuss. Dotted around the tiger's home you will probably find the odd trophy of some sporting, academic, or other achievement. These are arrayed to impress guests.

TIGER AT WORK

Tigers are formidable business leaders. With their risk-taking natures and natural good luck, tigers make fine entrepreneurs. Tigers' creative minds are full of ideas of how to make money. Although they do not desire riches for their own sake, tigers love the chase. To be really successful, though, a tiger may need the steadying influence of another. Dragons make ideal business partners for tigers, but a tiger will never be happy taking orders from someone else. This can create problems unless tiger's ego is regularly boosted. Even then, it won't take tigers long to work their way up the ranks to the top. Alternatively, tigers can often be found among the literary and artistic professions as noted writers, poets, or artists, for example. As they yearn for recognition they may feel the need to communicate their ideas to others—usually with great success.

SOME TYPICAL TIGER OCCUPATIONS

- entrepreneur
- military officer
- head of state
- politician
- publicist
- musician
- writer/poet
- advertising executive
- designer
- film/theater director
- stockbroker
- athlete
- film star
- union leader
- company director
- stunt person
- rebel leader
- explorer
- lion tamer
- teacher

? TIGER PREFERENCES

Likes
- success
- to be their own person
- comfort, though not too sumptuous
- big parties
- appreciation and recognition of their prowess
- spending money
- honesty in others and themselves
- change and anything new or unusual
- to buy the best quality goods they can afford
- a challenge
- being in charge
- flattery
- surprises

Dislikes
- failure
- feeling caged in by circumstances or people
- rules and laws made by others
- everyday life and its responsibilities
- paying attention to detail
- scandalmongering
- taking orders or criticism
- nursing others
- jewels and trinkets
- being ignored
- established authority
- hypocrisy

STRETCHING THE TRUTH

Tigers' disdain for established law manifests itself in countless antisocial ways. For example, a full ninety-six percent of tigers actually make prior arrangements to ensure that their cell phones go off in the movie theater.

GOOD FRIENDS FOR TIGERS

The diagram on page 273 shows the compatibility of tiger with other animals. There is no fixed rule, however, because there are other influences on both the tiger and any potential friend. These influences are:

- the companion in life (see page 231)
- the dominant element (from the year of birth)

Also, for any relationship to succeed, the tiger must be the center of attention and at least appear to take the lead.

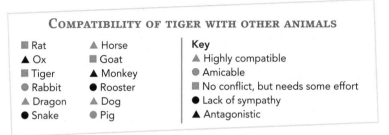

COMPATIBILITY OF TIGER WITH OTHER ANIMALS

■ Rat	▲ Horse	**Key**
▲ Ox	■ Goat	▲ Highly compatible
■ Tiger	▲ Monkey	● Amicable
● Rabbit	● Rooster	■ No conflict, but needs some effort
▲ Dragon	▲ Dog	● Lack of sympathy
● Snake	● Pig	▲ Antagonistic

♡ TIGER IN LOVE

Thanks to their charismatic personalities, tigers are not short of admirers. Led by the heart, tiger is quick to fall in love. When in love, tiger will at first be intense and passionate. After the initial thrill has passed, however, tiger often loses interest. Therefore, the love life of a tiger may be hard to keep up with—full of ups and downs, bursts of passion, and many "conquests." If tiger's love partner is clever, they will let tiger know that they would be quite happy alone. This will ensnare tiger, who hates an easy prey. Tiger can make a romantic, affectionate, but sometimes inattentive partner.

SECRET TIP

By "inattentive" we mean they will probably barely notice when you drop off the edge of the cliff.

✚ HEALTH

Tiger's element, wood, is associated with the liver, so tigers should pay particular attention to keeping this organ in working order.

Emotionally, tiger should let off steam occasionally to release any pent-up anger or passion. Otherwise tiger may become too anxious and obsessive.

🏃 LEISURE INTERESTS

Tiger people tend to engage in the more energetic and daring varieties of any activity. So skiing, hang gliding, stock-car racing, or surfing are ideal sports for the tiger. For vacations, tigers like to travel to distant places. Package tours, though, are not their style; trekking, mountaineering, going on safaris, white-water rafting, and so on are more suitable. On a tamer level, tigers love a good party where they can cause a stir.

DON'T BE A JERK

No matter how much the demanding tiger suggests their favorite party game "let's hang from the window ledge," do not indulge them.

🎲 THE TIGER YEARS AND THEIR ELEMENTS

The tiger is a Yang wood animal. Each of the tiger years, however, is associated with an element which is said to have its own influence. These elements are wood, fire, earth, metal, and water. They influence tiger in a regular sequence, which is repeated every sixty years. In the table on page 275, for example, the tiger year 1902 is a water year. The next tiger water year is sixty years later in 1962, and the next will be 2022. Tiger's natural element is wood; the influence of this combines with those of the element of the year of birth. The possible effects of the year elements are listed on pages 275–276:

1902	Feb. 8, 1902–Jan. 28, 1903	water
1914	Jan. 26, 1914–Feb. 13, 1915	wood
1926	Feb. 13, 1926–Feb. 1, 1927	fire
1938	Jan. 31, 1938–Feb. 18, 1939	earth
1950	Feb. 17, 1950–Feb. 5, 1951	metal
1962	Feb. 5, 1962–Jan. 24, 1963	water
1974	Jan. 23, 1974–Feb. 10, 1975	wood
1986	Feb. 9, 1986–Jan. 28, 1987	fire
1998	Jan. 28, 1998–Feb. 5, 1999	earth

Tiger Wood–Water (1902, 1962)

This reserved tiger is endowed with compassion and is more sensitive to the needs of others than a typical tiger. Full of noble ideas, combined with an ability to control passionate whims and look before leaping, this tiger can make a just and wise leader. A water tiger's life will be more calm than other tiger's. There is a tendency, though, for water tigers to be slightly pompous.

Tiger Wood–Wood (1914, 1974)

This sociable tiger is particularly charming and witty—a real party animal. Wood tigers are very enterprising and good at thinking up grand schemes; the details, however, will be left to others to sort out. Apparently superficial emotionally, double wood tigers can actually become quite anxious—so they should try to keep stress under control.

Tiger Wood–Fire (1926, 1986)

Tigers are already inherently Yang; fire is also Yang. This doubling of the Yang force makes fire tigers incredibly active people. They are animated, exciting yet changeable characters. Sensitive to perceived slights, the fire tiger often has a very quick temper and can soon become explosive. Fortunately, bursts of temper never last long with this tiger. To really enjoy life, fire tiger needs to try and relax and take things at a more controlled pace.

DON'T BE A JERK

Don't even try to take the remote from a wood-fire tiger.

Tiger Wood–Earth (1938, 1998)

Unlike most other tigers, earth tiger is hardly impulsive at all, naturally less excitable, and not averse to stability and continuity. This tiger is very practical and fond of comfort. For such reasons, earth tigers tend to be more successful at long-term relationships than other tigers. There is a danger, however, that unless they give free rein to their dynamic Yang element, earth tigers can become real stick-in-the-muds. This should be avoided, and, instead, a more forward-looking mind should be cultivated.

STRETCHING THE TRUTH

A huge percentage of wood-earth tigers live in their parent's basements.

Tiger Wood–Metal (1950, 2010)

This tough, outspoken tiger can sometimes be too bossy. Metal tiger is less ruled by the heart than typical tigers. Unfortunately, sometimes this only serves to make them unscrupulous. Metal tigers can be high achievers as they are very ambitious and self-disciplined. Advice to a metal tiger would be to try to listen to the wishes of others, practice tact, and be more flexible.

TIGER AND THE ZODIAC OF WESTERN ASTROLOGY

To work out your zodiac sign see page 233. General character traits of tigers of the twelve zodiac signs are given below and on pages 278–279. Bear in mind that the Western zodiac sign modifies the basic tiger nature—especially in the area of personal relationships.

Aries tiger

This is the most reckless and impetuous of all tigers. Aries tiger is well loved for sincerity, frankness, and kindheartedness. Although not very reflective, Aries tiger is very talented and often conscientious.

Taurus tiger

Careful but bold, a realist but brave, passionate but reliable, Taurus tiger combines the attributes of these two signs to great effect. This tiger is practical and determined, so will often achieve great material prosperity.

Gemini tiger

Impulsive tiger and mercurial Gemini make this person a mental and physical nomad. Hard to pin down to one idea or place, Gemini tigers are nonetheless highly creative people. What they lack in stamina, they make up for with inventiveness.

Cancer tiger

The combination of these opposites makes an enigmatic and at times overly sensitive person. Cancer tigers are often eccentric but likable characters. Self-discipline is vital to ensure that tasks are achieved, as Cancer tigers have a tendency toward introspection.

Leo tiger

Both Leos and tigers seek the limelight, a Leo tiger doubly so. Also, the Leo tiger is naturally arrogant, so at times this tiger can be unbearable. Nevertheless, they are generous, loyal, and charming people as well.

Virgo tiger

Hesitant Virgo and foolhardy tiger actually go very well together. A Virgo tiger is trustworthy, self-disciplined, diligent, and resourceful—an unbeatable combination. On the negative side, this variety of tiger may be a snob.

SECRETS TO MAKE YOU LOOK GOOD

You'd be a snob, too, if you were trustworthy, self-disciplined, diligent, and resourceful.

Libra tiger

Noble tiger's sense of justice is enhanced by the altruistic Libran sign. Libra tigers are often very attractive personalities. They combine a hardworking trait with a charming and compassionate nature.

Scorpio tiger

These tigers display all the tiger traits in the extreme; they have fearsome tempers, huge amounts of energy, and are dangerously reckless. As a friend, loyal Scorpio tiger is a great advantage; as an enemy, beware!

Sagittarius tiger

The Sagittarian tiger is an unpredictable dreamer. Basically gentle and easygoing, they can at times be infuriatingly changeable. Perhaps extroverted then withdrawn, generous then miserly—these people do not like to be taken for granted.

Capricorn tiger

Capricorn endows these tigers with the ability to avoid their usual pit-falls—in particular thoughtlessness. Capricorn tigers are not as at ease socially as others, though, and tend to be moody. They are, however, dependable and good-natured.

Aquarius tiger

This is the most idealistic of tigers. Intellectual Aquarius complements active tiger well; great things could be accomplished. Gullibility and lack of steadfastness can prove a problem. Aquarian tigers are fascinated by the latest gadgets.

Pisces tiger

This tiger is sympathetic, loving, very creative, but often woefully indecisive. The Pisces tiger will only achieve inner peace when the tiger is fully under control.

WELL LOOK WHO FINALLY MADE THE RODEO

In conclusion, tigers are willful, aggressive people who need lots of space. And, judging from what we learned in this chapter, most of us are only too happy to give it to them.

16. The Rabbit:
The Yin Wood Animal

The rabbit is associated with longevity and the moon. Some astrologers identify this sign as the cat, not rabbit, but Chinese astrologers always refer to it as the rabbit or hare.

LUNAR YEARS RULED BY THE RABBIT

1903	Jan. 29, 1903–Feb. 15, 1904
1915	Feb. 14, 1915–Feb. 2, 1916
1927	Feb. 2, 1927–Jan. 22, 1928
1939	Feb. 19, 1939–Feb. 7, 1940
1951	Feb. 6, 1951–Jan. 26, 1952
1963	Jan. 25, 1963–Feb. 12, 1964
1975	Feb. 11, 1975–Jan. 30, 1976
1987	Jan. 29, 1987–Feb. 16, 1988
1999	Feb. 6, 1999–Feb. 4, 2000

THE RABBIT PERSONALITY

Seemingly unexceptional, rabbits provoke extreme reactions. They inspire either adoration or hate, but never indifference. Rabbits are mysterious yet practical, timid but ruthless, articulate but inscrutable, and virtuous as well as cunning. They like their lives to be secure, comfortable, and calm, yet they are fiercely independent. Sensitive and intuitive by nature, rabbits are easily influenced by their emotions.

CHARACTERISTICS

Positive	Negative
• diplomatic	• indecisive
• circumspect	• unpredictable
• peaceful	• hesitant
• sensitive	• fainthearted
• intuitive	• easily shocked
• discreet	• touchy
• moderate	• conservative
• reflective	• conformist
• well-organized	• egotistical
• principled	• superficial
• refined	• cruel
• hospitable	• gossipy
• intelligent	• cunning
• expressive	• secretive
• honorable	• pedantic

SNAP OF THE FINGER

Rabbits are conservative and easily shocked. Boy, it's going to be fun telling them you're gay.

Element

Rabbit is linked to the ancient Chinese element of wood. Wood can be flexible like a sapling or sturdy as an oak. How its energy is expressed depends on how well a wood person can both control and indulge their natural tendencies.

For a rabbit, the tendencies to be wary of are the urge to avoid change or trouble at all costs, self-indulgence, and timidity.

Balance

The behavior of a rabbit can be unpredictable as it varies according to current circumstances. During peaceful times, rabbits will be at ease and relaxed. Sudden changes, unforeseen events, or conflicts will unbalance rabbits and make them irritable, confused, and even aggressive. Rabbit people will not be happy at such times until they are back in control of the situation. Also, rabbit personalities need to balance their self-preoccupied Yang natures and occasionally try to see things from another's point of view.

SECRETS TO MAKE YOU LOOK GOOD

Overall, rabbits do not function well in environments that are unpredictable or liable to change at a moment's notice. Since this basically describes life, you can draw your own conclusions.

Best associations

Traditionally, the following are said to be associated with rabbits:

Taste	acid	Plant	fig tree
Season	spring	Flower	Queen Anne's lace
Birth	summer	Food	wheat, poultry
Color	white	Climate	windy

THE MALE RABBIT

If a man has a typical rabbit personality, he will generally display the behavior listed below.

- is not a victim of fashions
- is careful when spending money on necessities
- is extravagant with his money when buying luxuries
- is neat and well dressed
- has a tendency to be superficial
- is interested in the arts and culture
- is not a family-minded man
- is faithful and loving
- is a careful listener
- is happy and content
- has a traditional outlook
- is protective towards his peace and quiet
- is flamboyant
- is in touch with his feminine side but not effeminate

SECRET TIP

Male Rabbit = That one guy in the dorm you always wondered about.

THE FEMALE RABBIT

If a woman has a typical rabbit personality, she will generally display the behavior listed below:

- is not overtly maternal
- is good at entertaining
- is sophisticated

- is tender and wistful
- is very determined
- is good at giving practical advice
- makes herself at home in most social circles
- is attentive to her material needs
- is able to strike a good bargain
- is naturally elegant and always stylishly dressed
- is wary of commitment
- has a sharp sense of humor
- is emotional
- prefers a comfortable to an adventurous life
- can be manipulative to get her own way
- prefers company to solitude
- is well mannered and conscious of etiquette

BARE FACTS

Female Rabbit = Got an MBA to help her give better Tupperware parties.

THE RABBIT CHILD

If a child has a typical rabbit personality, he or she will generally display the behavior listed below and on page 285:

- is not argumentative
- is shy and sometimes nervous
- is obedient and well-disciplined
- is happy at school
- enjoys team sports
- is usually more academic than athletic

- needs stimulation and motivation
- can be lacking in imagination
- is prone to nightmares
- succeeds through hard work
- enjoys fairy tales and fantasy stories

SNAP OF THE FINGER

It's never too early to teach your rabbit youngster to defend him or herself. Honestly, the poor thing is going to need all the help he can get.

RABBIT AT HOME

Rabbits are sensitive to environments and like to create cozy, intimate homes. Furnishings will be beautiful and comfortable; antiques or classic designs are preferred. Rabbits are meticulous and cannot bear to have an untidy or unclean home; a spill of red wine could move a rabbit to hysteria. Rabbits prefer to entertain at home rather than venture out into the cold. They make fine hosts and hostesses as they go to great lengths to make guests feel at home. Rabbits put a lot of effort into arranging their environments. Once established and satisfied with their homes, rabbits hate the disruption of moving.

RABBIT AT WORK

Although rabbits are not authoritative, they can make good leaders and organizers as they are skilled diplomats. A rabbit can win a battle without anyone knowing one has been fought. Not being ambitious, rabbits rarely reach the top of their chosen professions. They excel in administrative or clearly defined positions. Once rabbits know what needs to be done, they are thorough and diligent in carrying out their tasks. They are good at team work, but often prefer to work alone or be self-employed. Job security is important, so stable professions are preferred. With their ability to charm, rabbits are good at wheeling and dealing. However, their basically honest nature stops them from taking too much advantage of this. In business, rabbits should try and use their instinctive good taste, careful nature, and ability to evaluate a situation well to good advantage.

SOME TYPICAL RABBIT OCCUPATIONS

- antique dealer
- diplomat
- administrator
- interior decorator
- politician
- historian
- art collector
- attorney
- tailor
- receptionist
- chemist
- landlord
- pharmacist
- beautician
- accountant
- librarian

YOU'RE WELCOME FOR THE TIP

On occasion, the timid, nonconfrontational rabbit will rise to a leadership position. In such cases, you can say hello to a good long run of three-hour lunches and all the personal calls you care to make.

RABBIT PREFERENCES

Likes
- privacy
- conversation, including gossip
- routines
- to use their wits to solve a problem
- romantic films
- secrets and mysteries
- long hairstyles
- prefers company of good friends and family to going out
- comfortable surroundings
- beautiful paintings
- paying attention to detail

Dislikes
- arguments
- seeing or using violence
- drastic change
- taking risks
- surprises
- saying anything
- unpleasant
- being forced to make a decision
- complicated plans
- changing their mind
- witnessing suffering
- commitment
- open criticism

GOOD FRIENDS FOR RABBITS

The diagram below shows the compatibility of rabbit with other animals. There is no fixed ruling, however, because there are other influences on both the rabbit and any potential friend. These influences are:

- the companion in life (see page 231)
- the dominant element (for the year of birth)

COMPATIBILITY OF RABBIT WITH OTHER ANIMALS

- ● Rat
- ▲ Ox
- ■ Tiger
- ■ Rabbit
- ● Dragon
- ▲ Snake
- ▲ Horse
- ▲ Goat
- ● Monkey
- ▲ Rooster
- ● Dog
- ● Pig

Key
- ▲ Highly compatible
- ● Amicable
- ■ No conflict, but needs some effort
- ● Lack of sympathy
- ▲ Antagonistic

♡ RABBIT IN LOVE

Rabbits are wary of commitment as it involves change and making a major decision. This does not mean that they are fickle, just careful about choosing their partners. Rabbits would rather be alone than in unsatisfactory relationships; they highly prize their peaceful lives. Once committed, rabbits put a lot of effort into their relationships. Always willing to listen and loathe to argue, they make attentive, tender, and loving partners. Despite this, it is sometimes hard to know what rabbit partners are feeling or thinking as they are very private people. Rabbits listen better than they confide. This can be exasperating for others unless they learn how to read the signs. Rabbits need a lot of attention and love—but most are clever enough to have learned that, if given, these will be returned.

✚ HEALTH

Rabbit's element, wood, is associated with the liver, so rabbits should pay particular attention to keeping this organ in working order. Rabbits should make sure that they get enough exercise, otherwise their love of a quiet, comfortable life could damage their long-term health. Psychologically, rabbits need to try not to be too self-absorbed and concerned with themselves. Also, they should take care that their methodical, tidy natures do not become obsessively fastidious.

🏃 LEISURE INTERESTS

Rabbits will enjoy a wide range of activities, as long as they are not responsible for organizing them. For this reason, package tours are perfect for rabbits. Although not especially sporty, they can make good team players. Being lovers of art and culture, rabbits can often be found visiting museums and art galleries. Even though they are usually music lovers, rabbits would rather listen to a good recording in the comfort of their own home than go to a crowded, live concert. Rabbits like to be alone at times and may go on long nocturnal walks to indulge this. Great lovers of the good things in life—fine wine, gourmet food, and conversation—rabbits like to throw dinner parties for friends. Entertaining at home is always preferred to wild parties.

SECRETS TO MAKE YOU LOOK GOOD

For the reserved rabbit, eating is actually a substitute for sex. As anyone will tell you who has come home to find their rabbit partner in the shower, rinsing off the tuna casserole.

 THE RABBIT YEARS AND THEIR ELEMENTS

The rabbit is a Yin wood animal. Each of the rabbit years, however, is associated with an element which is said to have its own influence. These elements are wood, fire, earth, metal, and water. They influence rabbit in a regular sequence, which is repeated every sixty years. In the table on page 290, for example, the rabbit year 1903 is a water year. The next rabbit water year is sixty years later in 1963, and the next will be 2023. Rabbit's natural element is wood; the influence of this combines with those of the element of the year of birth. The possible effects of the year elements are listed on pages 290–292.

LUNAR YEARS RULED BY THE RABBIT AND THEIR ELEMENTS

Year	Date Range	Element
1903	Jan. 29, 1903–Feb. 15, 1904	water
1915	Feb. 24, 1915–Feb. 2, 1916	wood
1927	Feb. 2, 1927–Jan. 22, 1928	fire
1939	Feb. 19, 1939–Feb. 7, 1940	earth
1951	Feb. 6, 1951–Jan. 26, 1952	metal
1963	Jan. 25, 1963–Feb. 12, 1964	water
1975	Feb. 11, 1975–Jan. 30, 1976	wood
1987	Jan. 29, 1987–Feb. 16, 1988	fire
1999	Feb. 6, 1999–Feb. 4, 2000	earth

Rabbit Wood–Water (1903, 1963)

Water enhances rabbit's natural sensitive nature. Unfortunately, these rabbits can empathize with others so much that they become unproductive and shy away from harsh reality. All rabbits dislike conflicts, but water rabbits go to extremes to avoid confrontation. A natural passivity combined with a reflective nature can make them victims of remorse and "If Only" thoughts.

LISTEN UP, THIS IS IMPORTANT

Now that you know the facts about wood-water rabbits, you may be capable of a little more understanding toward that guy who works in the comic book store.

Rabbit Wood–Wood (1915, 1975)

Wood is rabbit's natural element, but it is a two-sided symbol. On the one hand, wood rabbits can be content to the point of placidity. Alternatively, they may be of the more adventurous type. In these cases, wood opens rabbits up to their emotions—which can also make them vulnerable. Double–wood rabbits tend to be easygoing, generous people. They should beware of others trying to take advantage of them. Wood releases the creative powers of rabbit people and enhances their aesthetic taste; therefore, these people are artistic and creative.

Rabbit Wood–Fire (1927, 1987)

Wood and fire is a curious, flammable mixture that can make rabbit warm and friendly, or moody and bad tempered. Rabbits are naturally Yin, and fire is Yang. One balances the other, so fire can help rabbits use their skills to reach the top. It also helps them to be more expressive. Fire rabbits are more likely to become leaders as they have many admirers and inspire confidence. They should try to follow their true rabbit natures and let reason control passion.

Rabbit Wood–Earth (1939, 1999)

Earth endows this rabbit with a more realistic and pragmatic character. Earth rabbits are more able to deal with the downside of life than other rabbits, who typically try to hide from it. Better equipped to make decisions, the earth rabbit will do so carefully and after great deliberation. They tend to be humble and aware of their limitations. Independent and fond of solitude, earth rabbits can achieve much through hard work.

YOU'RE WELCOME FOR THE TIP

Wood-earth rabbits, more equipped for life's downsides, make excellent therapists, or bartenders. The latter, of course, serves the same purpose and works for tips, while the former has you to thank for their recently-purchased vacation home.

Rabbit Wood–Metal (1951, 2011)

Metal gives the naturally timid rabbit greater courage. Rabbits born in metal years will be forthright and self-confident, and some say even visionary. They are more ambitious and can be ruthless underneath their charming exteriors. Metal rabbits tend to be polite but cold, and they can be indifferent to the feelings of others. For these reasons, they are often loners. Metal lends strength to a character but can also make it rigid. It can make rabbit's naturally conservative nature inflexible to the point of being reactionary.

RABBIT AND THE ZODIAC OF WESTERN ASTROLOGY

To work out your zodiac sign see page 233. General character traits of rabbits of the twelve zodiac signs are given below and on pages 293–295. Bear in mind that the Western zodiac sign modifies the basic rabbit nature—especially in the area of personal relationships.

Aries rabbit

Aries brings courage to rabbit, who adds grace to the equation. Aries rabbits are emotionally both expressive and vulnerable. Unlike other rabbits, however, they don't mind taking risks. Success is important to Aries rabbits.

Taurus rabbit

Both Taureans and rabbits are peace-loving, calm, stay-at-home people; Taurus rabbits doubly so. Their liking of the good things in life can make them materialistic, and they should be wary of ostentatious behavior.

Gemini rabbit

Mercurial Gemini and steady rabbit make an odd mixture. On the surface, a Gemini rabbit seems to be a superficial, turbulent kind of person; in fact, they are constantly on the alert and very analytical. These rabbits are persuasive and like to appear sophisticated and cultured.

Cancer rabbit

The close similarities between these two signs can accentuate certain facets of rabbit's nature. Cancer rabbits are doubly cautious and can be weak. On the whole, they are nice, hospitable people who make good friends.

COMMUNICATION

Anyone who doesn't think it sucks being described as a nice, hospitable person who makes a good friend deserves everything they get.

Leo rabbit

At times deceptively calm, Leo rabbits are potentially great achievers. Open in expressing their desires, flamboyant and popular, these people find it hard to be self-restrained or objective. A tendency to be self-centered and pompous is offset by mild manners and a generous nature.

Virgo rabbit

Analytical Virgo and careful rabbit combine to create a tendency to worry. These attributes can be beneficial though, and many Virgo rabbits are wise, considerate types. If their nervous energy is left unused, they can be fidgety.

Libra rabbit

Sweet talking and melancholic, these rabbits may appear slightly effeminate. They have very inquiring minds and make good scholars or communicators. Libra rabbits like to surround themselves with the best of everything and can be extravagant; but they work hard to get what they want. A tendency to be snobbish should be watched.

Scorpio rabbit

Scorpio rabbits are earnest people—they take themselves very seriously. Scorpio brings great willpower to the rabbit. They are secretive about intimate matters, but not dispassionate. In private, they can be passionate and have a high sex drive; but if they feel insecure, Scorpio rabbits can become deceitful and pedantic.

BARE FACTS

Even worse is the deceitful and pedantic Scorpio rabbit with a high sex drive. They like nothing more than to lecture you in the bedroom, while putting the other person they're sleeping with on speaker phone.

Sagittarius rabbit

This combination makes for the most balanced and easygoing rabbit. Unusually interested in the more exotic side of life, these rabbits are exceptional in that they like to experience adventure. They are not as diplomatic or tactful as other rabbits but are loyal and loving people.

Capricorn rabbit

Capricorn rabbits seem to be insensitive due to their brusque natures; underneath, however, they are kind and considerate, supportive and protective towards their family and loved ones. Physically graceful, these rabbits are surprisingly impractical.

Aquarius rabbit

Thirsty for knowledge and eager for new experiences, these rabbit are true intellectuals—they often make good writers. Not so much in need of stability and security, Aquarian rabbits like to keep their distance.

Pisces rabbit

The most difficult of all rabbits to read; spiritual and perceptive, Pisces deepens rabbit's inherently mysterious nature—such people can even be psychic. Accomplished in the arts, refined and companionable, Pisces rabbits have the ability to live happy, well-ordered lives. Their insecurities can make them appear stubborn at times.

WELL LOOK WHO FINALLY MADE THE RODEO

To wrap up, the rabbit is a cautious person, unlikely to take big risks, and not prone toward leadership. Or, as they are known in political circles, "dream voter."

17. The Dragon:
The Yang Wood Animal

The dragon is the only mythical animal in the Chinese zodiac. In China, dragons are associated with strength, health, harmony, and good luck; they are placed above doors or on the tops of roofs to banish demons and evil spirits.

LUNAR YEARS RULED BY THE DRAGON	
1904	Feb. 16, 1904–Feb. 3, 1905
1916	Feb. 3, 1916–Jan. 22, 1917
1928	Jan. 23, 1928–Feb. 9, 1929
1940	Feb. 8, 1940–Jan. 26, 1941
1952	Jan. 27, 1952–Feb. 13, 1953
1964	Feb. 13, 1964–Feb. 1, 1965
1976	Jan. 31, 1976–Feb. 17, 1977
1988	Feb. 17, 1988–Feb. 5, 1989
2000	Feb. 5, 2000–Jan. 23, 2001

THE DRAGON PERSONALITY

Dragons have magnetic, persuasive personalities and are capable of great success or spectacular failure. Normally, however, whatever they set their hearts on doing, they do well; the secret is their great faith in themselves. On the negative side, dragons are renowned for not finishing what they start. The frank and open way in which they approach people and situations can be disconcerting; but their innate sincerity and enthusiasm make up for this.

CHARACTERISTICS

Positive
- visionary
- dynamic
- idealistic
- perfectionist
- scrupulous
- lucky
- successful
- enthusiastic
- sentimental
- healthy
- voluble
- irresistible
- intelligent

Negative
- demanding
- impatient
- intolerant
- gullible
- dissatisfied
- overpowering
- irritable
- abrupt
- naive
- overzealous
- eccentric
- proud
- tactless
- short-tempered

COMMUNICATION

Dragons are gullible. This explains why they actually believe they have any positive qualities.

Element

Dragon is linked to the ancient Chinese element of wood. Wood is an ambivalent element. As a crutch it lends support; as a spear it can be used as a weapon. Consequently, dragons are full of both positive and negative energies that will surface in, for example, strong emotions. For instance, emotionally, wood is associated with both anger and kindness. Wood is also responsible for growth and renewal, so dragons tend to be creative people.

Balance

Dragons spend a lot of time racing from one experience to another. Always set on the latest goal, they are blind to failures and try to forget any that occur. Only successes are considered significant. Dragons seem impressive only because they believe that they are, and this amazing self-confidence makes others believe in them also. You could say that the dragon's image is all done with mirrors. According to Chinese tradition, dragons must confront their image and recognize its illusory nature. Dragons will only be truly content when they accept their vulnerability and use it to balance their exuberance.

BARE FACTS

Getting a dragon to accept their vulnerability is like getting a fan of 80s music to accept their loser-dom.

Best associations

Traditionally, the following are said to be associated with dragons:

Taste	acid	Plants	mandrake, sage
Season	spring	Flower	lotus
Birth	anytime, except during a storm	Food	wheat, poultry
Colors	yellow, black	Climate	windy

THE MALE DRAGON

If a man has a typical dragon personality, he will generally display the behavior listed below:

- is a natural showman
- is seductively attractive
- will have many admirers
- has a few close friends
- believes he is irreplaceable
- is good at sports
- does not believe he can make mistakes
- is sentimental and passionate about loved ones
- can be impulsive but not a daredevil
- will harbor a grudge for years
- is good-humored
- enjoys shopping
- has many hobbies and interests

SECRET TIP

Male Dragon = Only guy who can use Scrabble as foreplay.

 # THE FEMALE DRAGON

If a woman has a typical dragon personality, she will generally display the behavior listed below and on page 300:

- will not be happy as a housewife
- is generous with both time and money
- can instill confidence in others
- desires perfection in herself and others
- is always attractive, even if not beautiful

- takes revenge on enemies, even if it takes years
- craves attention
- likes to be flattered
- hates to be manipulated or deceived
- tells good jokes
- likes children
- is very straightforward
- needs to feel irreplaceable

BARE FACTS

Female Dragon = Saving up for the sex change.

THE DRAGON CHILD

If a child has a typical dragon personality, he or she will generally display the behavior listed below:

- is prone to boredom
- dislikes authority
- needs motivating but potentially a good student
- dislikes demonstrations of affection
- is insolent with teachers
- enjoys and is good at sports
- is undemanding as far as attention is concerned
- dislikes timetables
- is inventive
- needs to be given ample freedom to blossom
- has a short attention span
- is gifted but difficult
- feels he or she is misunderstood (often true)

DRAGON AT HOME

Dragon people suffer from mild claustrophobia—they need space, fresh air, and freedom. To live in one place for long is a chore for a dragon. If they have settled down, dragons like to live in ultramodern houses, onboard a houseboat, or near the coast, where they can hear the thunder of the ocean. If such options are not available, a dragon will at least try to redecorate frequently to keep boredom at bay. However pleasant their home environment, though, dragons will spend more time out and about than sitting at home.

DRAGON AT WORK

Dragons are not power-hungry people, but they tend to end up at the top of their profession, simply because this is what they do best—lead. They are terrible at carrying out mundane tasks but excel at solving problems that others have found unsolvable. They make great directors and troubleshooters. Dragons inspire confidence in others and are good promoters or sellers; their integrity lends credibility to whatever they do. Dragons need to feel vital at work and be in a position that allows them to innovate or create.

SOME TYPICAL DRAGON OCCUPATIONS

- managing director
- salesperson
- advertising executive
- president or prime
- minister

- prophet
- attorney
- film producer
- photojournalist
- architect
- professional speaker

- philosopher
- astronaut
- artist
- film star
- war correspondent

YOU'RE WELCOME FOR THE TIP

Very few dragons will deign to work in the retail or service industry. And, if they do, you need to make them think it was their innovative idea to change the grease in the fryolater more frequently.

DRAGON PREFERENCES

Likes

- any sort of celebration such as parties and festivals
- to wear casual, comfortable clothes
- going on vacation and traveling
- to be taken seriously
- picnics
- jazz music
- amusement parks, especially the roller coaster
- watching fireworks
- being asked for help
- giving advice
- to feel irreplaceable
- to be in charge
- championing causes

Dislikes

- having to be calm and patient
- waiting for anything or anyone
- a lack of vision in others
- having nothing to do
- manipulative people
- listening to advice
- dishonesty and hypocrisy
- lack of energy or willpower in others
- being patronized
- compromise

It is clear from page 302 that the dragon is a restless soul, for whom only loose-fitting clothing and a picnic can hope to quell the raging beast within.

GOOD FRIENDS FOR DRAGON

The diagram below shows the compatibility of dragon with other animals. There is no fixed rule, however, because there are other influences on both the dragon and any potential friend. These influences are:

- the companion in life (see page 231)
- the dominant element (from the year of birth)

COMPATIBILITY OF DRAGON WITH OTHER ANIMALS

		Key
▲ Rat	■ Horse	▲ Highly compatible
▲ Ox	● Goat	● Amicable
▲ Tiger	▲ Monkey	■ No conflict, but needs some effort
● Rabbit	■ Rooster	● Lack of sympathy
● Dragon	▲ Dog	▲ Antagonistic
▲ Snake	● Pig	

DRAGON IN LOVE

Dragons are never short of admirers and never suffer from unrequited love. They are passionate but never blinded by this. Dragons are very self-reliant and know that they could live without their partner. Although they are often loved, dragons fall in love rarely. Once in love, dragons are very loyal and loving. In fact, their partners are put on pedestals. If a dragon discovers that his or her partner is unworthy of their devotion, the dragon will be hurt and soon end the relationship.

Otherwise, it is difficult to break a dragon's heart because first you have to damage their invulnerable egos.

SNAP OF THE FINGER

Ostensibly, there is nothing you can do to break your dragon's heart, as they are inherently aware of being able to live without you.

HEALTH

Dragon's element, wood, is associated with the liver, so dragons should pay particular attention to keeping this organ in working order. Despite being associated with health and vitality, dragons often suffer from insomnia and respiratory problems. All dragons, however, take care of themselves to their best ability so they rarely get very sick. If they do, dragons normally recover quickly. When feeling vulnerable, dragons have a tendency to overeat and should watch out for this.

LEISURE INTERESTS

Dragons have many interests but often lack the staying power to learn the necessary skills. A typical dragon will be enthusiastically learning yoga one week, judo the next, and the saxophone for a while as well. Anything exciting, bold, or adventurous appeals. It cannot be something that involves too much training, but dragons will be keen to go on short breaks, where tuition or guidance is provided—a skiing vacation or safari, for example—and where they can still feel daring without taking many risks, as long as they can master the skills quickly and not spend too much time on the beginner's slopes. Otherwise, they love to go backpacking some-where like the Himalayas, where they feel at home in the lofty peaks.

Dragons singlehandedly support the worldwide khaki industry.

 THE DRAGON YEARS AND THEIR ELEMENTS

The dragon is a Yang wood animal. Each of the dragon years, however, is associated with an element which is said to have its own influence. These elements are wood, fire, earth, metal, and water. They influence dragon in a regular sequence, which is repeated every sixty years. In the table below, for example, the dragon year 1904 is a wood year. The next dragon wood year is sixty years later in 1964, and the next will be 2024. Dragon's natural element is wood; the influence of this combines with those of the element of the year of birth. The possible effects of the year elements are listed on pages 306–307.

LUNAR YEARS RULED BY THE DRAGON AND THEIR ELEMENTS		
1904	Feb. 16, 1904–Feb. 3, 1905	wood
1916	Feb. 3, 1916–Jan. 22, 1917	fire
1928	Jan. 23, 1928–Feb. 9, 1929	earth
1940	Feb. 8, 1940–Jan. 26, 1941	metal
1952	Jan. 27, 1952–Feb. 13, 1953	water
1964	Feb. 13, 1964–Feb. 1, 1965	wood
1976	Jan. 31, 1976–Feb. 17, 1977	fire
1988	Feb. 17, 1988–Feb. 5, 1989	earth
2000	Feb. 5, 2000–Jan. 23, 2001	metal

Dragon Wood–Wood (1904, 1964)

Wood dragons are in their natural element. Wood, a symbol of growth and renewal, allows dragons to be a creative, innovative person fond of improvisation. They love harmony, elegance, and all beautiful things. Relaxed and at ease socially, these dragons do not like to offend people. Wood can bring pessimism to a character, but dragons temper this tendency with their dynamism. They are progressive people, and, atypically, curious about affairs not centered on them. Dramatic and generous, wood dragons are fun and considerate people.

SECRETS TO MAKE YOU LOOK GOOD

To put it another way, the wood dragon is the only dragon anyone can stand.

Dragon Wood–Fire (1916, 1976)

Potentially a highly combustible combination of fire and wood, fire dragons are actually warmhearted and honest. They are temperamental and have no patience at all. Ambitious and proud, fire dragons tend to be authoritarian. They are perfectionists and will be highly critical if someone does not have the same standards or even opinions as they. All dragons are charismatic, fire dragons are inspirational—many are famous or infamous people.

Dragon Wood–Earth (1928, 1988)

Like all dragons, earth dragons like to dedicate themselves to a cause or project. Earth allows dragons to be more cooperative and open to teamwork than typical dragons, who are just as likely to embark on a solitary quest. Earth dragons don't mind paying attention to the details of a plan. Earth brings patience to the dragon, so they are not in such a hurry. Stability and security are important to these dragons, who will probably equate them with financial independence.

Dragon Wood–Metal (1940, 2000)

Metal strengthens many of dragon's qualities. Metal dragons are very theatrical and have enormous egos. Already resolute, they are argumentative to the point of aggression, but always honest. If a metal dragon believes in a cause, he or she will single-mindedly champion it against all odds. Bordering on the heroic, these dragons have the natures of gladiators. Visionary but still practical, efficient and hardworking, metal dragons are often successful.

Dragon Wood–Water (1952, 2012)

Normally, water would make a character calm and reflective. On dragons, however, the opposite can be true unless the dragon learns to balance the water tendency with his innate dragon excessiveness. Nevertheless, water dragons are more diplomatic than average dragons and very creative. They are pacifists and interested in social problems. This, combined with their intuitive wisdom, makes water dragons idealistic and compassionate.

DRAGON AND THE ZODIAC OF WESTERN ASTROLOGY

To work out your zodiac sign see page 233. General character traits of dragons of the twelve zodiac signs are given on pages 308–310. Bear in mind that the Western zodiac sign modifies the basic dragon nature—especially in the area of personal relationships.

Aries dragon

Two energetic signs make Aries dragons almost hyperactive. Their enthusiasm is infectious, but they need to learn to finish what they start. Selfish and impulsive, these dragons lead turbulent lives and tend to be excessively arrogant.

BARE FACTS

An excessively arrogant dragon is almost an impossible concept; sort of like an excessively dishonest lobbyist.

Taurus dragon

Taurean dragons are more down-to-earth than typical dragons while still being forward-looking and creative. They have great staying power and are more likely to finish a project and achieve fame easily. Taurus dragons are sentimental and sensuous people.

Gemini dragon

Airy Gemini and enthusiastic dragon combine to make a real character. These people have a razor-sharp wit and are verbally adroit. Gemini dragons are not fools; they use humor to make a serious point and are very principled.

Cancer dragon

Cancer dragons are profound in their thoughts and feelings, but they can be too sensitive. Cancer tones down some of the dragon's qualities, making them less brash and reckless and more cautious. These dragons are very good at rousing and inspiring others to achieve their aims.

Leo dragon

Leo dragons are exhausting, excessive, and superior—with good reason though. They are, however, noble at heart and basically good humored. Leo dragons love to bestow their generosity on others less fortunate than themselves. They are hospitable but need to be the center of everyone's attention.

Virgo dragon

Analytical Virgo and brash dragon do not always make a harmonious combination. They are precise, cannot resist an intellectual challenge, and love solving puzzles. As dragons, these people are not so "make-believe"; they are more realistic. Underneath their harsh exteriors, however, they are well-meaning people.

Libra dragon

Manipulative Libra allows dragon to be a more reassuring person, but deceptively so. Unusually diplomatic, they find it easy to rally support and take the lead. Libra dragons are refined and intelligent; style, taste, and quality are important to them.

Scorpio dragon

Passionate and unpredictable, Scorpio dragons often provoke strong reactions and create intense dramas. They never compromise or give up. Dragons are suspicious anyway, but combined with Scorpio's jealous and vengeful nature, this is not a person to have as an enemy.

COMMUNICATION

Like Al Pacino in *Scarface*, only less relaxed.

Sagittarius dragon

Friendly and relatively quiet, Sagittarius dragons are fun-loving optimists. They are proud of their ability to get along with anyone and, unlike most dragons, they do not suffer from arrogance. Expressive but not sentimental, Sagittarius dragon is not afraid to take great risks.

Capricorn dragon

Although eloquent about worldly matters, Capricornean dragons find it difficult to express their personal feelings. At times they seem hard and ambitious, but underneath they are really compassionate and sensitive.

Aquarius dragon

Aquarius allows the dragon to be calm and lucid and even capable of self-criticism—unique among dragons. They have inquisitive and versatile minds but find it difficult to relax. Despite being popular and sociable people, at heart Aquarian dragons are pessimists.

Pisces dragon

Watery Pisces dampens many of the dragon's fiery qualities. Pisces dragons are wise and inspired, but they are also enigmatic, making it hard to understand their motives. Often, they appear to have their head in the clouds but are in fact very shrewd people. On the whole, these dragons are loving and charming, but they will be defensive and demanding if insecure.

WELL LOOK WHO FINALLY MADE THE RODEO

To sum up, a dragon is amazingly self-confident, and will do anything to avoid failure. Which usually includes hanging around with the likes of you.

18. The Snake:

The Yin Fire Animal

There are few animals with more symbolic associations than the snake. Chinese mythology holds that a half-human snake was the father of the Chinese emperors.

LUNAR YEARS RULED BY THE SNAKE

1905	Feb. 4, 1905–Jan. 24, 1906
1917	Jan. 23, 1917–Feb. 10, 1918
1929	Feb. 10, 1929–Jan. 29, 1930
1941	Jan. 27, 1941–Feb. 14, 1942
1953	Feb. 14, 1953–Feb. 2, 1954
1965	Feb. 2, 1965–Jan. 20, 1966
1977	Feb. 8, 1977–Feb. 6, 1978
1989	Feb. 6, 1989–Jan. 26, 1990
2001	Jan. 4, 2001–Feb. 11, 2002

THE SNAKE PERSONALITY

In the West, the snake is often seen as evil. The snake of Chinese astrology, however, is associated with beauty and wisdom. Snakes may appear languid and serene, but they are always mentally active. Snakes are deep thinkers and give very good advice—but they cannot take it. Snakes are capable of lying to get out of a scrape. Linked with esoteric knowledge and spiritual discovery, snakes are sacred to many peoples. Snakes are often people who are "psychic," or who are interested in the psychic, the mystical, or the religious.

COMMUNICATION

Beauty and wisdom my butt. That so-called psychic who told you were going to make something of yourself ten years ago was still a snake.

CHARACTERISTICS

Positive
- distinguished
- elegant
- self-contained
- shrewd
- profound
- perceptive
- lucid
- sophisticated
- wise
- gregarious
- sensual
- curious
- reflective
- organized

Negative
- extravagant
- vengeful
- obstinate
- calculating
- mean with money
- cruel
- self-doubting
- suspicious
- crafty
- remote
- possessive
- anxious
- jealous
- dishonest

Element

Snake is linked to the ancient Chinese element of fire. Fire is a dynamic, exciting sign, which is balanced by snake's innate Yin tendency. The energy of fire can be expressed positively and negatively. It brings warmth, comfort, and light, and it protects. But fire can also burn and destroy. For example, emotionally fire is associated with cruelty and intolerance as well as love and respect. Fire people are always attractive.

Balance

Snakes and dragons are especially karmic signs. Put simply, karma is a person's destiny. Each action performed affects the next and so on, into infinity. The Chinese believe that snakes particularly must deal with their karmic problems within their lifetime to achieve balance. This should not be too much of a problem as snakes are generally well-balanced people. Their natural wisdom grants them the ability to deal with life gracefully, and they are usually unperturbed by life's ups and downs. Tendencies to watch out for are their highly individual approach to morality and honesty—that is, snakes do or say whatever is most convenient for them.

Best associations

Traditionally, the following are said to be associated with snakes:

Taste	bitter	Plant	ferns
Season	summer	Flowers	heather, thistle
Birth	warm, summer day	Food	rice, lamb
Colors	green, red	Climate	hot, sunny

THE MALE SNAKE

If a man has a typical snake personality, he will generally display the behavior listed below:

• is a bad loser
• does not tolerate insults
• is influential
• does not understand fidelity
• will be handsome and well groomed
• is a hedonist
• may be a snob at times
• is romantic and passionate
• has a subtle sense of humor
• relies on first impressions
• is an unlucky gambler

LISTEN UP, THIS IS IMPORTANT

Male Snake = James Bond without the roulette.

THE FEMALE SNAKE

If a woman has a typical snake personality, she will generally display the behavior listed below and on page 315:

• is witty and humorous
• takes failure personally
• gives good advice
• will be captivatingly beautiful
• is not prone to false modesty
• likes her home comforts
• is eager to please others

- will exact her revenge on enemies
- is more faithful than male snakes
- is uncannily perceptive

COMMUNICATION

Female Snake = A heady combination of swimsuit model and Martha Stewart.

THE SNAKE CHILD

If a child has a typical snake personality, he or she will generally display the behavior listed below:

- is tranquil and problem free
- is basically happy
- needs to learn how to share toys
- is sensitive to family quarrels
- is good at art subjects at school
- performs erratically at school
- is calm—if family is settled
- seeks to please parents
- likes secrets and confidences
- does not mind responsibility
- is jealous of parents' attentions
- demands a lot of affection

SNAKE AT HOME

Home is snake's favorite place. They will try to create a calm and peaceful environment but in an imaginative way. Snakes can naturally combine colors and designs in a tasteful way. Furnishings are chosen to indulge the snake's sensuous nature—they will be sumptuously comfortable. The larder will always be well stocked with the finest foods and drinks, and there will be plenty of books to read. A snake home is likely to have expensive items such as antiques and works of art on display. If so, they will not be fakes. In some way, snakes' homes will reflect their perception of themselves. For example, snakes will make their surroundings elegant, witty, or austere depending on their personalities. Snakes' need to stamp their personality on their homes makes them difficult people to live with.

SNAKE AT WORK

Snakes are very efficient and adaptable people. They will do something quickly with the minimum of fuss and in the most cost-effective way. They are also quite capable of quietly eliminating the competition. Although they are willful and well organized, snakes are not so good at long-term planning. A snake is more likely to rely on chance and wits. This does not mean, however, that they take risks. Snakes are opportunistic and ambitious but combine this with deliberation, not recklessness. Wisdom allows snakes to be objective about their goals and aspirations. Snakes can be very determined and persevering if they are morally or materially inspired. If they are not motivated or have nothing to do, they will revert to their natural reflective pose—which others may interpret as laziness.

SOME TYPICAL SNAKE OCCUPATIONS

- professor
- linguist
- philosopher
- teacher
- psychiatrist

- psychologist
- ambassador
- anything related to the arcane
- astrologer
- clairvoyant

- personnel officer
- diviner
- public relations
- executive
- mediator
- interior designer

STRETCHING THE TRUTH

The most deadly combination is a clairvoyant personnel officer, who will somehow always predict the exact moment that you are going to get canned.

? SNAKE PREFERENCES

Likes
- to please others
- ornaments
- dressing to impress
- confiding and hearing confessions
- deserts and wild landscapes
- to impress others with their knowledge
- to make gestures of good will
- a good debate
- to spend extravagantly on themselves
- abstract art
- applause
- harmony and stability
- to be asked for help

Dislikes
- people getting out of control
- to be found gullible
- prejudiced people
- to be made an example of
- disputes and violence
- to lend or give others money
- superficial people
- vulgarity
- to be abandoned
- fake anything

GOOD FRIENDS FOR SNAKES

The diagram below shows the compatibility of snake with other animals. There is no fixed rule, however, because there are other influences on both the snake and any potential friend. These influences are:

• the companion in life (see page 231)
• the dominant element (from the year of birth)

COMPATIBILITY OF SNAKE WITH OTHER ANIMALS

		Key
● Rat	● Horse	▲ Highly compatible
● Ox	● Goat	● Amicable
● Tiger	▲ Monkey	■ No conflict, but needs some effort
▲ Rabbit	▲ Rooster	● Lack of sympathy
▲ Dragon	■ Dog	▲ Antagonistic
■ Snake	▲ Pig	

SNAKE IN LOVE

Snakes are intense and passionate people. They have to feel they are the center of their lover's life. Often, this will smother a relationship. Snakes, however, will not curb their naturally flirtatious habits—they like to check that their sex appeal is still operational. Before they settle down, snakes will have many love affairs, liaisons, and intrigues; this may not stop once they are married. Snakes expect fidelity but may not be faithful themselves. Partners of snake people should try and remain a little independent to gain the snake's respect. Snakes will not like this but will admire them for it and will try harder to be faithful.

HEALTH

Snake's element, fire, is associated with the heart and the small intestine, so snakes should pay particular attention to keeping these organs in working order. They should have regular medical checkups for their heart. Stomachaches are a common snake complaint, so try to cut down on rich, indigestible foods. Snakes need to learn to control their passions and indulgent natures. Sensitive and highly strung, snakes have a tendency to nervous disorders.

LEISURE INTERESTS

Snakes like nothing better than to curl up with a good book in their favorite chair with some classical music in the background. Relaxing in the country on the weekend is another favorite snake pastime. When they go out, snakes like to frequent the theater and love opera. These pursuits allow them to indulge their love of dressing up as well as their enjoyment of the "finer" things in life. Snakes are great strategists, and they excel at games like backgammon and chess. At home, if they are not relaxing, snakes will undertake home improvements such as painting and decorating or just rearranging the ornaments.

THE SNAKE YEARS AND THEIR ELEMENTS

The snake is a Yin fire animal. Each of the snake years, however, is associated with an element which is said to have its own influence. These elements are wood, fire, earth, metal, and water. They influence snake in a regular sequence, which is repeated every sixty years. In the table below, for example, the snake year 1905 is a wood year. The next snake wood year is sixty years later in 1965, and the next will be 2025. Snake's natural element is fire; the influence of this combines with those of the element of the year of birth. The possible effects of the year elements are listed below and on pages 321–322.

LUNAR YEARS RULED BY THE SNAKE AND THEIR ELEMENTS		
1905	Feb. 4, 1905–Jan. 24, 1906	wood
1917	Jan. 23, 1917–Feb. 10, 1918	fire
1929	Feb. 10, 1929–Jan. 29, 1930	earth
1941	Jan. 27, 1941–Feb. 14, 1942	metal
1953	Feb. 14, 1953–Feb. 2, 1954	water
1965	Feb. 2, 1965–Jan. 20, 1966	wood
1977	Feb. 18, 1977–Feb. 6, 1978	fire
1989	Feb. 6, 1989–Jan. 26, 1990	earth
2001	Jan. 24, 2001–Feb. 11, 2002	metal

Snake Fire–Wood (1905, 1965)

Fire and wood can sometimes be a flammable combination. Normally, however, wood snakes are laid-back, easygoing and not as ruthless or vindictive as other snakes. Unusual for snakes, they can even be sympathetic and will work for the benefit of others, not just themselves. Wood is a creative element and allows the snake's imagination to run free. Wood snakes are often inventive or creative people who work to combine beauty of form with space. Many are poets, painters, or musicians.

Snake Fire–Fire (1917, 1977)

Snakes born in fire years are in their natural element. Double fire means double Yang, so they are very dynamic, almost unstoppable people of action. Fire inflames the energies but can be destructive. They are passionate in the intensity of their feelings towards both their lovers and their enemies. In other animal signs, fire can be destructive, but snakes are Yin and, therefore, have the wisdom to control their excesses and use their energies positively. Like all fiery people, fire snakes are dramatic, appealing, and very sexy. These snakes are not as profound as other snakes.

Snake Fire–Earth (1929, 1989)

Earth is a very good element for the snake. They undergo a deep transformation that allows a ripening of many of the snake's qualities. Snakes born in earth years are less mysterious and easy to get to know. Friendly and calm, these snakes try to see the best in people and are not so quick to use others for their own ends. Earth snakes prefer harmony to status. They are not as ambitious as other snakes—they will still achieve their goals, but these will not be so grand. Earth can make these snakes introverted; they are so busy recalling dreams or remembering the past that they do not look to the future.

Snake Fire–Metal (1941, 2001)

Metal brings strength of character to any animal sign. In the snake, this strength wavers between beauty and destruction. Metal snakes are energetic and self-disciplined people, often perfectionists. They have a very strong sense of self and are the most independent of all snakes. Always reflective, metal makes these snakes very serious people; the rigidity of metal can incline them to fanatical thinking, though. These snakes are intolerant, proud, and ruthless, but, unlike other snakes, metal ones are always honest.

YOU'RE WELCOME FOR THE TIP

Intolerant, proud and ruthless, but honest. Great. That means they screw you out of a promotion, but don't bother to lie about how happy it made them.

Snake Fire–Water (1953, 2013)

Reflective water combines with mysterious snake to produce one of the most enigmatic of all signs. Both water and snake are intuitive, so this snake can be intuitive to the point of clairvoyancy. The Yin of water balances the Yang of fire but water snakes should not let this element douse their inner fires. Snake's natural element, fire, stops these water people from being too passive, although the water does express itself as a pacifist streak. A case of still waters running deep, these snakes are calm, wise, and reflective. They are more just and honest than other snakes but still practical and intelligent.

SNAKE AND THE ZODIAC OF WESTERN ASTROLOGY

To work out your zodiac sign see page 233. General character traits of snakes of the twelve zodiac signs are given below and on pages 324–325. Bear in mind that the Western zodiac sign modifies the basic snake nature—especially in the area of personal relationships.

Aries snake

Two fire signs, talented Aries and intelligent snake, combine to make a more powerful, pythonesque snake. They are more impulsive and less reserved than other snakes.

SECRETS TO MAKE YOU LOOK GOOD

The pythonesque snake is also known for its droll British humor.

Taurus snake

Taurus brings industriousness to the snake. Unusually faithful, they are still charming. Do not be fooled by their decadent air, though, as snake's wisdom and Taurean practicality keeps them down-to-earth.

Gemini snake

Quick-witted Gemini and profound snake combine these two traits—dazzling others with eloquence on any sophisticated or intellectual subject. They should beware of being too clever and missing obvious truths.

Cancer snake

Cancerians are prone to depression, but snake relieves this trait. These snakes can recognize their own weaknesses and thus avoid indulging them. Although Cancer snakes can be temperamental, they are basically well-meaning.

Leo snake

Both fire signs, they combine to make an energetic and well-balanced individual. Noble lion makes this snake more generous and open. Leo snakes are endearing and have a lusty and adventurous approach to life but they can be self-righteous and competitive.

Virgo snake

Virgo snakes are both analytical and intuitive. Often theatrical, but always sophisticated and stylish, they can appear intimidating or calculating to others. More cautious about romance, Virgo snakes are serious about matters of the heart.

BARE FACTS

Sorry for the emotional pain, Virgo, but someone has to pay for all the other snakes who can't keep it in their pants.

Libra snake

Idealistic Libra and wise snake make a magnetic combination. They are polite and great diplomats. Do not be deceived by their placid appearance though. All snakes dislike vulgar outbursts, but if a Libra snake is roused then beware.

Scorpio snake

Suspicious Scorpio accentuates the snake's crafty, scheming side. They are always competitive, even at times when it is inappropriate. This makes their lives unnecessarily complicated.

Sagittarius snake

Honorable snakes who have a sense of morality that other snakes lack, they feel more social responsibility and are generous with money. They are not as bothered with their appearance as other snakes, which makes them more approachable.

Capricorn snake

Resolute Capricorn and ambitious snake make highly materialistic and status-seeking people. They are good providers and like to create a solid family base. They are even more profound than typical snakes but are too reserved. Capricornean snakes should relax a bit.

Aquarius snake

Born under two intuitive signs, these snakes are almost too visionary and esoteric. Very individualistic, Aquarian snakes appear eccentric, but they are not bothered by others' opinions and make friends quickly.

Pisces snake

On the surface, Piscean snakes are self-composed and appear cool. Underneath, they are kind but not courageous. The snake's great intellect is unfocussed in those born under Pisces; these snakes are dreamers and idealists and are consequently often disillusioned.

WELL LOOK WHO FINALLY MADE THE RODEO

To review, the snake personality is sophisticated and efficient, but can also be ruthless and cruel. Before you act on this knowledge, you should check to make sure that the statute of limitations is up on the last time you punched one of them.

19. The Horse:

The Yang Fire Animal

The horse is associated with grace, elegance, bravery, and nobility. In China, the horse is the symbol of freedom.

LUNAR YEARS RULED BY THE HORSE	
1906	Jan. 25, 1906–Feb. 12, 1907
1918	Feb. 11, 1918–Jan. 31, 1919
1930	Jan. 30, 1930–Feb. 16, 1931
1942	Feb. 15, 1942–Feb. 4, 1943
1954	Feb. 3, 1954–Jan. 23, 1955
1966	Jan. 21, 1966–Feb. 8, 1967
1978	Feb. 7, 1978–Jan. 27, 1979
1990	Jan. 27, 1990–Feb. 14, 1991
2002	Feb. 12, 2002–Jan. 31, 2003

THE HORSE PERSONALITY

Horses approach life with contagious enthusiasm. They are usually happy and will have many friends. They love to chat, converse, or orate. Horses have good images—others see in their zest for life bravery and independence—but they are actually quite cowardly. Although they love freedom, horses are not truly independent as they rely on others for support and encouragement that is vital to their well-being.

YOU'RE WELCOME FOR THE TIP

Looking for a pal who's excessively needy *and* won't shut up? Horse is for you!

CHARACTERISTICS

Positive
- loyal
- noble
- cheerful
- enthusiastic
- enterprising
- flexible
- sincere
- frank
- versatile
- talkative
- gregarious
- generous
- unselfish
- realist
- energetic

Negative
- unstable
- temperamental
- impatient
- insecure
- hot tempered
- irresponsible
- superficial
- ambitious
- careless
- spendthrift
- contradictory
- vain
- easily panicked
- vulnerable
- anxious

COMMUNICATION

It's good that horses are realists; it helps them accept that they're inferior.

327

Element

Horse is linked to the ancient Chinese element of fire. Fire is a dynamic, exciting sign, which is enhanced by the horse's innate Yang tendency. The energy of fire can be expressed both positively and negatively. It brings warmth, light, and protection as well as the ability to burn and destroy. In horses, fire expresses itself erratically, making them both dynamic and temperamental.

Balance

Horses are both fire and Yang. Therefore, they naturally have great reserves of strength. Yet people born under this sign, although seemingly self-confident, are too easily affected by the opinions of others. Criticism or hostility, no matter how slight, shatters their vulnerable egos. Horses will only have access to their full strengths when they have learned to balance their need for approval with faith in themselves.

SNAP OF THE FINGER

It only takes one, well-chosen snide comment to completely demoralize horse. Think of what ten of them could do!

Best associations

Traditionally, the following are said to be associated with horses:

Taste	bitter	Plant	palm tree
Season	summer	Flower	hawthorn
Birth	winter	Food	rice, lamb
Colors	orange	Climate	hot, sunny

THE MALE HORSE

If a man has a typical horse personality, he will generally display the behavior listed below:

- is not very good with money
- is secretly a pessimist
- will always try to look good
- is egocentric
- will offend others without realizing it
- is independent
- needs approval
- likes the sound of his own voice
- appears to be cheerful and easygoing
- is sloppy at home

SECRET TIP

Male Horse = That one guy at the party who is still wearing Members Only.

THE FEMALE HORSE

If a woman has a typical horse personality, she will generally display the behavior listed below:

- does not like authority
- will never tolerate a subordinate role
- has no time for the problems of others
- craves flattery and attention
- is elegant and well groomed
- is always late
- enjoys dramatic scenes
- needs her own space
- is a good persuader

THE HORSE CHILD

If a child has a typical horse personality, he or she will generally display the behavior listed below:

- is prone to temper tantrums
- is independent
- has a lazy tendency
- is impetuous
- gives up difficult tasks quickly
- is carefree and lively
- dislikes responsibility
- is untidy and disordered
- prefers playing to learning
- is easy to love
- is difficult to discipline

STRETCHING THE TRUTH

Parents of horse children often have bumper stickers reading: "My Child Was Student of the Month . . . In Another Life."

HORSE AT HOME

Horses are not great home lovers. Often, they prefer to spend time at other people's houses. Nevertheless, a stable home base is actually very important to the horse. They need one to bolster their fragile self-confidence. Horses will appreciate their homes more if they go away occasionally. Horses like to be proud of their home environments, but a horse's decorations in the house are unlikely to be imaginative or original. Also, they are not very good at housework. The home of a

horse will be clean but untidy. Horses are not particularly materialistic people. They will decorate their homes with things of sentimental
rather than real value.

COMMUNICATION

What we can conclude from the above is that all
horses need is a damn stable.

HORSE AT WORK

Horses tend to be talented people rather than particularly intelligent. They need to have a job with variety to keep them interested
and to exploit their versatile natures. Horse people are fast-talking and
fast-thinking but are not good at long-term planning or organization.
They are not suited to bureaucratic positions as horses hate routine
and are unable to pay attention to details. They are skilled communicators, however, and very imaginative. Horses are great to have at
brainstorming sessions as they will come up with many ideas—but
don't expect them to carry out the ideas. Impatient for results, they
are better at initiating projects than performing them. Initially, horses
inspire confidence in others as they appear to be supremely confident
and enthusiastic about their work. This enthusiasm crumbles at the
least mishap, though, and a horse's colleagues will soon lose their faith
in these inconstant creatures.

SOME TYPICAL HORSE OCCUPATIONS

- athlete
- cowboy
- technician
- administrator
- chauffeur

- inventor
- truck driver
- salesperson
- teacher
- reporter
- painter

- advertising executive
- poet
- hairdresser
- tax collector
- tour guide

SNAP OF THE FINGER

Fun! Combine "cowboy" with any of the other professions above and let your imagination run wild! (Cowboy hairdresser is our personal fave!)

 HORSE PREFERENCES

Likes

- beginning a new project
- to be complimented
- dancing
- to make people laugh (but not at their own expense)
- a change of scenery
- going on a voyage
- meeting new people
- any conversation, chat, or gossip
- to feel like a pioneer
- to discuss his or her emotions
- to eat at expensive restaurants

Dislikes

- silence
- schedules and timetables
- disapproval
- bureaucrats
- unenthusiastic or disinterested people
- uncommunicative
- people
- being told what to do
- having too many material possessions
- listening to others
- criticism or complaint
- solitude
- being bored

GOOD FRIENDS FOR HORSES

The diagram below shows the compatibility of horse with other animals. There is no fixed rule, however, because there are other influences on both the horse and any potential friend. These influences are:
- the companion in life (see page 231)
- the dominant element (for the year of birth)

COMPATIBILITY OF HORSE WITH OTHER ANIMALS

		Key
▲ Rat	■ Horse	▲ Highly compatible
● Ox	▲ Goat	● Amicable
▲ Tiger	▲ Monkey	■ No conflict, but needs some effort
▲ Rabbit	● Rooster	● Lack of sympathy
■ Dragon	▲ Dog	▲ Antagonistic
● Snake	■ Pig	

HORSE IN LOVE

Horses love to be in love. In fact, they can be more in love with the idea of being in love than with the actual recipient of their affections. Horse people are the type to fall in love at first sight. Once smitten, they put all their energies into seducing that person. As partners, horses are exciting but difficult. They are moody and like their freedom while still demanding support. They are highly romantic and live at the mercy of their emotions. For love, a horse will change everything—buy a house, change job or emigrate, for example. They are flighty people, however, and will fall out of love as quickly as they fell in love. To keep horses interested, partners should try ignoring them. Any lasting relationship with a horse will be punctuated by major crises. Strangely enough, these actually help to prolong the relationship as they keep the horse interested—horse people thrive on dramatic scenes.

✚ HEALTH

Horse's element, fire, is associated with the heart and small intestine, so horses should pay particular attention to keeping these organs in working order, in particular by watching their diets and establishing healthy eating patterns. Horses are highly strung and need to expend their energies in some kind of exertion. This nervous energy will otherwise affect the horse both physically and mentally, therefore making them prone to psychosomatic disorders—those brought about by mental stress—such as anxiety attacks, insomnia, and eating disorders.

🏃 LEISURE INTERESTS

Horses enjoy all kinds of sport and especially competitive ones. Although they are not very good at cooperating, team sports such as football or hockey appeal to horses. This is because they allow the horse to shine while still providing the necessary support that the horse needs to succeed. Horses also love most outdoor pursuits—basically anything that gets them out of the house. On vacation, camping is enjoyed by horses as it allows them to feel independent and pioneering without actually being too daring. Hiking and canoeing appeal to their carefree natures.

THE HORSE YEARS AND THEIR ELEMENTS

The horse is a Yang fire animal. Each of the horse years, however, is associated with an element which is said to have its own influence. These elements are wood, fire, earth, metal, and water. They influence horse in a regular sequence, which is repeated every sixty years. In the table below, for example, the horse year 1942 is a water year. The next horse water year is sixty years later in 2003, and the next will be 2063. Horse's natural element is fire; the influence of this combines with those of the element of the year of birth. The possible effects of the year elements are listed to the below and on pages 336–337.

LUNAR YEARS RULED BY THE HORSE AND THEIR ELEMENTS

1906	Jan. 25, 1906–Feb. 12, 1907	fire
1918	Feb. 11, 1918–Jan. 31, 1919	earth
1930	Jan. 30, 1930–Feb. 16, 1931	metal
1942	Feb. 15, 1942–Feb. 4, 1943	water
1954	Feb. 3, 1954–Jan. 23, 1955	wood
1966	Jan. 21, 1966–Feb. 8, 1967	fire
1978	Feb. 7, 1978–Jan. 27, 1979	earth
1990	Jan. 27, 1990–Feb. 14, 1991	metal
2002	Feb. 12, 2002–Jan. 31, 2003	water

Horse Fire–Fire (1906, 1966)

Fire horses are exceptional people. To be born during the year of the fire horse is considered either very advantageous or disastrous. In China, many people try to avoid giving birth during fire horse years as they do not want to risk bringing bad luck into the family. Fire multiplies both the good and bad attributes of the horse. These people are extreme and excessive. More adventurous, passionate, unruly, and talented than other horses, they will lead thrilling lives. Fire horses are destined for great success or spectacular failure.

Horse Fire–Earth (1918, 1978)

Earth brings stability to the horse. The capability and resourcefulness of this element makes earth horses less flighty. They are more able to see a project through to the end. These horses are more responsible and cautious, yet they are not as much fun as typical horses. Normally, earthy types are very conventional, but horse breathes fresh air into this element and prevents inflexibility. Earth horses will express their nervous energies by paying attention to details and by displaying minor eccentricities.

Horse Fire–Metal (1930, 1990)

Metal is a good element for horse. It compensates for some of horse's failings. They can be more resolute and persevering than other horses—but only if they are motivated. Metal horses need stimulation to stop them from getting bored. They are headstrong and irrepressible. Metal can also restrain horses, smothering their passionate natures. This is not necessarily a good thing as horses need to give vent to their emotions.

Horse Fire–Water (1942, 2002)

Water facilitates the horse's dormant creativity and brings these people success in the arts. Elusive water and easily distracted horse combine to produce people with very short attention spans. Water is a communicative element and enhances the horse's already verbose nature. It allows them to be humorous and witty in their conversation. Although inconsiderate and self-centered, water horses endear themselves to others by being charming. They cultivate daredevil personae that allow others to excuse their shortcomings. Water exploits the horse's nervous energy and these horses keep active and like to live by their wits.

Horse Fire–Wood (1954, 2014)

Wood has a calming influence on the horse. Wood horses are more cooperative and helpful than other horses. They should watch out for others trying to take advantage of them, though, as wood diminishes the horse's perceptive abilities, making them too gullible at times. Wood helps to settle the horse's nervous energies. Emotionally, therefore, this horse is not so prone to depression and bad moods and will be mostly happy and good-tempered.

BARE FACTS

Happy and good-tempered fire-wood horses often indulge their inherent fondness for gabbing and chatting the day away. We'll take the bad moods and depression any day.

HORSE AND THE ZODIAC OF WESTERN ASTROLOGY

To work out your zodiac sign see page 233. General character traits of horses of the twelve zodiac signs are given below and on pages 338–340. Bear in mind that the Western zodiac sign modifies the basic horse nature—especially in the area of personal relationships.

Aries horse

Aries exacerbates the horse's wild side. These horses are aggressively competitive and very enterprising. Aries horses are more capable of devotion than other horses and are good company.

Taurus horse

Pragmatic Taurus allows the horse to plan ahead. These horses are less temperamental and more stable but they can be too rigid. Taurean horses are not averse to taking advice from others.

Gemini horse

These two signs share many similar traits which are, therefore, multiplied under this sign. Gemini horses are even more enthusiastic, curious, rebellious, and sociable than usual.

Cancer horse

Cancer makes this horse able to appreciate the needs and wishes of others. Being more sensitive, these horses are very dependent on the love and support of close family and friends.

LISTEN UP, THIS IS IMPORTANT

Sorry, Cancer horse, old buddy. After what we found out in this chapter, if you're relying on the love and support of pretty much anybody, you're S.O.L.

Leo horse

To these horses, the world is their playground. The Leo horse loves adventure, craves admiration, and is not beset by the self-doubts that normally plague the horse.

Virgo horse

Virgoan horses are well-balanced people. Virgo cures some of the horse's shortcomings, such as lack of precision, lack of self-discipline, irresponsibility, and unruliness.

Libra horse

Libran horses are level-headed and realistic yet surprisingly indecisive. Not as independent as other horses, they are honest about how important their loved ones are to them.

Scorpio horse

Headstrong, stubborn, and wild, these horses never compromise. They direct their considerable energies into fulfilling their desires—which govern the lives of Scorpio horses.

YOU'RE WELCOME FOR THE TIP

That couple in the next room, making it very difficult for you to get any sleep? Don't fret. It's simply a couple of Scorpio horses, directing their considerable energies into fulfilling their desires.

Sagittarius horse

The symbol of Sagittarius is itself a horse. In many ways, these people are almost stereotypical horses. Easygoing and carefree, they are fun people but typically unpredictable.

Capricorn horse

Capricorn makes these horses relatively materialistic. A Capricorn horse is not afraid of working hard to achieve financial security. They are more serious in their demeanor than one would expect from a horse.

Aquarius horse

Two unpredictable signs combine to produce an eccentric but talented horse. More than any other horses, Aquarian horses love the company of new friends.

Pisces horse

Self-conscious Pisces heightens the horse's basic insecurities. When they are not being anxious, Piscean horses are loving, eager to please, and warmhearted.

WELL LOOK WHO FINALLY MADE THE RODEO

To summarize, horse people are enthusiastic and energetic, but rather unstable and irresponsible, too. Not so great for everday life, but, hey, if you're ever considering a cross-country crime spree . . . .

20. The Goat:
The Yin Fire Animal

The goat is associated with harmony, creativity, peace, and pleasure. In China, the goat is seen as a harbinger of peace.

BARE FACTS

Quite different from America, where the goat is seen as a harbinger of goat droppings.

LUNAR YEARS RULED BY THE GOAT	
1907	Feb. 13, 1907–Feb. 1, 1908
1919	Feb. 1, 1919–Feb. 19, 1920
1931	Feb. 17, 1931–Feb. 5, 1932
1943	Feb. 5, 1943–Jan. 24, 1944
1955	Jan. 24, 1955–Feb. 11, 1956
1967	Feb. 9, 1967–Jan. 29, 1968
1979	Jan. 28, 1979–Feb. 15, 1980
1991	Feb. 15, 1991–Feb. 3, 1992
2003	Feb. 1, 2003–Jan. 21, 2004

THE GOAT PERSONALITY

Charming, amiable, and sympathetic, goats are genuinely nice people. They hate to criticize and always look for the best in people—including themselves. A goat will prefer to forget grievances rather than brood over them and will bottle up resentments to keep the peace. Goat people live in the present, which they enjoy to the best of their abilities. Thanks to their sensitive natures, goats are one of the most artistic and creative of all the Chinese horoscope signs.

YOU'RE WELCOME FOR THE TIP

If you are a pushy loudmouth who needs someone that will shut up and take it, consider getting together with a goat.

CHARACTERISTICS

Positive	Negative
• creative	• eccentric
• imaginative	• illogical
• ingenious	• vulnerable
• honest	• irresponsible
• capricious	• irrational
• sensitive	• naive
• faithful	• unsatisfied
• sincere	• disorganized
• peaceful	• impulsive
• adaptable	• lazy
• independent	• gullible
• ardent	• fickle
• elegant	• careless
• gentle	• anxious
• easygoing	• impractical

Element

Goat is linked to the ancient Chinese element of fire. Fire is a dynamic, exciting, and energetic sign. In the case of goats, fire expresses itself in their imaginative and creative abilities. Normally, fire people are as fiery as the sign suggests. The easygoing and carefree nature of the goat, however, dampens their fiery sides, which are kept well hidden until times of crisis.

Balance

Normally, people are advised to look to themselves to balance the strengths and weaknesses of their characters. For example, the goat would be advised to try and take more care of the practical side of life—such as paying the bills—and not rely on others to support them as they pursue their own interests. Chinese tradition, however, holds that goats are mostly unable to change this aspect of their natures. Therefore, they will need to find a patron to take care of the "administration" of their life and allow them the freedom to make the most of their creative talents. This role could be filled by, for example, a devoted husband or wife, a manager, or even a loyal accountant!

Best associations

Traditionally, the following are said to be associated with goats:

Taste	bitter	Plants	wormwood, anise
Season	summer	Flower	honeysuckle
Birth	rainy day	Food	rice, lamb
Colors	sky-blue	Climate	hot

THE MALE GOAT

If a man has a typical goat personality, he will generally display the behavior listed below:

• is dependent on his family
• will be a fun but irresponsible parent
• is fretful and indecisive
• has a highly developed aesthetic sense
• is unusually sensitive for a man
• has a natural flair for hospitality
• is reflective and gentle
• will remember birthdays and anniversaries
• is easily put off by obstacles

COMMUNICATION

Male Goat = One of the few men who has no qualms about driving a Volkswagen Jetta.

⚲ THE FEMALE GOAT

If a woman has a typical goat personality, she will generally display the behavior listed below:

- is indifferent to conventions
- is angered by injustice
- is talented
- leads a carefree existence
- is never hostile
- is impressionable and easily led
- likes to be the center of attention
- fears rejection and criticism
- needs security to blossom
- likes to be noticed

SECRETS TO MAKE YOU LOOK GOOD

Female Goat = The reason most guys decided to audition for the school play.

THE GOAT CHILD

If a child has a typical goat personality, he or she will generally display the behavior listed below and on page 346:

- is delicate and sickly
- needs to be indulged
- is fickle and unstable
- is timid and uncertain at times
- blossoms with a supportive family
- must be allowed to find their own way
- enjoys creating things

- makes up fantasies and fairy tales
- will give away their toys to friends

GOAT AT HOME

Goats love the creature comforts of life but are not practical enough to go out and get them. It is usually left to their partner or family to decorate and furnish the home. Nonetheless, goats are very acquisitive—they are attracted to beautiful or novel things. A goat house will be full of knickknacks, souvenirs, and odd bits of furniture that have caught the goat's fancy. They love junk shops, charity shops, and markets where they can find new and interesting goods at low prices. If they have enough money, they will indulge themselves by rummaging around the better department stores as if they were flea markets. At heart, though, goats are indifferent to material possessions and will be as happy in another's home that is full of beautiful objects as their own. A goat may have one beautiful item, perhaps made by himself or herself, installed in the home that negates the drab surroundings.

GOAT AT WORK

Goats would never work if they had the choice, if only money was not a necessity. They are not especially active or hardworking and will be lazy and erratic at work. Despite this, if goats do undertake a job, they will carry it out properly or not at all. Goats can be both scrupulous and perfectionists. They have a profiteering side and hate to support themselves—they will try to profit from the hard work of others. This does not mean that they are ambitious, as they will not better themselves at the expense of others. If they do have some money, goats will be better off seeking advice on how to invest it wisely rather than using it to start their own business. Goats are inspired by the arts and love anything concerned with harmony and beauty. They come into their own in art if they have a mentor or patron who can recognize and encourage their talents.

SOME TYPICAL GOAT OCCUPATIONS

- actor/actress
- story writer
- painter
- musician
- landscape gardener

- weaver
- potter
- courtesan
- television presenter
- gigolo
- dancer

- tramp
- fortune-teller
- escort
- investor
- shareholder

BARE FACTS

Observant readers will notice that both "courtesan" and "gigolo" are suitable goat occupations. This is perfect, because they are too damn lazy to make it in any of the other professions, and usually have no choice but to fall back on the world's oldest ones.

GOAT PREFERENCES

Likes
- to please others
- beauty
- to make people curious
- tranquillity
- to forgive and forget
- parks with fountains
- marble statues
- costume dramas
- to be taken care of
- beautiful people

Dislikes
- to be made to choose
- unwanted responsibility
- routines
- to be involved in others' problems
- obligations
- hostile atmospheres
- to offend others
- emotional scenes
- doing the accounts
- taking the initiative

GOOD FRIENDS FOR GOATS

The diagram below shows the compatibility of goat with other animals. There is no fixed ruling, however, because there are other influences on both the goat and any potential friend. These influences are:
- the companion in life (see page 231)
- the dominant element (from the year of birth)

COMPATIBILITY OF GOAT WITH OTHER ANIMALS

● Rat
● Ox
■ Tiger
▲ Rabbit
● Dragon
● Snake

▲ Horse
● Goat
● Monkey
● Rooster
■ Dog
▲ Pig

Key
▲ Highly compatible
● Amicable
■ No conflict, but needs some effort
● Lack of sympathy
▲ Antagonistic

♡ GOAT IN LOVE

Goats cannot be objective, and they think that the world revolves around them and their loved ones. Effectively it does, as they will simply blind themselves to matters not concerning them. Emotional and sensitive, goats have great expectations of romance but they will also give a lot in return. A goat will adapt to please a loved one and does not mind making concessions to keep the peace. They are polite and affectionate partners. Although goats are sympathetic, they are not particularly compassionate, so partners should not expect to burden the goat with their problems. Goats do not like to be depended on. Conversely, the goat will expect their partner to be always there for them and never even to be tempted by another. Above all else, partners must accept goats as they are and not try to change them.

YOU'RE WELCOME FOR THE TIP

You can date a goat, or you can date a soap dish. It's entirely up to you.

✚ HEALTH

Goat's element, fire, is associated with the heart and small intestine, so goats should pay particular attention to keeping these organs in working order. Being of the Yin tendency, goats are advised to try and prevent, rather than cure, illnesses. It is probably the case that most goats, being nervous about their health, are already practicing this by having regular checkups with the doctor. Yin people tend to have delicate constitutions. Goats should make sure they keep warm during the winter months and remember to relax occasionally. Meditation would probably be beneficial for goats as it would help them focus their energies and develop an inner sense of well-being.

Goats consume more Airborne than any other zodiac sign.

LEISURE INTERESTS

Goats are not particularly energetic people. They would rather visit an art gallery than go swimming. Parks, botanical gardens, historic houses, and flower gardens will all have many goat visitors. Goats love anything in which they can find beauty and harmony. Alternatively, goats spend a lot of their time visiting friends. They are never short of invitations as goat people bring a pleasant ambience to any gathering. On the whole, goats are better as guests than hosts. As guests, they only have to be their agreeable selves, but as hosts they would have to organize and plan the event—not goat strong points.

THE GOAT YEARS AND THEIR ELEMENTS

The goat is a Yin fire animal. Each of the goat years, however, is associated with an element which is said to have its own influence. These elements are wood, fire, earth, metal, and water. They influence goat in a regular sequence, which is repeated every sixty years. In the table on page 351, for example, the goat year 1907 is a fire year. The next goat fire year is sixty years later in 1967, and the next will be 2027. Goat's natural element is fire; the influence of this combines with those of the element of the year of birth. The possible effects of the year elements are listed on pages 351–353.

LUNAR YEARS RULED BY THE GOAT AND THEIR ELEMENTS

1907	Feb. 13, 1907–Feb. 1, 1908	fire
1919	Feb. 1, 1919–Feb. 19, 1920	earth
1931	Feb. 17, 1931–Feb. 5, 1932	metal
1943	Feb. 5, 1943–Jan. 24, 1944	water
1955	Jan. 24, 1955–Feb. 11, 1956	wood
1967	Feb. 9, 1967–Jan. 29, 1968	fire
1979	Jan. 28, 1979–Feb. 15, 1980	earth
1991	Feb. 15, 1991–Feb. 3, 1992	metal
2003	Feb. 1, 2003–Jan. 21, 2004	water

Goat Fire–Fire (1907, 1967)

Fire is the goat's natural element. Double fire goats are blessed with courage and intuition. These goats are dramatic and innovative, yet they have a knack for making their wild ideas seem safe and logical. They do, however, have a tendency to be reckless and of not looking before they leap. Goats are never very good at managing their money, and double fire goats are even worse. Money almost burns a hole in their pockets. As with all fire types, these goats are attractive and appealing people. They are gentle and sympathetic but intolerant of those they consider fools.

COMMUNICATION

Unfortunately, a goat considering someone a fool is like a musician considering someone a deadbeat.

Goat Fire–Wood (1955, 2015)

Wood is a creative element associated with growth, renewal, and innovation. Combined with the goat's imagination, this makes wood goats highly artistic. It also heightens the goat's sensitive nature. Unlike water goats, however, wood makes goats very compassionate people and not worriers. These people are generous with their time and money for good causes that they believe in; but they are more likely to be working in the local charity shop than far away in a refugee camp.

Goat Fire–Earth (1919, 1979)

Earth grounds the goat. It brings them down to earth and keeps their heads out of the clouds for too long. Earth bestows on the goat steadfastness and the ability to work hard. These goats are more materialistic than the rest of the breed. Atypically, earth goats are capable of fulfilling their own material needs and are not so dependent on others to organize them. Earth goats are basically cheerful and optimistic people but when wronged they can complain too much. Earth signs can, at times, be so cautious and practical that they stagnate.

Goat Fire–Metal (1931, 1991)

Metal strengthens the goat. It brings determination and perseverance to an otherwise work-shy type of person. Fire combines with metal to give these people more presence than typical goats. Metal goats are still sensitive but not as vulnerable as usual. In fact, other people do not realize how sensitive and affectionate these goats really are underneath their harsh exteriors. As with all metal types, these are very ambitious people, but their ambitions will be directed toward typically goatlike goals—achieving in the arts, for example.

SECRETS TO MAKE YOU LOOK GOOD

Also, as with all metal types, they have a tendency toward big hair, loose women and seriously hard rocking.

Goat Fire–Water (1943, 2003)

Fluid water makes the goat even more capricious than usual. Water goats are incredibly sensitive people and very perceptive emotionally. This can hamper them as they will internalize other people's problems and may become worriers. Fire aligned with water makes these people able to get their own way—but very subtly. Surprisingly, water goats are conservative people; they are fearful of change and do not like to take risks.

 # GOAT AND THE ZODIAC OF WESTERN ASTROLOGY

To work out your zodiac sign see page 233. General character traits of goats of the twelve zodiac signs are given below and on pages 354–355. Bear in mind that the Western zodiac sign modifies the basic goat nature—especially in the area of personal relationships.

Aries goat

The goat and the ram share many traits. So those born under both these signs are almost stereotypical goats. Yet they are more independent and are even headstrong. Aries makes the goat stubborn and, unlike other goats, these people hold grudges and will exact revenge on their enemies.

Taurus goat

Taurean goats crave domestic and financial security. They are cautious and never take risks. Although still easygoing, if pushed to the limit a Taurus goat will soon break into a fury.

Gemini goat

Mercurial Gemini and capricious goat combine to make easily distracted people. They are intelligent and curious and always have something on their minds.

Cancer goat

Moody Cancer serves to make the goat temperamental as well as fickle. These goats are very concerned about what others think of them. If they feel secure, then Cancerian goats will be kind and gentle; if they feel neglected, they can be vindictive and stubborn.

Leo goat

Leo brings a much-needed measure of common sense to the goat. Leo goats are both sensitive and resolute. They are the most charismatic of all the goats, and it is easy for them to find willing supporters of their latest idea or scheme.

Virgo goat

Virgo goats are perfectionists and apply this in their drive to help others. Although they can be too critical, Virgoan goats are basically well meaning. They are more intellectual than other goats and need a job that exploits this to prevent boredom.

Libra goat

Libra goats are intelligent and refined. They like to make a good impression and will take care of their appearance. Capable of making great compromises to keep people's affection, these goats need constant companionship.

Scorpio goat

Scorpio endows the goat with huge reserves of willpower. Their sensitive natures take second place to their ambitions. Yet these goats are not practical. They are erratic and eccentric but have bursts of wisdom and are very gifted artistically.

Sagittarius goat

Sagittarian goats have enough self-confidence to support themselves and do not need to look for others to care for them. They are more adventurous yet less sensitive than other goats.

Capricorn goat

Capricorn goats are practical and opportunistic. Financial wealth and status are important to them, and they are usually successful in their chosen careers. These goats do find it difficult to be open emotionally with others, though.

Aquarius goat

Visionary Aquarius and imaginative goat combine to give great potential. These people are gifted planners, oblivious to criticism, and often idiosyncratic. Aquarian goats are innovative but need to learn to evaluate risks.

Pisces goat

Born under two sensitive signs, Pisces goats are almost too sensitive for their own good. Their emotions will reflect the atmosphere of their surroundings. These goats are inspired people but need a stable home base before they can express their creativity.

WELL LOOK WHO FINALLY MADE THE RODEO

To review, the goat is sweet and very creative, but rather unmotivated and irresponsible. You know, when actors play mentally-challenged people like this, they usually win Oscars.

21. The Monkey:

The Yang Metal Animal

In some parts of China, the monkey is worshipped as the "Great Sage Equal to Heaven." Monkeys are also associated with adultery, justice, and, emotionally, with sorrow.

LUNAR YEARS RULED BY THE MONKEY	
1908	Feb. 2, 1908–Jan. 21, 1909
1920	Feb. 20, 1920–Feb. 7, 1921
1932	Feb. 6, 1932–Jan. 25, 1933
1944	Jan. 25, 1944–Feb. 12, 1945
1956	Feb. 12, 1956–Jan. 30, 1957
1968	Jan. 30, 1968–Feb. 16, 1969
1980	Feb. 16, 1980–Feb. 4, 1981
1992	Feb. 4, 1992–Jan. 22, 1993
2004	Jan. 22, 2004–Feb. 8, 2005

THE MONKEY PERSONALITY

Highly competitive and insatiably curious, monkeys are very shrewd. They are intelligent and ingenious and try to make the best of any situation. Monkeys are quick-witted and never at a loss for words. They have a reputation for trickery. Although monkeys can be scheming and are good at manipulating people, they use these skills wisely. Despite this, monkeys are quick to stop others who manipulate them. Monkeys try to be honest but will tell a lie if it is convenient.

CHARACTERISTICS

Positive
- independent
- astute
- sociable
- vivacious
- enthusiastic
- tolerant
- lively
- quick-witted
- sensitive
- generous
- optimistic
- entertaining
- audacious
- gregarious
- inventive

Negative
- opportunistic
- restless
- manipulative
- scheming
- unpredictable
- secretive
- deceitful
- mischievous
- vain
- fickle
- dishonest
- selfish
- cunning
- opinionated
- devious

YOU'RE WELCOME FOR THE TIP

The key negative trait here is "unpredictable," which means that one minute the typical monkey will be horrible to deal with, and the next minute will be really, amazingly horrible to deal with.

Element

Monkey is linked to the ancient Chinese element of metal. This is a very strong element. It can be seen positively as a valuable resource, such as gold;

or negatively as a weapon, such as a sword. In monkeys, the energy of metal expresses itself as their imaginative, ambitious, and independent streaks.

Balance

Monkeys are curious people who find something of interest anywhere. They are attracted to the new and unknown. This can make them broad-minded and knowledgeable people, but their energies can be dissipated by these many interests. Monkeys need to learn how to channel their energies into one particular goal at a time. If they can balance their need to search for fresh pastures by bringing some routine or stability into their life, they will find that they can achieve considerable success.

Best associations

Traditionally, the following are said to be associated with monkeys:

Taste	pungent	Plant	Chinese wolfberry
Season	fall	Flower	bird of paradise
Birth	summer	Food	cloves
Colors	white	Climate	dry

BARE FACTS

Anyone who has spent time around their favorite monkey will note that taste is not the only thing pungent about them.

THE MALE MONKEY

If a man has a typical monkey personality, he will generally display the behavior listed below and on page 359:

- breaks the rules
- lacks self-discipline

- likes to gamble
- is accommodating
- appears to be shallow
- is very good with children
- gets on well with women
- likes to tease his friends
- can lie cheerfully
- is warmhearted and generous
- has a sharp sense of humor

COMMUNICATION

Male Monkey = First twit voted off the island.

 ## THE FEMALE MONKEY

If a woman has a typical monkey personality, she will generally display the behavior listed below:

- provokes jealousy
- is flirtatious
- needs to be independent
- is witty
- likes to have her own space
- prefers not to marry
- is very good with children
- does not have conventional morals
- is more honest than the male
- is very practical
- is good at fixing things

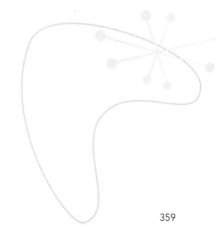

THE MONKEY CHILD

If a child has a typical monkey personality, he or she will generally display the behavior listed below:

• has a tendency to become overexcited
• needs to be encouraged to calm down
• is impatient and hotheaded
• has a lively imagination
• adapts easily to new environments
• is very critical of peers
• will not suffer bullying for long
• has a short attention span
• can stand up for himself or herself

SNAP OF THE FINGER

Thankfully, the parents of a monkey do not need to schedule a lot of extracurricular activities for their child. Their youngster will be caught up in an endless cycle of futile violence and detention which will leave little time for soccer.

MONKEY AT HOME

Monkeys are not stay-at-home types. Nevertheless, a stable home environment is important. It gives them a sound base from which to venture forth on their latest adventure. Monkeys hate the status quo. They will always be planning to move to a better house or, if this is not possible, then they will be organizing a major redecoration of their home. Monkeys are real do-it-yourself enthusiasts; they are practical people and enjoy making things, repairing, and decorating. Even when restricted by funds, a monkey will find ingenious ways to furnish and decorate a house. For example, tables and chairs will be made from odds and ends and lots of brightly colored objects of interest displayed as ornaments.

COMMUNICATION

Monkeys' ability with makeshift arts and crafts allows them a seamless transition from their home to activity room at the mental hospital.

MONKEY AT WORK

Monkeys can always find work as they are versatile and quick-thinking. They are highly flexible people who can turn their hand to virtually anything. Monkeys hate routine. For monkeys to stay in a job, it must provide them with plenty of variety as well as challenge. If they are overstimulated, however, their minds will wander. When this happens, or alternatively, if they are bored, the monkey's notoriously short attention span will cause them to change careers. Also, a monkey will feel trapped in a predictable career. So, one year a monkey may be teaching English and the next driving a bus. Whatever their job, though, monkeys are at their best when they are breaking or stretching the rules. To be happy at work, monkeys need a position where they are allowed to use their discretion and need to use their wits.

SOME TYPICAL MONKEY OCCUPATIONS

- counselor
- therapist
- installation artist
- bus driver
- occupational therapist

- nurse
- judo instructor
- English teacher
- art critic
- stockbroker

- theologian
- foreign correspondent
- town planner
- writer
- journalist

STRETCHING THE TRUTH

Monkey's penchant for breaking the rules can lead to some disastrous results on the job. Those of you in jail may have taken the advice of your monkey stockbroker, and those of you who are dead may have listened to your monkey nurse.

 # MONKEY PREFERENCES

Likes

- a challenge
- to listen to others' problems and worries
- to care for people
- charting horoscopes
- alternative belief systems
- to travel
- practical jokes
- decorating the house
- reading tarot cards
- visiting friends
- ethnic art
- games of chance
- nightclubs

Dislikes

- routine
- bars and alcohol
- established religions
- being manipulated
- depending on others
- doing without money
- purely physical work
- the achievements of others
- conventional people
- compromising their independence

GOOD FRIENDS FOR MONKEYS

The diagram below shows the compatibility of monkey with other animals. There is no fixed rule, however, because there are other influences on both the monkey and any potential friend. These influences are:

• the companion in life (see page 231)
• the dominant element (from the year of birth)

COMPATIBILITY OF MONKEY WITH OTHER ANIMALS

		Key
▲ Rat	● Horse	▲ Highly compatible
■ Ox	● Goat	● Amicable
▲ Tiger	● Monkey	■ No conflict, but needs some effort
● Rabbit	■ Rooster	● Lack of sympathy
▲ Dragon	● Dog	▲ Antagonistic
▲ Snake	● Pig	

MONKEY IN LOVE

Monkeys approach love in their typically vivacious and enthusiastic way. In the beginning, they are heady with passion and will be infatuated with their new-found love. As the novelty wears off, however, their excitement fades, and monkeys may instead start to criticize their partner. The relationship has to be lively to keep a monkey interested. If happy and stimulated, a monkey can be a tolerant and understanding partner, although tears are just as likely as laughter in a relationship with a monkey—they are excitable and unpredictable people. Monkeys are usually charming and love to please. In return, they expect their partner to be alert and attentive to their needs.

✚ HEALTH

Monkey's element, metal, is associated with the lungs and large intestine, so monkeys should pay particular attention to keeping these organs in working order. Also, monkeys should take care of their kidneys by not consuming too much coffee and salt. Despite the fact that they are not great athletes or health-club fans, monkeys are usually surprisingly fit and healthy people well into their old age. They tend to be naturally slight people. Monkeys should not neglect their diets—either through distraction or illness—as they may become too thin.

COMMUNICATION

The fact that their main worry is that they might be too thin is another reason to hate these simian bastards.

🏃 LEISURE INTERESTS

The leisure interests of monkeys are typically varied. Friendly and gregarious, monkeys inevitably spend a lot of time socializing. Either visiting or entertaining at home, a monkey can always be found at the hub of any social activity. For entertainment, they like to see the latest film or play the latest game. Monkeys like games of chance but will probably cheat! For exercise, they are attracted to all sports that involve speed, especially water sports. Monkeys indulge their taste for the unusual and the exotic by visiting exhibitions of art from different cultures. Many monkeys are keen amateur photographers. This gives them an excuse to explore new places and acts as a cover for their curious natures.

 THE MONKEY YEARS AND THEIR ELEMENTS

The monkey is a Yang metal animal. Each of the monkey years, however, is associated with an element which is said to have its own influence. These elements are wood, fire, earth, metal, and water. They influence monkey in a regular sequence, which is repeated every sixty years. In the table below, for example, the monkey year 1908 is an earth year. The next monkey earth year is sixty years later in 1968, and the next will be 2028. Monkey's natural element is metal; the influence of this combines with those of the element of the year of birth. The possible effects of the year elements are listed below and on pages 366–367.

LUNAR YEARS RULED BY THE MONKEY AND THEIR ELEMENTS		
1908	Feb. 2, 1908–Jan. 21, 1909	earth
1920	Feb. 20, 1920–Feb. 7, 1921	metal
1932	Feb. 6, 1932–Jan. 25, 1933	water
1944	Jan. 25, 1944–Feb. 12, 1945	wood
1956	Feb. 12, 1956–Jan. 30, 1957	fire
1968	Jan. 30, 1968–Feb. 16, 1969	earth
1980	Feb. 16, 1980–Feb. 4, 1981	metal
1992	Feb. 4, 1992–Jan. 22, 1993	water
2004	Jan. 22, 2004–Feb. 8, 2005	wood

Monkey Metal–Earth (1908, 1968)

Earth is a sympathetic and balancing element for the metal-dominated monkey. It grounds these otherwise flighty people. Atypically, earth

365

monkeys are studious, dutiful, hardworking, and thorough. They are patient and scientific in their approach to solving problems. Earth enhances the monkey's natural intelligence, making them more intellectual. Earth monkeys have cutting tongues. They can be harsh in their criticisms of others. For this reason, these monkeys may have difficulties in their personal relationships.

Monkey Metal–Metal (1920, 1980)

Metal is the monkey's natural element. Double metal multiplies the monkey's intelligence but also increases aggressiveness. Metal monkeys are extremely independent people, simply because they feel superior to their peers. Metal monkeys are materialistic and, fortunately, have a knack for making money. With their nerves of steel, metal monkeys like to take risks and can be successful gamblers, as they are fortunate people.

SNAP OF THE FINGER

If you can put up with their innate superiority and aggressiveness for ten years or so, you could probably get a hell of a house in the settlement.

Monkey Metal–Water (1932, 1992)

Water and metal are a harmonious combination. Water monkeys are cooperative and understanding people. They are almost too sensitive and will see implied criticism where none is meant. Water enhances the monkey's already gregarious nature. Yet water monkeys are complex characters. Enigmatic and secretive, they keep their true feelings well hidden. These monkeys are prone to mood swings and are notoriously fickle.

Monkey Metal–Wood (1944, 2004)

Wood is a fortunate element for monkeys. It helps to focus and stabilize them. Wood monkeys are friendly and approachable people. Coupled with metal, wood makes the monkey very resourceful and a great problem solver. In fact, wood monkeys are remarkable people. Wood is a creative element, so monkeys born in these years are likely to be artistic. They are also gifted communicators who have a strong sense of ethics.

YOU'RE WELCOME FOR THE TIP

The metal-wood monkey seems to possess all the friendly, stable and ethical qualities not usually associated with this sign, making them more placid and predictable. You may want to seek sex outside the relationship.

Monkey Metal–Fire (1956, 2016)

Strong metal combined with passionate fire creates powerful and dominant but aggressive people. Fire also makes this monkey the most competitive of all monkeys. They are driven to succeed. Yet fire and metal bring conflict to the monkey. Fire monkeys have great potential but they tend to overstretch themselves. They do not always respond to challenges in the best way. These monkeys need to accept their own limitations and act accordingly.

 # MONKEY AND THE ZODIAC OF WESTERN ASTROLOGY

To work out your zodiac sign see page 233. General character traits of monkeys of the twelve zodiac signs are given on pages 368–370. Bear in mind that the Western zodiac sign modifies the basic monkey nature—especially in the area of personal relationships.

Aries monkey

Aries monkeys are some of the most talkative and forthright people around. They are uncannily perceptive and people can always recall the words of an Aries monkey. Both enterprising and opportunistic, they are also very successful.

Taurus monkey

Determined Taurus facilitates the monkey's remarkable mental abilities. These people are capable and resourceful. Unusually persevering, they can apply themselves successfully to one task at a time.

LISTEN UP, THIS IS IMPORTANT

And that one task that they apply themselves successfully to? Annoying the hell out of you.

Gemini monkey

Mercurial Gemini and the trickster monkey have a lot in common. People born under both these signs are incredibly quick-witted but lack focus and direction. They are the mental gymnasts of the Chinese zodiac.

Cancer monkey

Cancer brings extra sensitivity to the monkey. In fact, Cancer monkeys are moody as well as unpredictable. If they feel secure, then they can become more like the typical, happy-go-lucky monkey personality.

Leo monkey

Leo monkeys are direct and candid people. They are very witty and are great raconteurs. Happy when they are the center of attention, Leo monkeys get irritable when they are ignored.

Virgo monkey

Analytical Virgo and clever monkey combine to make very profound people. Virgo monkeys can be too calculating and emotionally distant, however. Busy looking for hidden agendas, they can miss the more obvious facts.

Libra monkey

Eloquent and sociable, these monkeys have the "gift of gab." They pride themselves on their ability to get along with anyone. But Libran monkeys can be manipulative and tend to exploit weaker people.

Scorpio monkey

Mystery-loving Scorpio and devious monkey are a dangerous combination. They are secretive people who are suspicious of everyone. Always planning and scheming, these monkeys assume that others are equally ambitious.

Sagittarius monkey

Sagittarian monkeys are almost stereotypical monkeys. They are broad-minded and curious people. They love to travel and explore new horizons. If they are not stimulated, these monkeys will act mischievously.

COMMUNICATION

Let's be honest: they act even more mischieviously when they *are* stimulated.

Capricorn monkey

This sign brings conflict to the monkey. Austere Capricorn and witty monkey combine to produce seemingly debonair people. In fact, Capricornean monkeys are often hiding great personal anguish beneath their smooth exteriors.

Aquarius monkey

This sign is very good for monkeys. It allows their creativity to blossom and Aquarius lends a visionary aspect to their work. They may appear independent, but, at heart, Aquarius monkeys need to be loved and appreciated.

Pisces monkey

Pisces is spiritual; the monkey is clever. Together, they create intuitive and impressionable people. Pisces monkeys often appear eccentric, when, in fact, they just have rather unique thought processes.

WELL LOOK WHO FINALLY MADE THE RODEO

In summary, the monkey is an impulsive creature, incredibly intelligent but also prone to dishonesty. If there isn't a twelve-step program for this kind of crap, there sure as hell ought to be.

22. The Rooster:
The Yin Metal Animal

In China, the rooster is associated with the five virtues: fortune, courage, goodness, confidence, and military honor.

STRETCHING THE TRUTH

A recently-added sixth virtue is trying not to crow about how you're all that.

LUNAR YEARS RULED BY THE ROOSTER

1909	Jan. 22, 1909–Feb. 18, 1910
1921	Feb. 8, 1921–Jan. 27, 1922
1933	Jan. 26, 1933–Feb. 13, 1934
1945	Feb. 13, 1945–Feb. 1, 1946
1957	Jan. 31, 1957–Feb. 17, 1958
1969	Feb. 17, 1969–Feb. 5, 1970
1981	Feb. 5, 1981–Jan. 24, 1982
1993	Jan. 23, 1993–Feb. 9, 1994
2005	Feb. 9, 2005–Jan. 28, 2006

THE ROOSTER PERSONALITY

Roosters are flamboyant people. Appearance is very important to them, and roosters are constantly improving themselves, as they are never satisfied with how they look. Roosters are also friendly, pleasant, and obliging people. At times of crisis, they prove themselves to be resourceful and talented. Roosters have the wisdom to take life as it comes and keep their attitudes relaxed. They are genuinely independent and rely on no one but themselves for moral support and for solutions to their problems.

LISTEN UP, THIS IS IMPORTANT

Of course, the rooster's reliance on themselves can mean they never come to you with any of their problems. Sweet!

CHARACTERISTICS

Positive	Negative
• honest	• vain
• obliging	• thoughtless
• courageous	• self-preoccupied
• flamboyant	• arrogant
• resilient	• vulnerable
• enthusiastic	• critical
• relaxed	• superior
• cultivated	• argumentative
• loyal	• harsh
• sincere	• boastful
• capable	• dissipated
• generous	• ostentatious
• charitable	• pretentious
• entertaining	• embellishes the truth

Element

Rooster is linked to the ancient Chinese element of metal. This is a very strong element. It can be seen positively as a valuable resource, such as gold, or negatively as a weapon, such as a sword. For example, the energy of metal expresses itself supportively and inspirationally as well as destructively and inflexibly. Metal people are also intuitive and ambitious.

COMMUNICATION

Metal roosters are also often pressed into service as weathervanes.

Balance

Chinese tradition holds that the lives of roosters will be filled with ups and downs. They will experience both the joys and sorrows that life has to offer; for example, sometimes poor and at other times rich. Roosters should aim to achieve emotional stability. They must balance their larger-than-life images with their vulnerable inner selves. Only then will their lives become calm and productive.

Best associations

Traditionally, the following are said to be associated with roosters:

Taste	pungent	Plants	orange and palm trees
Season	fall	Flower	sunflower
Birth	spring	Food	cereals
Colors	yellow, white	Climate	dry

♂ THE MALE ROOSTER

If a man has a typical rooster personality, he will generally display the behavior listed below:

- is charming
- is attracted to difficult situations
- has a tendency to be a braggart
- is brutally frank
- has a good memory
- is jealous of rivals
- appears indifferent
- is a real spendthrift
- may be a dandy
- tells great stories
- is entertaining and witty
- likes the company of women

YOU'RE WELCOME FOR THE TIP

Male Rooster = One cocky son of a bitch.

♀ THE FEMALE ROOSTER

If a woman has a typical rooster personality, she will generally display the behavior listed below and on page 375:

- is not malicious
- does not tell white lies
- is reasonable
- is social and communicative
- applies herself totally to whatever she does
- is not as secretive as male roosters

- keeps her promises
- is secretly a jealous person
- appears frivolous
- is good at dealing with catastrophes
- is generous with friends

 THE ROOSTER CHILD

If a child has a typical rooster personality, he or she will generally display the behavior listed below:

- is alert and curious
- responds to reasoning
- has many interests and hobbies
- is rebellious if discouraged
- is easy to live with
- will be a daredevil
- is secretive
- likes being independent
- is good with brothers and sisters
- dislikes solitude
- is well organized

Ironically, although these youngsters are good with brothers and sisters, they rarely have any, since after about a year dealing with a rooster child, mommy usually has her tubes tied.

ROOSTER AT HOME

A typical rooster is very adaptable and can feel at home anywhere. If they can, roosters will indulge their extravagant tastes in their homes. Although expensive, furniture is likely to be simple in design. On the whole, roosters will try to create a harmonious and comfortable home. They love gadgets and novelties. Anything that makes life easier or more comfortable, roosters will install in their home. Roosters are obsessive about cleanliness and order in their home, and they keep even little-used cupboards neat and tidy. Ideally, roosters should have a room, den, or at least a corner of a room set aside for their sole use. Roosters need a space purely for themselves, where they can gather their wits.

ROOSTER AT WORK

As they are not blessed by good fortune, roosters have to work hard to achieve success. This is not a problem as roosters give their all to their work and are conscientious. Roosters can succeed in any profession that requires nerve, self-confidence, and charisma. Therefore, they are suited to anything concerned with selling and also commercial professions. Roosters are too conspicuous to be doing anything discreet and too tactless to be diplomats. They are interested in topical events and dislike routine. Roosters would enjoy working in the media, perhaps on a news-based television show or as a journalist for a newspaper.

Roosters are reasonably ambitious and do not like subordinate positions. They are more likely to be head of a department than managing director, though, as roosters prefer to avoid undue stress.

SOME TYPICAL ROOSTER OCCUPATIONS

- TV anchor
- salesperson
- sales director
- restaurant owner
- hairdresser
- public relations officer
- actor
- farmer
- aesthete
- critic
- manicurist
- teacher
- town crier
- waiter
- journalist
- travel writer
- beautician
- dentist
- surgeon
- soldier
- fireman
- security guard
- police officer

 # ROOSTER PREFERENCES

Likes
- seductions
- receiving admiring looks
- serious conversations
- ostentatious displays of wealth
- putting on a show
- tidiness
- occasional periods of solitude
- flattery
- to dream
- to give advice
- spending money
- to make an entrance

Dislikes
- losing their composure
- to be asked direct, personal questions
- poorly dressed people
- to display their knowledge
- interference in their affairs
- keeping their opinions to themselves
- to confide in anyone
- practical jokes played on them

Whether or not a rooster would bother to seduce a poorly dressed person is a question for greater minds than ours.

GOOD FRIENDS FOR ROOSTERS

The diagram below shows the compatibility of rooster with other animals. There is no fixed rule, however, because there are other influences on both the rooster and any potential friend. These influences are:

- the companion in life (see page 231)
- the dominant element (from the year of birth)

COMPATIBILITY OF ROOSTER WITH OTHER ANIMALS

		Key
■ Rat	● Horse	▲ Highly compatible
▲ Ox	● Goat	● Amicable
● Tiger	■ Monkey	■ No conflict, but needs some effort
▲ Rabbit	▲ Rooster	● Lack of sympathy
■ Dragon	● Dog	▲ Antagonistic
▲ Snake	● Pig	

ROOSTER IN LOVE

To a rooster, love is a responsibility and a challenge, not a casual matter. The organized and analytical approach they have towards love makes them prey to disappointment. After all, things rarely happen as planned in a love affair. Roosters are intense and devoted to their loved ones, but they have a tendency to be domineering. Preoccupied with their own needs, desires and longings, roosters do not always make the most sympathetic of partners. They expect their partners to know what mood they are in and act accordingly—to know when to be silent or chatty, for example. The rooster's dislike of confidences is an obstacle to real intimacy. Also, the fact that roosters like to sort out their problems by themselves leaves little room for mutual support in a relationship.

YOU'RE WELCOME FOR THE TIP

The reason the rooster's organized and analytical approach to love makes them prey to disappointment is that most people can barely resist the urge to strangle someone who has an organized and analytical approach to love.

HEALTH

Rooster's element, metal, is associated with the lungs and the large intestine, so roosters should pay particular attention to keeping these organs in working order. Roosters are often afflicted by respiratory problems and should make sure that they keep fit. This will improve both their health and their psychological balance. To maintain a healthy emotional life, roosters should put aside time to just relax and think, preferably on their own.

LISTEN UP, THIS IS IMPORTANT

Is is not a coincidence that the rooster's element is associated with the lungs and the intestines, since everything they say is a bunch of crap.

🏃 LEISURE INTERESTS

The favorite pastimes of roosters are socializing and reading. These very different pursuits are typical of the rooster, who is prone to extremes. Roosters have a busy social life, as they are agreeable and entertaining guests. Occasionally, they like to get away from it all and visit some quiet, comfortable hideaway. This gives them a chance to replenish their energies and renew their vigor.

THE ROOSTER YEARS AND THEIR ELEMENTS

The rooster is a Yin metal animal. Each of the rooster years, however, is associated with an element which is said to have its own influence. These elements are wood, fire, earth, metal, and water. They influence rooster in a regular sequence, which is repeated every sixty years. In the table below, for example, the rooster year 1909 is an earth year. The next rooster earth year is sixty years later in 1969, and the next will be 2029. Rooster's natural element is metal; the influence of this combines with those of the element of the year of birth. The possible effects of the year elements are listed on pages 381–382.

LUNAR YEARS RULED BY THE ROOSTER AND THEIR ELEMENTS

1909	Jan. 22, 1909–Feb. 18, 1910	earth
1921	Feb. 8, 1921–Jan. 27, 1922	metal
1933	Jan. 26, 1933–Feb. 13, 1934	water
1945	Feb. 13, 1945–Feb. 1, 1946	wood
1957	Jan. 31, 1957–Feb. 17, 1958	fire
1969	Feb. 17, 1969–Feb. 5, 1970	earth
1981	Feb. 5, 1981–Jan. 24, 1982	metal
1993	Jan. 23, 1993–Feb. 9, 1994	water
2005	Feb. 9, 2005–Jan. 28, 2006	wood

Rooster Metal–Earth (1909, 1969)

Steadfast earth and ambitious metal combine to make very resourceful and determined people. These people do not shy away from taking on responsibilities and can quickly get to the root of a problem. Earth, however, lessens the rooster's immediate, dramatic appeal. On closer inspection, though, the rooster's penchant for finery reveals itself in small touches—discreet but bizarre jewelry, for instance. Earth roosters are not as talkative as other roosters. This does not mean that they are less outspoken, just not as verbose. The few words they do say are guaranteed to by typically blunt.

SECRETS TO MAKE YOU LOOK GOOD

"Discreet but bizarre jewelry" = a piercing somewhere around where the sun don't shine.

Rooster Metal–Metal (1921, 1981)

Double metal roosters are trouble. They are the most headstrong of all the roosters. Well organized and precise, metal roosters are great sticklers for detail. They have high expectations of themselves and others. These roosters can be harshly critical of those who fail to live up to their standards. The vitality of roosters can be constrained by the rigidity of double metal. Roosters are not naturally restrained, so metal roosters can, at times, feel confused and ill-at-ease with themselves. On such occasions, they need to seek out solitude to regain their harmony.

Rooster Metal–Water (1933, 1993)

Transparent water combines with clear-thinking metal to add clarity to the already considerable intellectual capabilities of the rooster. Water roosters are capable and adaptable people, proficient in many fields.

Less authoritarian than others, they gain support by persuasion rather than by intimidation. Water also helps the rooster's innate sensitivity to surface. Roosters born in water years, therefore, are more sympathetic and easier to relate to than other roosters. The metal in their characters, however, stops them from being overwhelmed by these sympathies and helps them to focus on worthwhile causes.

Rooster Metal–Wood (1945, 2005)

Wood roosters are enthusiastic and progressive people. Wood releases the rooster's dormant creativity and, with their fine imaginations, wood roosters can do well in arts such as poetry and painting. Wood is also, however, an element that is prone to excesses. Roosters are already aggressive and susceptible, and wood can serve to make these qualities more pronounced. On the positive side, both wood and metal are associated with integrity. Wood tempers the moral rigidity of metal with kindness. Roosters born in wood years are completely trustworthy and are even capable of discretion.

BARE FACTS

Great. So you can count on a metal-wood rooster never to betray the trust of the person they're cheating on you with.

Rooster Metal–Fire (1957, 2017)

Fire and metal combine to make strong, dramatic characters. Although eccentric, fire roosters are always convincing people. Rash, audacious, and argumentative, they are never inconspicuous. These roosters are high fliers. Fire roosters are often exceptional: people of action, leaders, heroes, or pioneers. Usually with great success, they single-mindedly pursue their goals. Fire enables the rooster to look ahead to the long-term future and not get lost in details on the way. Fire also strengthens the belligerent nature of roosters.

ROOSTER AND THE ZODIAC OF WESTERN ASTROLOGY

To work out your zodiac sign see page 233. General character traits of roosters of the twelve zodiac signs are given below and on pages 384–386. Bear in mind that the Western zodiac sign modifies the basic rooster nature—especially in the area of personal relationships.

Aries rooster

Aries and rooster are similar in many respects, so these roosters have the qualities and defects of typical roosters, but multiplied many times. Above all else, Aries roosters are courageous people who put all their talents into getting what they want out of life.

Taurus rooster

Taurus brings stability to these roosters who are less flamboyant. Steady and dependable, they are always willing to help others. Taurus roosters are not as adaptable as other roosters but make up for this by being good planners.

Gemini rooster

Mercurial Gemini and extravagant rooster combine to make these people both inconstant and hyperactive. Cultured and knowledgeable, they have a tendency to be intellectual poseurs.

Cancer rooster

All roosters are susceptible to the opinions of others and are easily swayed by criticism or flattery. Cancer roosters take this tendency further and are ruled by their emotions. When feeling insecure, they are depressing, vain, and egotistical.

Leo rooster

Leo roosters are honest, noble, proud, vain, and only happy when they are the center of attention. They are clever at disguising this egotism with acts of generosity, which are actually done to make the rooster feel good rather than the recipient.

Virgo rooster

Precise and critical, Virgo roosters are argumentative perfectionists—their comments are usually accurate, though. Underneath, Virgo roosters are full of self-doubt and lack confidence.

Libra rooster

These roosters are talkative people, yet they are not outspoken—they are capable of diplomacy. Libran roosters are proud, indecisive, and have a highly developed aesthetic sense.

Scorpio rooster

Scorpio roosters have the "gift of gab" and are very persuasive people. Combined with their competitive natures, these are not people to get into a verbal sparring match with. They will be high achievers in any profession they choose.

Sagittarius rooster

Sagittarius makes these roosters less ostentatious than their fellows. These roosters are still enthusiastic and excitable, of course, but not as pretentious. They have a more holistic approach to life and like to travel.

Capricorn rooster

The least boastful of all roosters, Capricornean ones know that a conservative image is more suitable to achieve the material success they crave. They make loyal and devoted lovers, but their intellectual lives are fuller than their love lives.

Aquarius rooster

More flamboyant and eccentric than any other rooster, Aquarian roosters are unique people. Despite this, they are not arrogant and despise this trait in others. These roosters are broadminded idealists who are sincere and generous.

Pisces rooster

Pisces makes the rooster more sensitive and vulnerable. Pisces roosters are lacking in self-confidence and cannot relax and be happy until they have reached a state of financial and domestic security.

WELL LOOK WHO FINALLY MADE THE RODEO

To wrap-up, roosters are outgoing, entertaining people who nonetheless can be vain and brash, even to the point of criticizing what you are wearing. We hate to say it, but after seeing what you wore last night, we're siding with the rooster here.

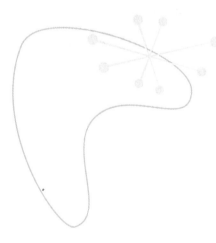

23. The Dog:

The Yang Metal Animal

In China the dog is associated with justice and compassion. Dogs are often described as being the "champions of the underdogs."

STRETCHING THE TRUTH

If a dog can be a champion of the underdogs, was Gandhi a champion of the underhumans?

LUNAR YEARS RULED BY THE DOG

1910	Feb. 10, 1910–Jan. 29, 1911
1922	Jan. 28, 1922–Feb. 15, 1923
1934	Feb. 14, 1934–Feb. 3, 1935
1946	Feb. 2, 1946–Jan. 21, 1947
1958	Feb. 18, 1958–Feb. 7, 1959
1970	Feb. 6, 1970–Jan. 26, 1971
1982	Jan. 25, 1982–Feb. 12, 1983
1994	Feb. 10, 1994–Jan. 30, 1995
2006	Jan. 29, 2006–Feb. 17, 2007

THE DOG PERSONALITY

Essentially, dogs are honest and noble creatures. They are renowned for being champions of justice and have a tendency to see things in black and white. Dogs are respected for their lively minds and quick tongues, which they use in defense of their chosen cause. Yet dogs are cynics as well as idealists, which produces characters with high moral standards, but they are beset by doubts and anxieties.

COMMUNICATION

Most of the anxieties felt by idealistic dogs stem from their ill-informed decision to work for a nonprofit.

CHARACTERISTICS

Positive
- loyal
- tolerant
- idealistic
- understanding
- dutiful
- moralistic
- faithful
- unselfish
- noble
- imaginative
- honest
- courageous
- responsible
- witty
- trustworthy
- sensitive

Negative
- cynical
- anxious
- pessimistic
- suspicious
- timid
- strict
- discouraging
- doubtful
- dissatisfied
- fatalistic
- obstinate
- distrustful
- shy
- introverted
- unadventurous
- tasteless

Element

Dog is linked to the ancient Chinese element of metal. This is a very strong element. It can be seen positively as a valuable resource, such as gold, or negatively as a weapon, such as a sword. The energy of metal expresses itself in dogs as their strong-minded, idealistic traits. Metal people are usually ambitious; dogs, however, are not personally ambitious. Instead, they are more concerned with the advancement of the downtrodden.

Balance

The main character fault of dogs is their constant worrying and self-doubting natures. A certain amount of stress or anxiety can be useful as it helps motivate the dog, who lacks motivation. But dogs can worry to the extent that it stops them doing anything useful. This interferes with their ability to lead happy and productive lives. Anxious of the future and regretful of the past, dogs need to learn how to live in the present. If they can take each day as it comes, dogs will find that their anxieties lessen. They need to reach a balance between necessary and useful worrying and self-defeating anxiety.

Best associations

Traditionally, the following are said to be associated with dogs:

Taste	pungent	Plants	poppies, water lilies
Season	fall	Flowers	orange blossoms, red poppy
Birth	daytime	Food	oats
Colors	black, dark blue	Climate	dry

THE MALE DOG

If a man has a typical dog personality, he will generally display the behavior listed below:

- will be a protective father
- is loyal and faithful to friends and family
- can be unnecessarily defensive
- makes a good ally
- is slow to make close friends
- is quick to criticize the wrongdoings of others
- has an ironic sense of humor
- is prone to depression
- loves to gossip
- can be stubborn
- rarely shows his true feelings

LISTEN UP, THIS IS IMPORTANT

Male Dog = Woody Allen coaching high school football.

♀ THE FEMALE DOG

If a woman has a typical dog personality, she will generally display the behavior listed below:

- has a very black sense of humor
- is more ambitious than male dogs
- is gifted and creative
- is lacking in perseverance
- does not compromise
- is impatient
- is attractive
- likes conversation
- will be critical of those who do not have her high standards

BARE FACTS

Female Dog = Goth chick CEO.

THE DOG CHILD

If a child has a typical dog personality, he or she will generally display the behavior listed below:

- is sensitive and affectionate
- needs attentive and understanding parents
- is scared of the dark
- will be stable if parents are protective
- resents younger siblings at first
- is obliging and devoted
- has difficulty adapting to school
- is well behaved and obedient
- likes fantasy and monster stories

DOG AT HOME

Dogs are not renowned for their sense of taste. They are not materialistic people and would rather not spend all their time and money on perfecting their home. Dogs will decorate and furnish their homes according to personal preference, budget, and convenience. They are not ones to be dictated to by fashion, unless they actually like the latest design. This does not mean that the home of dog will be badly decorated and furnished. In fact, the overall effect is often welcoming, pleasant, and personal. It may not be the home of an interior designer, but it will have been put together with care and attention to detail.

DOG AT WORK

Dogs are very capable people. The only obstacle to their success is a lack of motivation. They lack the aggression and ambition needed to put their unique skills to work. Dogs can overcome this by choosing a profession that inspires their idealistic natures, something worthwhile and altruistic, for example, to which they can commit themselves. They will then prove themselves to be hardworking, conscientious, and honest. Dogs make good managers as they are able to wield authority with tact and will remain accessible to all their staff. They consider collective interests before personal concerns.

SOME TYPICAL DOG OCCUPATIONS

- priest
- missionary
- nun
- union leader
- teacher
- charity worker
- nurse
- doctor
- judge
- lawyer
- scientist
- researcher
- critic
- social worker
- legal aid lawyer
- community worker

 DOG PREFERENCES

Likes
- anything arcane or concerned with the occult
- horror movies
- natural fabrics
- detective novels
- to remember birthdays
- writing letters to friends
- learning about other cultures
- silver jewelry
- reunions with old friends

Dislikes
- pedants
- hypocrites
- selfish behavior
- deceit and dishonesty
- family reunions
- smart cocktail parties
- superficial and ambitious people
- psychological game playing
- manmade fabrics
- counting the financial cost of an activity

LISTEN UP, THIS IS IMPORTANT

The dog's inherent dislike for family reunions, combined with their taste for horror and the occult, has led to some rather gruesome moments at weddings and funerals. Who knew ushers and bridesmaids could projectile vomit something so colorful?

GOOD FRIENDS FOR DOGS

The diagram below shows the compatibility of dog with other animals. There is no fixed rule, however, because there are other influences on both the dog and any potential friend. These influences are:

• the companion in life (see page 231)
• the dominant element (for the year of birth)

COMPATIBILITY OF DOG WITH OTHER ANIMALS		
● Rat	▲ Horse	**Key**
● Ox	■ Goat	▲ Highly compatible
▲ Tiger	● Monkey	● Amicable
● Rabbit	● Rooster	■ No conflict, but needs some effort
▲ Dragon	● Dog	● Lack of sympathy
■ Snake	▲ Pig	▲ Antagonistic

DOG IN LOVE

Dogs are easy people to love. They are warm, kind, and generous. Dogs, however, are not quick to fall in love themselves. They are suspicious and distrustful of people at first. If they meet someone who lives up to their high ideals, dogs will allow themselves to slowly fall in love with that person. Once committed, a dog will want to share everything with their partner and will be affectionate and tender. In return, dogs expect their partners to be everything to them: lover, best friend, confidant, parent, and muse. Dogs are not always happy in love as they have such high expectations. Also, they are anxious people who need constant reassuring. Although they are stable characters themselves, their pessimism and anxiety make it difficult for their partners to feel secure with them.

HEALTH

Dog's element, metal, is associated with the lungs and the large intestine, so dogs should pay particular attention to keeping these organs in working order. Dogs are anxious people and therefore prone to insomnia and stress-related illnesses. Dogs should try and maintain a balanced approach to life and not become eaten up by worry. Being Yang people, dogs are generally of sound physical health. They should make sure, however, that they watch their weight.

LEISURE INTERESTS

Dogs are sociable and enjoy spending time with friends. They are not particularly adventurous people: a dog is happier going to the movies or to a good restaurant than rock climbing. They enjoy visiting restaurants that serve foreign cuisine—although it has to be authentic—or just going for a coffee and a chat to the local café. Somewhere peaceful and friendly where they can discuss the wrongs of the world and how to put them right is preferred. For exercise, dogs like simple sports that they can incorporate easily into their lifestyle, swimming in the morning or bicycling to work, for example.

QUICK FIX

For years, your dog friends have been dragging you out to coffee shops to discuss the wrongs of the world, simply because they couldn't find any other depressing weirdos to talk to. Man, wasn't buying them that laptop the smartest thing you ever did?

THE DOG YEARS AND THEIR ELEMENTS

The dog is a Yang metal animal. Each of the dog years, however, is associated with an element which is said to have its own influence. These elements are wood, fire, earth, metal, and water. They influence dog in a regular sequence, which is repeated every sixty years. In the table below, for example, the dog year 1922 is a water year. The next dog water year is sixty years later in 1982, and the next will be 2042. Dog's natural element is metal; the influence of this combines with those of the element of the year of birth. The possible effects of the year elements are listed below and on pages 397–398.

LUNAR YEARS RULED BY THE DOG AND THEIR ELEMENTS

1910	Feb. 10, 1910–Jan. 29, 1911	metal
1922	Jan. 28, 1922–Feb. 15, 1923	water
1934	Feb. 14, 1934–Feb. 3, 1935	wood
1946	Feb. 2, 1946–Jan. 21, 1947	fire
1958	Feb. 18, 1958–Feb. 7, 1959	earth
1970	Feb. 6, 1970–Jan. 26, 1971	metal
1982	Jan. 25, 1982–Feb. 12, 1983	water
1994	Feb. 10, 1994–Jan. 30, 1995	wood
2006	Jan. 29, 2006–Feb. 17, 2007	fire

Dog Metal–Metal (1910, 1970)

Dogs born in metal years are in their natural element. In China, metal dog years are approached warily as they will either be very bad or very good, but never mediocre. In the same way, metal dogs themselves are capable of extreme behavior. Dogs are already idealistic, and double metal multiplies this tendency twofold. Metal dogs are therefore very principled to the point of being inflexible. This can make metal dogs towers of strength, but their inability to compromise may be their downfall.

Dog Metal–Water (1922, 1982)

Dogs come into their own in this element. Yin water balances with the dog's own innate Yang tendency. Chinese tradition holds that water dogs are the most beautiful and sensual of all the animal signs in the Chinese zodiac. Water erodes the harder edges from dogs, making them charming as well as sexy. These dogs are more contemplative and intuitive than other dogs. They are less rigid than their natural element, metal, usually dictates and are instead very liberal.

Dog Metal–Wood (1934, 1994)

Wood and metal together produce popular and charismatic individuals. Wood allows the dog to appraise situations with more open minds than otherwise. They do not see everything in black and white as most dogs do. They can devote themselves to a cause without becoming obsessive. Wood allows the dog's dormant creativity to blossom. These people are interested in the arts even if they are not creative themselves.

Dog Metal–Fire (1946, 2006)

Yang fire enhances the dog's innate Yang tendency. Fire quells their doubts and helps them to be optimists rather than pessimists. Fire dogs are unusually charismatic and flamboyant dogs, but in a friendly and approachable way. These dogs are less egalitarian than other dogs and are not afraid to put themselves first. Fire dogs are enthusiastic and curious. They should make sure, however, that they control their excessive tendencies and do not become addictive personalities.

COMMUNICATION

Finally! A dog that doesn't give a crap about the poor!

Dog Metal–Earth (1958, 2018)

Earth dogs are well-balanced people. They are generally happy and stable. Earth gives dogs the ability to take each day as it comes and not to be so anxious about the future. These dogs are, of course, still idealists, but earth imparts efficiency which enables them to put their ideals to some practical use. Earth dogs are materialistic for dogs, but only relative to others of the breed.

 # DOG AND THE ZODIAC OF WESTERN ASTROLOGY

To work out your zodiac sign see page 233. General character traits of dogs of the twelve zodiac signs are given below and on pages 399–400. Bear in mind that the Western zodiac sign modifies the basic dog nature—especially in the area of personal relationships.

Aries dog

In some ways, Aries helps to balance the dog. Those born under this sign are more relaxed, less serious, and more energetic. In other ways, Aries accentuates some of the dog's traits. Arien dogs are incredibly strong minded and extremely idealistic.

Taurus dog

Dogs born under this sign benefit from the sensible and constructive talents of Taurus. These dogs, however, are the most materialistic of all, and the males can be chauvinistic.

Gemini dog

Intellectual Gemini and ethical dogs are prone to theorizing about the causes of the world's problems. Gemini also increases the dog's already nervous disposition, and these people can be unstable.

Cancer dog

Cancer dogs often appear cold and indifferent, but underneath they are among the most sensitive and vulnerable of all the animal signs. They are primarily family-oriented people.

Leo dog

The most direct and honest of all the dogs, Leo ones despise being manipulated. They are spontaneous and energetic people who are unusually flamboyant and even egotistical, for dogs.

Virgo dog

Critical Virgo adds bite to the dog's nature. These people are kind but not necessarily gentle. This applies to how they perceive themselves as well as others. Virgo dogs can be too critical of themselves, and this increases their anxiety.

Libra dog

Refined and intelligent, Libra dogs are sociable animals. They are open to compromise as they are not aggressive enough to get their own way.

Scorpio dog

Self-righteous and aggressive, Scorpio dogs are not sociable animals. They are nevertheless compassionate people at heart. These dogs find it hard to be faithful, as they cannot resist temptation.

Sagittarius dog

These dogs are intrigued by different cultures and viewpoints. Although others may find their broad-mindedness a bit impersonal, they are still passionate about justice.

Capricorn dog

Conservative and materially successful, Capricorn dogs are often pillars of the community. They have a strict sense of duty and responsibility and are very moralistic.

Aquarius dog

Eccentric Aquarius and constant dog combine to produce highly individualistic people. They each have a uniquely personal outlook on life. All of them have well-developed communication skills.

Pisces dog

Pisces dogs are a strange combination of strong minds with weak wills. All dogs are plagued by self-doubt, and Pisces dogs are at times incapacitated by this. They should beware of others taking advantage of this weakness.

WELL LOOK WHO FINALLY MADE THE RODEO

In summary, dogs have a strong social conscience, but are riddled with self-doubt and need guidance. That could be why they keep doing their business in the neighbor's yard.

24. The Pig:

The Yin Water Animal

In China, the pig is associated with fertility and virility. To bear children in the year of the pig is considered very fortunate, for they will be happy and honest.

SECRETS TO MAKE YOU LOOK GOOD

And morally divided about bacon.

LUNAR YEARS RULED BY THE PIG

1911	Jan. 30, 1911–Feb. 17, 1912
1923	Feb. 16, 1923–Feb. 4, 1924
1935	Feb. 4, 1935–Jan. 23, 1936
1947	Jan. 22, 1947–Feb. 9, 1948
1959	Feb. 8, 1959–Jan. 27, 1960
1971	Jan. 27, 1971–Feb. 14, 1972
1983	Feb. 13, 1983–Feb. 1, 1984
1995	Jan. 31, 1995–Feb. 18, 1996
2007	Feb. 18, 2007–Feb. 6, 2008

THE PIG PERSONALITY

Pigs are among the most natural and easygoing personalities around. They are pleasure-loving characters who seek out the good and the fun things in life. Pigs are sympathetic and will always be there for friends in times of trouble. In turn, they look to their friends for advice and support when difficult decisions have to be made. Pigs still like to maintain their independence, though, and privacy is very important to them.

STRETCHING THE TRUTH

Yes, privacy is important to pigs. Nothing makes them happier than having their own personal trough.

CHARACTERISTICS

Positive	Negative
• eager	• indulgent
• optimistic	• impatient
• fortunate	• excessive
• tolerant	• spendthrift
• careful	• gullible
• sensual	• debauched
• courteous	• fierce
• uncomplaining	• fearful
• determined	• hesitant
• generous	• materialistic
• peaceful	• naive
• honest	• defenseless
• diligent	
• cheerful	

Element

Pig is linked to the ancient Chinese element of water. Water is linked to the arts and inner expressiveness. Emotionally, water is associated with fear. It also endows sensitivity and understanding. In pigs, water expresses itself as their nurturing qualities and in their ability to compromise and avoid conflict.

Balance

The pig is a Yin animal that exemplifies the Yin principles of peace, rest, and harmony. On the whole, therefore, pigs are well-balanced people. Their lives will not suffer from the ups and downs typical of the more unbalanced animal signs such as the dragon and the horse. Indeed, the Chinese astrological symbol for the pig is a set of balanced scales.

Best associations

Traditionally, the following are said to be associated with pigs:

Taste	salt	Plant	ginseng
Season	winter	Flower	water lily
Birth	winter	Food	peas, meat
Colors	black	Climate	cold, wet

STRETCHING THE TRUTH

Since the advent of a more health-conscious diet, pigs born after 1970 have fifty percent less sodium.

THE MALE PIG

If a man has a typical pig personality, he will generally display the behavior listed below:

- is easily deceived
- has impeccable manners
- does not exact revenge on enemies
- is endowed with common sense
- enjoys good food and fine wines
- always sees the best in people
- is a pacifist
- will have a difficult youth

LISTEN UP, THIS IS IMPORTANT

Male Pig = The twerp you beat up in high school, and into whose Mercedes you are now pumping gas.

THE FEMALE PIG

If a woman has a typical pig personality, she will generally display the behavior listed below:

- is famous for her hospitality
- is often taken advantage of
- will always help her friends
- is naturally clever
- is always polite
- will not bear grudges
- is bright and alert
- is eager to learn
- forgives but does not forget

THE PIG CHILD

If a child has a typical pig personality, he or she will generally display the behavior listed below:

- is reasonable and peaceful
- daydreams
- is careless
- does not have tantrums
- will sulk if ignored
- needs gentle discipline
- enjoys privacy
- is enthusiastic when happy
- has a sweet tooth
- is even-tempered

PIG AT HOME

Pigs are very sensual as well as domestic people and their homes reflect this. Soft armchairs, deep-pile carpets and huge bathtubs are all favored by pigs. The home of a pig will not be ostentatious, though. They do not decorate to impress—only to please themselves. Pigs like to be able to relax at home. They do not want to be inhibited by thoughts of leaving marks on expensive furniture. All pigs are prone to excesses. At home, they can be either extremely houseproud, tidy people or very slovenly, messy types. One thing is certain, however; the kitchen will be well stocked and well equipped. Pigs are gourmets when it comes to food. They love to be creative in the kitchen.

SECRET TIP

Deep pile carpets and huge bathtubs. Pig homes are coveted by the adult film industry, who also "love to be creative in the kitchen."

PIG AT WORK

Pigs are not lazy. They are very hardworking and will rarely be unemployed. Although money, status, and power are not particularly important to pigs, they do want to achieve a comfortable lifestyle. So, they will do their best to ensure their financial security. Pigs are suited to most kinds of technical, scientific, and practical work. They are careful and diligent—skills which are ideal for such occupations. Pigs also excel as managers. Attentive and understanding but not weak, they are good at dealing with people. Pigs can take advice, and indeed actually seek it out when faced by a decision. The decisions they make are, therefore, carefully thought out and never rash.

SOME TYPICAL PIG OCCUPATIONS

- researcher
- scientist
- chemist
- technician
- musician
- restaurateur
- shoemaker
- social worker
- fundraiser
- builder
- delicatessen owner
- chef
- personnel manager
- administrative officer
- gourmet
- Samaritan
- civil servant

 ## PIG PREFERENCES

Likes
- making presents for people
- to be comfortable
- organizing parties
- reading a good book
- famous people
- to gossip
- the sound of applause
- to work as part of a team
- to be in a relationship

Dislikes
- arguments
- making difficult decisions alone
- possessive people
- to be reproached
- talking to people they dislike
- living by their wits alone
- being deceitful
- to feel confused
- to argue with friends
- inhospitable people
- not knowing where they stand

SECRET TIP

Clearly, pigs are most happy in a comfortable environment where they are always appreciated, and where there are no difficult people. Their insane belief that such a place actually exists is what makes them the clueless, happy-go-lucky numbnuts they are.

GOOD FRIENDS FOR PIGS

The diagram below shows the compatibility of pig with other animals. There is no fixed ruling, however, because there are other influences on both the pig and any potential friend. These influences are:

• the companion in life (see page 231)
• the dominant element (from the year of birth)

COMPATIBILITY OF PIG WITH OTHER ANIMALS

		Key
● Rat	■ Horse	▲ Highly compatible
■ Ox	▲ Goat	● Amicable
● Tiger	● Monkey	■ No conflict, but needs some effort
▲ Rabbit	● Rooster	● Lack of sympathy
● Dragon	▲ Dog	▲ Antagonistic
▲ Snake	● Pig	

PIG IN LOVE

Pig people are enthusiastic about love. Once they have met someone compatible, they fall in love quickly and deeply. It is obvious to everyone when a pig is in love, as they wear their hearts on their sleeves. Warmhearted and open people, pigs create peaceful and happy relationships. They will do anything to please the loved one. Pigs are sentimental and may overdo their displays of love and devotion. They should take care not to smother their partners, as not everyone appreciates constant attention. Conversely, pigs also like to maintain an aura of independence, even though at heart they are emotionally dependent on their partners. Pigs are vulnerable when they are in love. If they get hurt badly, then they may become bitter and will not risk the experience again.

HEALTH

Pig's element, water, is associated with the kidneys and the bladder, so pigs should pay particular attention to keeping these organs in good working order. Watch out for the symptoms of urinary tract infections and drink plenty of water. Pigs cannot resist good foods, so many have a weight problem. They should try to establish healthy eating patterns and eat fewer rich foods. For a change, pigs could treat themselves to exotic fruits instead of high-fat foods.

YOU'RE WELCOME FOR THE TIP

In other words, "that'll do, pig."

LEISURE INTERESTS

Pigs love to read and write. They always keep in touch with old friends, often by letter if they live far away. To relax, pigs like to visit remote and wild landscapes. They can indulge their need for privacy and get involved in some outdoor sports. Rock climbing, canoeing, and windsurfing all appeal to pigs, who have an adventurous streak. Pigs also enjoy less daring activities such as long country walks. Rambling is ideal for the relaxed and sociable pig. Of course, all pigs enjoy preparing good food. Consulting the latest cookbook, they will try their hand at new and unusual dishes. The preparation is as enjoyable as the consumption for a pig.

SECRETS TO MAKE YOU LOOK GOOD

And if you're lucky, you'll be able to consume some of it, too.

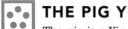 # THE PIG YEARS AND THEIR ELEMENTS

The pig is a Yin water animal. Each of the pig years, however, is associated with an element which is said to have its own influence. These elements are wood, fire, earth, metal, and water. They influence pig in a regular sequence, which is repeated every sixty years. In the table below, for example, the pig year 1911 is a metal year. The next pig metal year is sixty years later in 1971, and the next will be 2031. Pig's natural element is water; the influence of this combines with those of the element of the year of birth. The possible effects of the year elements are listed below and on pages 411–412.

LUNAR YEARS RULED BY THE PIG AND THEIR ELEMENTS

1911	Jan. 30, 1911–Feb. 17, 1912	metal
1923	Feb. 16, 1923–Feb. 4, 1924	water
1935	Feb. 4, 1935–Jan. 23, 1936	wood
1947	Jan. 22, 1947–Feb. 9, 1948	fire
1959	Feb. 8, 1959–Jan. 27, 1960	earth
1971	Jan. 27, 1971–Feb. 14, 1972	metal
1983	Feb. 13, 1983–Feb. 1, 1984	water
1995	Jan. 31, 1995–Feb. 18, 1996	wood
2007	Feb. 18, 2007–Feb. 6, 2008	fire

Pig Water–Metal (1911, 1971)

Normally, the element metal makes a person rigid and pessimistic. The easygoing and optimistic pig, however, relieves these tendencies. Instead, metal pigs are blessed with immense fortitude and a great deal of perseverance. Metal makes these pigs more ambitious and stubborn than any other. They are extroverts as well as socialites. Unusually for pigs, those born in metal years have sharp wits and incisive intellects. Metal pigs are more brash than other pigs. For these reasons, they are prone to offending people.

Pig Water–Water (1923, 1983)

Pigs born in water years are in their natural element. Double water makes these people incredibly diplomatic and highly persuasive. Water pigs are very sympathetic and refuse to hear anything bad about anybody. They need to learn to be more realistic about others. All pigs are sensual and physically indulgent—water ones doubly so. These people need to find more constructive outlets for this side of their nature. Otherwise, they will become degenerates.

Pig Water–Wood (1935, 1995)

Wood and water is a fortunate combination for the pig. Water allows the creative wood element to blossom. These people are communicative and will gather respect and support in whatever field they operate. Consequently, wood pigs often rise to prominent positions. They are wise people who give very good, though not always welcome, advice. Wood pigs should take care not to associate with less scrupulous people who will take advantage of them.

Pig Water–Fire (1947, 2007)

Fire increases the excessive tendencies of pig people. Positively aspected, fire pigs are the most brave, adventurous, and optimistic of all pig people, yet the huge energies they have are just as likely to be concentrated on indulging their pleasure-loving natures as plunged into some worthwhile cause. Pigs born in fire years are capable of reaching great heights of achievement or great depths of depravity.

SECRET TIP

Or, in the case of Congressmen, both.

Pig Water–Earth (1899, 1959)

Earth steadies the fluid element of water. It is a balancing medium for the pig. Those pigs born in earth years are likely to lead safe, comfortable, and secure lives. Most pigs suffer from fear and excessive caution, but earth pigs are not beset by such problems. Consequently, they are more self-confident and assured than pigs usually are. Earth pigs are hardworking and resourceful. They tend to have great physical strength and stamina.

 ## PIG AND THE ZODIAC OF WESTERN ASTROLOGY

To work out your zodiac sign see page 233. General character traits of pigs of the twelve zodiac signs are given on pages 413–415. Bear in mind that the Western zodiac sign modifies the basic pig nature—especially in the area of personal relationships.

Aries pig

Impetuous Aries and carefree pig combine to produce youthful, almost childlike people. They are enthusiastic and innocent characters who are well liked by everyone they meet. Aries pigs are also brilliant at both art and management.

Taurus pig

Taurus pigs are patient, materialistic, and cautious. They can be found in the upper echelons of society among the "beautiful people." Pigs born under this sign are not snobs, however; they are generous, kind, and understanding to a fault.

LISTEN UP, THIS IS IMPORTANT

Numbering themselves among the "beautiful people,"
Taurus pigs prove that they are generous, and not
snobbish, by constantly throwing charity events to
which losers like you will never be invited.

Gemini pig

Mercurial Gemini does not allow the pig to be as hesitant or indulgent as usual. Gemini pigs are more interested in cerebral matters than physical pleasure. They are outspoken and have a sardonic sense of humor.

Cancer pig

Cancer pigs are amazingly self-sufficient. They have self-discipline and great insight. Unfortunately, this assurance can crumble when they feel insecure. Cancer pigs are prone to mood swings and bouts of depression.

Leo pig

Leo pigs are larger-than-life characters. They are open, warmhearted, and very generous. A pig born under this sign positively enjoys helping others out. The only bad thing to be said about a Leo pig is that, at times, they are self-centered.

Virgo pig

Virgo pigs appear cold and calculating. They are still typically kind pig people, however, but just a little more discriminating than other pigs. Analytical Virgo makes them less ready with their favors. They will only help those whom they feel really deserve help.

Libra pig

Sophisticated Libra lends refinement to the pig. Libran pigs are talented and creative people. Dreamers as well, if they are not careful they will spend all their time with their heads in the clouds.

Scorpio pig

Scorpio brings a measure of depth to the pig. Typically, pigs are credulous people, but not those born under this sign. Scorpio pigs are very suspicious. Pushy and outspoken, these people are driven by the need to secure their financial success.

Sagittarius pig

Sagittarius pigs are happy-go-lucky adventurers. They have an enthusiastic and curious approach to life. Although they make loving partners, these pigs cannot stand to feel tied down.

Capricorn pig

Capricornean pigs are authoritarian and opportunistic. They want to both succeed materially and impress their contemporaries. Despite this, they are loyal and protective, if a little overpowering, with loved ones.

Aquarius pig

Honest and sincere, Aquarian pigs are popular people. They often appear eccentric, however. In fact, these pigs have such a unique perspective on life that they find it difficult to get close to anyone.

Pisces pig

Charming, sweet-natured, and loving, Pisces pigs are truly nice people. They are renowned for their hospitality but can be unexpectedly stingy with their money. Pisces pigs often have healing gifts.

WELL LOOK WHO FINALLY MADE THE RODEO

To conclude, pigs are affable, hardworking people who need to keep their taste for debauchery in check. Unless we won't see them again after that one night, in which case, debauche away, piggy.

INDEX